Seasonal Performances

Seasonal Performances
A *Michigan Quarterly Review* Reader

Edited by Laurence Goldstein

Ann Arbor
THE UNIVERSITY OF MICHIGAN PRESS

1994   1993   1992   1991   4   3   2   1

Distributed in the United Kingdom and Europe by
Manchester University Press, Oxford Road,
Manchester M13 9PL, UK

"The Waking," by Theodore Roethke, reprinted by permission from Theodore
Roethke, *Collected Poems,* Doubleday and Co., Inc.

"Bees: A Story to Be Spoken," by Arthur Miller, reprinted by permission of
Arthur Miller. Copyright © 1990 by Arthur Miller.

"Annus Mirabilis" from *High Windows* by Philip Larkin. Copyright © 1974 by
Philip Larkin. Reprinted by permission of Farrar, Straus and Giroux, Inc.

Library of Congress Cataloging-in-Publication Data

Seasonal performances : a Michigan quarterly review reader / edited by
    Laurence Goldstein.
        p.   cm.
    Includes bibliographical references and index.
    ISBN 0-472-10121-8 (alk.).—ISBN 0-472-08147-0 (pbk. : alk.)
        1. American literature—20th century.   I. Goldstein, Laurence,
    1943–   .   II. Michigan quarterly review.
PS536.2.S38   1991
810.8'0054—dc20   90-26384
                                                              CIP

British Library Cataloging in Publication Data

Seasonal performances : a Michigan Quarterly Review reader.
    1. United States. English literature
    I. Goldstein, Laurence 1943–   II. Michigan Quarterly Review
    810.80054

    ISBN 0-472-10121-8
    ISBN 0-472-08147-0 pbk

Acknowledgments

Unlike a monograph, or a collection of pieces by a single author, an anthology like this one has no business being dedicated to anyone but the authors and readers who have made the journal a living presence in the literary community. Nevertheless, I will take this chance to thank several people whose service to *MQR* has been crucial to its continuing existence. First and foremost my predecessors: Sheridan Baker, whose issues from 1962–70 I read with such pleasure in my undergraduate and graduate libraries, and Radcliffe Squires, who gave me the opportunity when I arrived in Ann Arbor in 1970 to assist in editing the journal, and who taught me the trade secrets of manuscript evaluation. Since 1977 Ned Creeth has been my invaluable friend and second-in-command, the unfailing source of good sense amidst the everyday editorial bustle. Finally, I am grateful to Rosemary Barfield and Therese Odlevak for undertaking the unglamorous aspects of preparing the manuscript for publication.

Contents

Four: The Artist's Perspective

Five: Six Short Stories

Introduction

In the winter of 1962 *The Michigan Alumnus Quarterly Review* fissioned into two distinctly different journals, *The Michigan Alumnus,* published by the Alumni Association of the University of Michigan, and *Michigan Quarterly Review,* published by the university. Frank E. Robbins served as interim editor of *MQR* for a brief period, but it was Sheridan Baker, appointed as editor the following year, who spelled out the nature and function of the new journal. He subtitled *MQR* "A Magazine of University Perspectives and General Intelligence" and claimed that giving the periodical "a local habitation" as well as a new name placed it in the tradition begun by Joseph Addison in the eighteenth century when he founded *The Spectator* in order to "transplant philosophy from the study to the coffee house." Baker wistfully mentioned *The New Yorker* as another model, but clearly a university journal could never have the urbane tone or vast circulation of either the London- or the Manhattan-based magazine. Baker saw a field of discourse entirely open before him, however. He wrote, "If we can make the university universal, the intellect amiable, and the magazine readable, we shall rest content."

Volume One, Number One of *MQR* had indicated just how useful and interesting such a journal could be. The lead essay by historian Arnold Toynbee argued with what now seems astonishing prescience that the Cold War needed to be conducted in an atmosphere of calm because communism, not being indigenous to Russia or congenial to its people, would eventually change its character. "If the Communist and the Western worlds can coexist for a while," he asserted, "it is possible that the present hostility between them will diminish and the gulf between them narrow." In the same issue Saul Bellow, writing about the future of fiction, argued that "a writer should aim to reach all levels of society and as many levels of thought as possible, avoiding democratic prejudice as much as intellectual snobbery." By saying as much he set the terms for a debate about the aims of the novel that is still flourishing. In both cases, and throughout the volumes of *MQR* ever since, there has been a consistent attempt by authors not only to describe the present in an engaging manner but to address the future by means of persuasive argument and example. This is what makes intellectual journals so fascinating. They are at all times contemporary.

This does not simplify the task of editing an anthology of writings from thirty years of *MQR,* though it has guaranteed much pleasure in the process of selection. I read through 120 issues with an eye for material that would intrigue and inform readers of the 1990s and beyond, and especially that totality of literate readers that Bellow identified as the necessary audience of all serious writers. Many fine but highly specialized essays were put by in favor of works that achieved that indefinable blending of the energetic personal style with the enduringly significant public subject. To locate such works, Sheridan Baker, his successor (my predecessor) Radcliffe Squires, and I read who-knows-how-many manuscripts in search of genuinely original writing, be it essay, fiction, or verse. Some several hundred thousand manuscripts have crossed the editorial desk since 1962, with only a minuscule percentage accepted for publication. What follows is one person's choice from that select gathering; needless to say, a different editor might have assembled an entirely different table of contents just as compelling and contemporary.

The final volume has the shape of a typical issue of *MQR:* a preponderance of essays, a section of fiction and one of poetry (though these are not compartmentalized in *MQR*), and some graphic artwork that has graced our pages. This book is roughly three times the length of an *MQR* issue and fairly represents the range and intellectual force of the journal since its founding.

Essays, of course, are the heart and soul of a quarterly, and it is this fact that distinguishes it from the literary magazine. Texts of all kinds have the power to change a reader's life by introducing a new way of feeling and thinking into his or her experience. In the "local habitation" of the academy, however, the essay form has always been privileged as the chief mode for the mind's excursive power, its fascination with *ideas* that can be refined and amplified through the challenge and response of debate. Indeed, it is the pleasurable obligation not only of intellectuals but of all people to argue new ideas in educational forums such as journals and classrooms and public meetings. This responsibility of people of good will informs the first section, "The Shape of a Postwar Culture," where the viability of language and the legitimacy of certain cultural ideas are focal points for the essays. None of the issues raised in Part 1 disappears from the book, for the other two sections of esays, and the fiction and poetry, sustain the important dialogue entered into by these philosphers of the contemporary human condition.

As a humanities journal *MQR* has always paid special attention to the arts, not only to their formal dynamics but to their origins and their reception by society. The second section of essays surveys four different media in order to formulate paradigms of participation between the producers and consumers of artworks. How artists create, how their creations compel enduring attention, how their chosen media perform their unique functions in contemporary culture—these are subjects of speculative, and polemical, attention. The third section of esssays, "The Personal Voice," has more of a miscellaneous cast, as it examines how ideas take living form in the experience of individuals. Because ideas of culture and the practice of art play an important part in these recreations of the self, the three sections of essays ultimately join together in mutual investigation, a dance of the intellect with more than usual harmony in its movements.

Editors of journals that publish fiction probably receive more short stories than any other form of writing. The winnowing of this great mass of imaginative prose requires enormous amounts of editorial time, which is why some academic journals keep a Fiction Editor on the staff. This has never been the policy at *MQR;* it is precisely because fiction fills a relatively small slot in the makeup of each issue that the editor has jealously guarded the prerogative of making the selections himself, lest any discovery, any splendid jewel of a story, elude his cultivated eye. The first story I accepted for *MQR* when I became editor was Lyn Coffin's "Falling Off the Scaffold," which was later reprinted to acclaim in *The Best American Short Stories* annual. The same welcome fate awaited Charles Baxter's story the following year, confirming my belief that an editor's most gratifying task is the discovery of new talent. The publication of a short story by a University of Michigan undergraduate, Mary Gaitskill, marked the boldest attempt to locate talent at an early stage; Gaitskill's later success with her book *Bad Behavior* was a welcome indication that the selection process can and does work to the benefit of emerging writers. One such writer, it might be added, was John Fowles, whose "tyro" story—as he calls it—appeared in 1965, long before it reappeared in a much revised form in the novel *Daniel Martin.* The search for new writers, of course, does not mean that we are inhospitable to writing on the high level of Joyce Carol Oates's and Arthur Miller's; we are not prejudiced against the eminent.

For poetry, even more than for fiction, personal taste overrides any other principle of selection. Freshness of language, precision of imagery, and profundity of theme have been our criteria for poetry, no matter what the subject matter. And yet here too, one can make a case for "cultural knowing" as a chief value in the assembled poems. Poems are contemporary before they are "immortal"; they address an audience whose sensibility is nourished daily by events and materials of extraordinary complexity. Poems that observe or witness these external forces have an obvious place in a review, and have been given a special role in this anthology. Poets who accommodate the imagery of computer technology, drugs, racial tension, space exploration, abortion, and any number of other topics, risk overlaying the poems with a "period" timeliness that can give the work a dated character. But the willingness to open their poems to history can and does enhance the complexity of these poems considerably, and puts them in the same constellation of intellectual pursuits as the other writings in the volume.

A description of what is included in such an anthology raises the question of what has been excluded. A large category is what might be called high-level reportage: the monitoring of people, places, and events in order to secure a precise sense of their quiddity, or essence. What is it like living in Nigeria during the civil war, or Vietnam during the late 1960s, or the South during the early days of the Civil Rights movement? What should we know about Raoul Wallenberg or Hannah Arendt or the Michigan farmers who watched their cows die from PBB poisoning? What is the current status of the artifical intelligence debate, of biblical research, of educational theory? A review must constantly issue progress reports and sightings that nourish the public imagination as it strives to reach a more sophisticated understanding of modern life, and in the process reshape and improve policy. Though such essays tend undeniably to sound a bit dated in later decades, they perform an essential task of periodical literature by refreshing our sense of wonder at being alive in the midst of the moveable feast of modern history.

Though interviews with famous personalities have been a regular feature of *MQR*, beginning with a previously unpublished conversation with Winston Churchill upon his visit to Ann Arbor in 1901, I have decided to omit this category of discourse also, if only because it would be impossible to choose from among them. The annual Hopwood Lecture by an eminent author is published in *MQR*, but since these lectures have recently been collected by Nicholas Delbanco and published by the

University of Michigan Press, these too have been excluded. Essays that have developed into books, such as Sidney Fine's study of the Detroit riots of 1967 or James Boyd White's on the invisible discourse of the law, were set aside as well, though these rank among the most widely admired contents of the journal. And I avoided taking material from our special issues, because they are virtually books in themselves, though I could not resist selecting one essay from the double issue devoted to "The Automobile and American Culture," our most successful ever. An addendum provides a list of fifteen other essays I would have liked to include in this anthology.

The proliferation of journals on the academic scene is a testimonial to their continuing service to general readers and specialists alike. They are part of an information explosion that has become deafening to some ears but is sweet music to those who believe that the complexity of modern experience requires constant analysis. "Analysis" might be too severe a term, for it suggests a highly methodical course of examination derived from textbook models, as in psychoanalysis or medical analysis. The readings from *MQR* that follow offer such a variety of methods, and such a diversity of rhetorics, that the stern connotations of "analysis" give way to that pleasure-in-reading that preceded analysis in the personal history of each reader. If the book is as much a banquet for the mind as I think it is, it should remind readers not only why periodicals like *The Spectator* flourished in the past but why the interdisciplinary journal remains an amiable and important part of our culture at century's end.

One: The Shape of a
Postwar Culture

A Poet between East and West

Czeslaw Milosz

> The Kingdom of art increases and that of health and innocence declines on this earth.
>
> —Thomas Mann, *Tonio Kröger*

A long time ago, in my youth, I read a story by Thomas Mann, *Tonio Kröger*. That story was written before World War I and was constructed upon a premise then quite generally accepted in artistic circles. According to that premise, art and literature are intimately connected with abnormality or sickness and are even its function. Mann remained faithful to that premise in all his *oeuvre*, from *Buddenbrooks* to *Doctor Faustus*. Undoubtedly that view on the sources of art also influenced my literary generation to some extent, but it seemed to offend us and we tended to reject it as too obviously marked by romantic irony—and decadent.

I am separated from the moment when I read *Tonio Kröger* not only by the passage of years. Unfortunately, I must say, and let me use a pathetic expression, my eyes have seen at least a part of that horror which belongs to the very essence of the twentieth century. And that experience did not relegate to the past the problem brought up by the story of Mann; on the contrary, it gave it a greater poignancy. Now I would agree with Tonio Kröger that literature is not a vocation but a curse; I can also add new arguments as to its unhealthy character. I am even ready to make a frontal attack against the art of the written word, particularly against its transformations in our time.

"The artist must be unhuman, extrahuman," says Tonio Kröger; "he must stand in a queer aloof relationship to our humanity; only so is he in a position, I ought to say only so would he be tempted, to represent it, to present it, to portray it to good effect. The very gift of style, of form and expression, is nothing else than this cool and fastidious attitude toward humanity; you might say that there has to be that impoverishment and devastation as a preliminary condition."

I believe all that is true, and I understand it better now than in the years of my youth. For then "humanity" was for me an abstraction, while now it has the shape of emaciated prisoners in their striped garb, of corpses in the streets of the Warsaw ghetto, of a hand with a pistol in a window that will be changed in a moment into a gaping hole by the fire of a tank. "A cool and fastidious attitude" in the face of such scenes is a moral monstrosity, but it is precisely that monstrosity which lies, in Mann's opinion, at the foundation of art. And to deny that there is truth in his premise would be of no use. It does not matter that a poet, an artist, may preserve that same cool attitude *toward himself,* that is, that he becomes double, a man who while being led to his own execution still remains, with one part of himself, a detached, ironic observer. From a moral point of view that distance is hard to accept and poetry, which owes everything to this distance, must be morally suspect.

But I do not intend to lead my attack in the name of ethical principles. Let us assume, following Mann, that art grows out of abnormality, out of a more or less hidden demonic possession, and that a kind of moral detachment makes up part of that abnormality. As we have often heard, art, by its very being, by its very *esse,* redeems the dark neurotic operations from which it stems. I prefer, by the way, to narrow the scope of my considerations and by "art" I will mean poetic art. It consists in joining words in such a manner that a unit called "the line" not only acquires a power of affecting contemporaries, but is felt by generations as something necessary and natural, like the spirals of a shell. Yet there is a prerequisite, and that is a relation, let us concede, an enigmatic one, between the words of a poem and reality, always a reality of a given place and time. An imitator of Horace would today create only rhetoric. Besides, the example of Horace may indicate that the laws of the relationship between poetry and reality are different in every period, since Horace was filling his poems with philosophical maxims that must have looked like clichés to his contemporaries. And yet, whatever those laws of relationship are, old theories proclaiming that art is *mimesis* always seem to preserve their validity, even if we no longer confer upon art, as was done in the Middle Ages, the highly honorable title of a grandchild of God—for art imitates the daughter of God, that is Nature. By now advancing a thesis unfavorable to the art of joining words, I take into account both my impressions as a reader and my meditations as a practitioner. My thesis is: poetry, and literature in general, prove to be less and less potent in the presence of what reveals itself in our century as reality, which means that it changes into an autonomous activity of the language, *écriture,* and as a consequence the very reason for its existence is open to question.

What do I consider reality? Probably not the same thing as an American poet does. I will choose a case which is perhaps extreme, but significant. When I came to California, I dedicated much time to the poetry of Robinson Jeffers. In my opinion he is a poet of great stature, unjustly thrown down into near-oblivion from the pedestal he occupied in the twenties. Jeffers deliberately opposed avant-garde fashions deriving from French Symbolism and, in clear-cut, transparent syntax, described in his poems what was for him most real, the shore of the Pacific near his home in Carmel. And yet, when reading Jeffers, I discovered that those orange-violet sunsets, those flights of pelicans, those fishing boats in the morning fog, as faithfully represented as if they were photographs—all that was for me pure fiction. I said to myself that Jeffers, who professed, as he called it, "inhumanism," took refuge in an artificial world which he invented using ideas taken from biology textbooks and from the philosophy of Nietzsche. I also realized to what extent I dislike Nature. I do not want to say that I am insensitive to the beauty of mountains, forests, oceans. Simply, Nature, very much present in the imagination of American poets and so often identified by them with reality—without doubt very real when we enumerate the elementary facts of our biological existence, "birth, copulation, and death," is for me, in this century of mine, a huge museum of inherited images. The struggle of poetry with the world cannot take place within a museum. Precisely in California, perhaps more acutely than in any other place, I have felt that the problem of my time should be defined as Poetry and History.

Thus, I hear a question: do I mean poetry confronted by History as a cycle of horrors: pacts between big powers dealing in human herds, battles, massacres, concentration camps? No, not at all, though it cannot be denied that such events are for poetry a sort of test: then it finds out how much reality it is able to bear. A countless number of anti-Nazi poems written in the years 1939–45 in Poland, in terrorized cities, in ghettos, in prisons, in extermination camps, gives new substance to the contention of Thomas Mann that "the artist must be unhuman, extra-human"—for the authors of those poems were merely human, and, to the extent that they were human, they lost artistically, so that their poems taken together make a huge and poignant document of several thousand pages, but a document is not art. I have seen in my own case that a serious conflict arises here. For today, from a distance, those poems of mine which moved my underground audiences in Warsaw seem to me weak, while those which then looked enigmatic as to their intentions and were cruel, full of offensive mockery, now seem strong. That conflict also manifested itself when, in Warsaw in 1942, I was preparing for print an underground anthology, *Invincible Song*. Fanatically attached to my standards of quality, I rejected those poems which were not up to my requirements because of their banal vocabulary or trite rhymes, but I knew at the same time that I was wrong, for it was precisely those bad poems which were most effective as an emotional charge, as a weapon.

It may now be a cause for surprise that I read into this a problem. After all, *Inter arma silent Musae*—the Muses fall silent at the time of war—and how slight is the trace left in poetry by the Napoleonic wars, by the American Civil War or World War I! To this I answer that historical analogies are misleading and that the problem definitely exists. And it can be formulated as follows: the written word encountered in our time a completely new phenomenon in the guise of a totalitarian State organization—and I do not refer here to the slaughter of populations by the will of a ruler of the Genghis Khan type. Nor do I feel that it is correct to place the events of the first half of our century in a rubric entitled "the past," for there is a strong possibility that "L'Univers Concentrationnaire," to use a term introduced by David Rousset, was only the first of *forms* taken by an emerging Leviathan, an apocalyptic Beast. People who were confronted with it for the first time, whether in its Nazi or Soviet variety, dimly perceived that all the known concepts of man and of society disintegrated and a *new dimension* unveiled itself, not because of the magnitude of the crime, but because of its impersonal nature. For that reason the behavior of language facing such a new social form, the inability or ability of language to cope with it, must be a basic problem for a poet.

This problem has been given attention in a book which reaches probably deeper than many sophisticated teatises of structural analysis. It was first presented at the Sorbonne as a Ph.D. dissertation in sociology by a colleague of mine from Poland, Michal Borwicz, and was published in 1954 under the title *Écrits des condamnés à mort sous l'occupation alle-mande*—Writings of people sentenced to death under the German occupation. The author, using materials gathered from all over Europe, analyzes the urge felt by those people to leave a testimony and to communicate their knowledge, which they sensed to be completely new, radically different from what was until then known about reality. But, as the author proves, they were doing it in a language inherited, *conventional,* proper to a social milieu which had shaped them before their key experience. If we take this as a struggle of language with reality, the data gathered by the author indicate that language was losing, retreating into ready-made *topoi* and formulas, and even behaving as if these provided a refuge. Probably similar conclusions to those of Borwicz will be reached by scholarly investigators of the rich literature (songs, poems, inscriptions) written in Soviet prisons and concentration camps.

But what has all this to do with poetry written here, in America, or in England, in France, now, in the last quarter of the twentieth century? In dealing with that poetry I should be loyal, that is, I should limit myself to a personal declaration: rarely do I find in it what *I myself* consider to be reality. I assume that in our century something has been born which we try in vain to name, and to which I give the provisional name of a new dimension of man and of society. I assume also that poetry, unless it is conscious of this and stays in that frontier area where it should strive to grasp the new dimension, by necessity lacks that vigor of being which is necessary to redeem the abnormality and moral ambiguity attending its birth. Relations between Poetry and History do not mean, in my view, that a poet should constantly visit in his imagination places of human suffering enclosed with barbed wire. I am against an obsessive turning back, and in my poems written in California I put much effort into leaving behind things past. Yet I cannot remain indifferent when I hear widespread opinions on the events of the first half of the century, often completely departing from historical truth. According to those opinions, there is a natural course of events, for man is everywhere the same in whatever State and system he lives. That natural course of events was disturbed by incomprehensible cataclysms unleashed by some monstrous dictators, but everything leveled off, or, if not yet, it will level off in the near future. As a bumper sticker I recently saw read: "One Earth, One Humanity, One Spirit." Such reasoning bypasses the possibility that the presumed "disturbance" was the first phase of something new and that we all, as a species, are menaced by implementations of an idea: that of the State conceived as an owner of human beings, both of their bodies and their souls. Since such a State must also be an owner of their language, that is, give to words such meaning as it desires, a moment may be near when the apparent similarity of people living in various political zones will be reduced to their having two eyes, two hands and two legs. For what above all is being undermined now is the millennia-old belief in the autonomy of a human molecule endowed with an orbit of its own—and an expression has even been coined: "death of man."

My attack is not directed against poets of the West but against poetry of today in general, therefore also against myself. Suppose I am right in my criticism. Yet, as a poet whom I dislike, Mallarmé, said, poetry is not written with ideas but with words. As are all my contemporaries, I am subject to the directives dictated by a certain style. Were I not looking upon myself as a good craftsman who has written a certain number of professionally satisfactory poems, the matter would be just academic. As it is, I feel I both have the right to attack and deserve to be an object of attack.

As Borwicz's book demonstrates, a paralyzing and incommunicable experience is conveyed by ordinary people, not artists, in a language of inherited stylistic conventions. Those conventions are periodically broken by art, thanks to, in the words of Mann, a "cool and fastidious attitude towards humanity." The history of poetry in our century has been a series of breakthroughs, one quickly succeeding another, so that the language of poetry is today very distant from that of the year 1900. Yet the speed with which new varieties of style succeed each other is matched by the speed with which they are set as conventions and changed into common property. Let us notice that the transformation of discoveries into clichés speaks in favor of the theory of art as *mimesis*. That is why today, any time we try to find a name for a new form of a bureaucratic Leviathan, we pronounce the words: "surrealism," "Kafka."

Kafka should be invoked here, for his appearance is simultaneous with a historical mutation that escapes our definitions, though philosophers and sociologists come forward with many terms. Whatever was the core of Kafka's neurosis (and his personality cofirms the theory of Mann), he had a strong resolve to remain faithful to reality. At the same time his *oeuvre* proves that so-called realistic description had come to its end, because it is possible only when there is a describing individual endowed, as I said, with an orbit of his own. Kafka, like his heroes, cannot act; he is acted upon. Moreover, he is in the power of forces characterized not only by omnipotence, but also by anonymity. One can describe things if they possess tangible shapes, while completely different tactics are indicated when we confront a dragon that is either invisible or if he becomes visible, may be this or that. And Kafka applied such new tactics, replacing a description of characters and events by parable and metaphor. And that is a change important for poets who write after him.

As a literary genre, poetry during the last couple of centuries had for its companion another literary genre, the novel. Suddenly poetry is alone. Everything points toward the demise of the novel, probably unable to survive the end of old-fashioned descriptive narrative. The solitude of poetry will bring about serious consequences, but we do not understand them as yet. Poetry does not supersede the novel to occupy the honorable place it held in the era when the novel was still a country-fair genre. Just the opposite is true, as if the blame incurred by the novel, less and less read by the cultivated public, extended to *belles lettres* as a whole. And yet the quantity of poems and publications of poetry, not read anymore by anybody, increases at a terrifying rate. Language, liberated from aims and duties, seems to speak by itself to itself. Not to act but to be acted upon—this Kafka perceived as a tragedy, but it is possible that half a century after his death we agree with a remark made by the Polish writer Witold Gombrowicz, much earlier than it was noticed by the French structuralists: that it is not we who speak the language but it is the language that speaks us.

Yes, it is undeniable, the power exerted over us by the language is a great discovery of our century. We can express no more than the language of our time and place allows us to, and this is known not only to poets, but also to rulers who change the meaning of words for their own purposes. But precisely resistance against that limitation, in the name of reality, prompts me now to attack the art of the written word. For, while realizing the autonomous tendencies of language, we may look beyond language for a tangible criterion. And this is not the same as to say with resignation that there is no such criterion. Of course, by bringing in reality, I expose myself to many misunderstandings, for years in a seminar in philosophy would not exhaust the implications contained in the term *mimesis*. Also, I risk inviting the phantom of realism together with all the epithets usually accompanying it. But most of the so-called realisms have little to do with reality, often no more than an inscription on the gate of a concentration camp: "*Arbeit macht frei.*"

To sum up, I rebelled in my youth against the portrait of the artist

I found in Thomas Mann's *Tonio Kröger,* against his connecting creative activity with neurosis, with internal "impoverishment and devastation." I believed in health, strength, and sometimes even imagined a model poet as a happy giant. Later on, I learned that the presumed health of happy giants was just an appearance masking demonic possession, and I myself stopped pretending to be a strong man. I experienced how painful it is to realize that it is not the most noble, most human impulses which are allies of the poet but rather his "cool and fastidious attitude"—even if he writes a poem against inhumanity. Out of that realization grows an exigency addressed to poetry: poetry should strive toward a sufficient degree of *being* and thus to redeem its original sin. To put it a different way, if I agree with Thomas Mann when in *Tonio Kröger* he says that poetry serves as "a sort of revenge on life," I would not like the revenge to be taken at the expense of our human world.

Buber and the Holocaust: Some Reconsiderations on the 100th Anniversary of His Birth

Richard L. Rubenstein

As we commemorate the hundredth anniversary of the birth of Martin Buber here in Würzburg, it is impossible not to reflect on what those years have meant in the history of Judaism, of Germany and of the western world. In 1878 the vast majority of the world's Jews were domiciled in Eastern Europe. There was a minuscule Jewish community in what is now Israel. There were no more than 300,000 Jews in the United States, almost all of whom were of German origin. In the same year on January 3, 1878, Pastor Adolf Stöcker, the Kaiser's Court Chaplain, founded Germany's first overtly anti-Semitic political party, renamed shortly thereafter the Christian Social Party. One year later Wilhelm Marr founded his Anti-Semite League. Stöcker's program was relatively mild compared to that of his successors. Nevertheless, the Pastor laid a more enduring foundation for the total annihilation of Germany's Jews than he knew. In 1881, three years after Buber's birth and the founding of Stöcker's party, the Jews of Czarist Russia were the object of government-instigated pogroms of unprecedented violence. In retrospect, these pogroms must be seen as providential. Without the goad of overt violence, it is doubtful that the emigration of Jews from Eastern Europe to the still-open United States would have assumed the large-scale proportions it did. We know what fate was in store for those who remained in Eastern Europe.

From the perspective of 1978, it is clear that Martin Buber was born into and eventually came to lead a hopelessly doomed community whose grim fate was inexorably to unfold during his lifetime. There is no other way to understand the history of European Judaism from 1878, when the clouds of doom were barely visible on the horizon, to 1945, when the full dimensions of the catastrophe were finally revealed. Martin

Buber was undoubtedly the most important and influential religious thinker produced by his doomed community. This is an exemplary achievement given the period in which he flourished. In its closing hours the European Jewish community produced an extraordinary number of world leaders in the fields of art, science, philosophy, and literature, but in the field of religion, only one Jew was able fully to transcend the limits of his own tradition and achieve preeminent status as a world leader. That man was Martin Buber.

Nevertheless, Buber's preeminence as a unique leader in his bitterly tragic era makes it all but inevitable that his career be re-examined in the light of the history and fate of his community. In recent years, all contemporary Jewish theology has become Holocaust theology, at least on the North American continent.[1] Although the debates between contemporary Jewish theologians have at times been embittered, there is absolutely no disagreement concerning the central issue confronting contemporary Jewish thought.[2] Almost every contemporary reflection about God, man, revelation, election, tradition, redemption, Israel, and Christianity starts with the Holocaust as the central event. After Auschwitz became the dominant issue for the reflective Jewish consciousness, it became exceedingly difficult to read Martin Buber save in the light of that event.

This does not mean that Buber can be faulted because he did not make the Holocaust his central theological concern. It was Buber's fate to help guide the spiritual destiny of the German Jewish community in its terminal agony. Like philosophic reflection, theological reflection tends to arise after the fact. It is a *Nachdenken*. Perhaps the words of Hegel in the preface to the *Philosophy of Right* were never more appropriate than as a description of the current state of Jewish theological reflection:

> When philosophy paints its grey in grey, then has a shape of life grown old. By philosophy's grey in grey it cannot be rejuvenated but only understood. The owl of Minerva spreads its wings only with the falling of the dusk.[3]

Holocaust theology begins its task only after night has fallen. It was Buber's lot to have lived through and to have been a principal actor in many of the events concerning which contemporary theology must now reflect. His greatness is inextricably linked to his time. He cannot be expected to have been both a participant in the events of his time and to have reflected on the meaning of that which he was compelled to endure. His insight and his vision have enlivened our understanding of the biblical, New Testament, and Hasidic periods in the history of Judaism and of western religion. It is inevitable that others would come after Buber whose task would be to reflect on the time and the teaching which were the substance of his life. This essay is hopefully a contribution to that labor.

Buber did, of course, survive the Holocaust by twenty years and his latter years, like those of Sigmund Freud and Paul Tillich, were among his most creative. Yet, when one turns to his writings from 1945 to 1965 there is little if any evidence of a confrontation with the Holocaust as a religious or theological issue. The Holocaust is mentioned in the address he gave at the *Paulskirche* in Frankfurt am Main on the occasion of his controversial acceptance of the Peace Prize of the German Book Trade, September 27, 1953, but the grim subject is not raised as a religious problem. It is only mentioned because of its obvious relevance to the issue of Buber's attitude toward Germany and Germans. In that address Buber is principally concerned with what appears to be a more universal problem, the Cold War, which he saw as a result of the inability of men truly to speak to each other. Characteristically, Buber expresses the faith that the international crisis, though fraught with danger, can result in healing because "despite all, . . . the peoples in this hour can enter into genuine dialogue with each other."[4] Thus, although the Holocaust was alluded to on the occasion of a highly significant postwar encounter between Buber and the German world of letters, Buber was fundamentally preoccupied with the absence of dialogue between nations as the source of international instability.

If Buber ever had any intention of dealing explicitly with the Holocaust as a religious or theological problem, one might have expected his reflections on the subject to have been included in the work that became known as *Eclipse of God* (1952), which dates from the same period as the *Paulskirche* speech.[5] While that book expresses concern for the collapse of faith in a transcendent deity in modern philosophy, the Holocaust is nowhere seen as relevant to that issue. Buber is sensitive to the philosophical critique of faith in Sartre, Heidegger and Nietzsche. He also argues against Feuerbach and his intellectual heirs that those who maintain that "every alleged colloquy with the divine is only a soliloquy" must inevitably conclude that "God is dead," a position Buber emphatically rejects.

For Buber, the fundamental reason for the absence of genuine meeting between man and the Eternal Thou in our time is that "the I-It relation, gigantically swollen, has usurped, practically uncontested, the mastery and the rule." In spite of this universal contemporary dominion of I-It and its consequence, the eclipse of God, Buber assures us that (*a*) the absence of God is a temporary phenomenon due in large measure to mankind's currently flawed capacity for dialogue, and (*b*) we can expect that the encounters between men and the Eternal Thou will be resumed in the future in ways that cannot yet be foreseen. This is expressed as follows:

> Something is taking place in the depths that as yet needs no name. Tomorrow it may happen that it will be beckoned to from the heights, across the heads of earthly archons. The eclipse of the light of God is no extinction; even tomorrow that which has stepped in between [man and the Eternal Thou] may give way.[6]

Having offered his readers a series of wholly unsupported oracular pronouncements, Buber nowhere states his reasons for either his diagnosis or his prophecy.

Nevertheless, Buber's silence on the Holocaust as a theological issue is altogether consistent with his view of the divine-human encounter. For Buber, that encounter is utterly removed from all of the categories of normal human experience. It is atemporal, nonspatial, noncausal, and, in fact, devoid of the kind of *any* content that could be shared in normal discourse. As Buber informs us, in the divine-human encounter we receive "not a content but a presence, a presence in strength."[7] Moreover, for those who enter into the absolute relationship with the Eternal Thou, "nothing retains any importance."[8] It would thus appear that, because of its wholly ineffable character, Buber's version of the divine-human encounter must prove indifferent to the vicissitudes of human history.

Moreover, since, according to Buber, there is nothing cumulative or structured about the meetings of God and man, each encounter is without identifiable precedent or consequent. The spontaneous and utterly unpredictable character of such meetings is devoid of that indispensable note of confidence and trust that could only develop in a relationship between partners whose behavior toward each other possesses a measure of consistency and predictability. This is as true of the relationship between God and man as it is between man and man. That is why normative Judaism and Christianity, in contrast to Buber, have always insisted that there is both structure and continuity in the relationship between God and his people. This also is why Jesus is depicted as addressing God as Abba, thereby expressing his confidence in the trustworthiness of his continuing relationship with God.[9] Such trustworthiness can never rest upon ineffable spontaneity. Indeed, it requires the assurance that only a sense of structure and continuity could make possible.

Buber, of course, recognized that men are as anxious to find elements of consistency in their relations with God as they are in their relations with earthly parents, but he regarded that quest as a fall from grace. It is, in fact, the closest analogue to the biblical doctrine of the fall we can discern in Buber's thought.

"This," he tells us, "is the sublime melancholy of our lot that every Thou must become an It in our world."[10] Here, in the demise of spontaneity and ineffability we find Buber's version of the "Fall." Man is alienated from God not only by some willful act of disobedience or self-assertion—there is, in fact, no way man could realistically disobey Buber's God—but by the transformation of an utterly unpredictable divine-human relationship into a predictable one. For Buber, this is taken to mean that even the ineffable presence of the divine Thou is destined to be lost within the objectifying categories of the world of I-It.

Given such a perspective, there is no reason why the Holocaust should have been regarded by Buber as a significant religious or theological problem. For those who believe in the biblical God of covenant and election, the Holocaust raises the obvious question: How could an all-powerful and all-righteous God . . . ? For Buber, the very spontaneity and utter unpredictability of the divine-human encounter precludes such a question. Within Buber's thought, one can interpret the Holocaust as the most radical extension of the domain of I-It. Nevertheless, even the Holocaust would not be incompatible with Buber's version of the Eternal Thou, that is, a divine Presence which cannot be contained within any humanly comprehensible meaning. Thus, there are important religious and theological reasons why Buber never raised the Holocaust as a central problem for contemporary Judaism.

Nevertheless, Buber's indifference to the Holocaust as a religious problem is indicative of the radical disjunction between his religious thought and that of the classical Judaeo-Christian mainstream. Although both Judaism and Christianity acknowledge that God as He is in Himself is beyond the comprehension of finite human thought, neither tradition knows of an *unmediated relationship* between God and man, such as that set forth by Buber. In Judaism men are never enjoined to meet the Absolute; they are enjoined to keep his commandments. Buber's rejection of the system of religous law in Judaism is well known and, given the centrality of the ineffable divine-human encounter in his thought, it is entirely understandable.[11] Were God present to us in the fashion described by Buber, no such system of law would be necessary or even possible. It is because normative Judaism knows nothing comparable to Buber's version of the divine-human encounter that it insists upon its system of religious law.

Similarly, Christianity knows no unmediated relationship with the Absolute. Jesus Christ is the Mediator *par excellence* between God and man. That is why Christian thinkers among Buber's contemporaries, such as Guardini, Gogarten and Barth, insisted that only in and through Christ is God available to man as the Eternal Thou. This is in the strongest possible contrast to Buber for whom the relationship between man and the Eternal Thou is utterly without mediation.

In contrast to Buber, in Judaism and Christianity the divine-human relationship requires mediation. Moreover, in both traditions sin consists in rejecting the divinely-bestowed mediations. Judaism and Christianity differ on the nature of the mediations but agree that the penalty for rejecting the divinely sanctioned mediations is dire. Indeed, the very fate of mankind is depicted as resting upon a proper response to the mediations.

It is at this point that contemporary Holocaust theology raises its fundamental issue: if God is more than Buber's ineffable Eternal Presence, but, as both traditions assert, the all-powerful Actor in the drama of human history who has elected Israel as his distinctive people, how shall we understand the divine role at Auschwitz? The response of classical Jewish and Christian tradition is identical: Auschwitz must be seen as God's chastisement against the Jews for having rejected the divinely sanctioned mediations. This is not necessarily the response of most contemporary Holocaust theologians in either tradition.[12] It certainly is not mine. Nevertheless, unlike Buber, contemporary Holocaust theology begins with a classical problem in Jewish and Christian religious thought, namely, the question of covenant, election, and God's action in history.

Moreover, Holocaust theology rests upon a premise that Buber is not prepared to grant, namely that the encounter between God and man is never unmediated. As a Jew of Polish origin, Buber presumably felt deeply the monumental tragedy of Auschwitz but, given his distinctive religious system, he could not identify God as the Actor in *any* concrete set of historical events. To do so would be to comprehend the Eternal Thou in the domain of I-It. Furthermore, Buber saw evil fundamentally as *absence of relationship*. Hence, he was not prepared to see in the Holocaust the *presence* of God.

Yet, when one contrasts Buber's position with that of the traditional believer who asserts that somehow God was mysteriously present at Auschwitz, one wonders whether there may not be greater realism in the believer's harsh and uncompromising faith. We may reject as simplistic the believer's attempt to ascribe cosmic significance to such grim happenings, but we ought to recognize that radical evil, sin, and suffering are issues of the greatest possible urgency to him.

By contrast, Buber's notion of evil as *absence* of relationship has the unintended consequence of radically underestimating evil's potency. As we shall see, Buber's tendency to underestimate the power of evil affected his politics as well as his theology. Given his view of evil as privation of dialogue, Buber was more concerned with attempting to restore the broken dialogue with the evil-doer than to face the tragic but compelling necessity of creating and sustaining political structures possessed of the power to contain evil. The human problems involved in the administration of a system of officially sanctioned coercion are, of course, a principal concern of nonutopian politics. By contrast, Buber's ventures into the realm of politics were almost always utopian and messianic.

Buber's insistence on the unmediated character of the divine-human encounter rendered him disinterested in the Holocaust as a religious problem. It also distorted his understanding of what was at stake in the two-thousand-year theological conflict between Judaism and Christianity. It is the consensus of a growing number of biblical scholars that the fall of Jerusalem to the Romans in 70 was a historical watershed of epoch-making proportions for both Judaism and Christianity.[13] Those who were the dominant religious authorities in both the Christian movement and Judaism before 66 were no longer so in the aftermath of the fall of Jerusalem. Before the war, the dominant authorities within Judaism were the priestly Sadducean aristocrats who controlled the sacrificial worship of the Jerusalem sanctuary. In the period between the ministry of Jesus and the Judaeo-Roman War, the Christian community and the Pharisees were essentially rival movements within Judaism which attempted to challenge the priestly party's monopoly of the central religious institutions. Put differently, before the Judaeo-Roman War the priestly party possessed a monopoly of the officially sanctioned *media of redemption,* a monopoly that was challenged by both the young Christian church and the Pharisees.[14]

But note the language we employ: we speak of "media of redemption," that is, the religious means by which men pay their debts to God and to their fellow men. Contrast this with Buber's insistence on the immediate and ineffable character of the presence of the indescribable Absolute as the content of authentic religion. Since Buber's meeting with the Absolute is devoid of content, it can hardly involve a concrete sense of indebtedness or sin. Thus, while Buber is concerned with the presence or absence of a relationship with God, he never takes seriously, as do the classic traditions, the decisive problem of how men are to make good their primal indebtedness to the Absolute.

Unlike Buber, we hold with the classic traditions that a fundamental preoccupation of *homo religiosus* is his profound sense of indebtedness both to God and to his fellow man. We further hold that in his religous life, *homo religiosus* seeks above all to annul that indebtedness. This, we believe, was clearly understood by Paul of Tarsus who held that Christ's gift consisted precisely in the redemption of mankind from the indebtedness it had inherited from its original progenitor.[15] By contrast, in his work *Two Types of Faith,* Buber saw Paul's *pistis,* his faith in Christ as Redeemer of mankind's primal indebtedness, as infinitely more Greek than Jewish.[16] Buber ignores the fact that both Paul and his Jewish contemporaries shared a common belief that the human condition had been flawed at the outset by Adam's original offense against the Creator and that both Paul and his Jewish contemporaries yearned for an identical release from the indebtedness.[17]

When we turn to the ancient rivalry between the priests, the Pharisees and the Christians in the period immediately before the fall of Jerusalem, we again note the extent to which Buber's view of religion distorts the past, and, insofar as the present is heir to the past, the present as well. In the period between the birth of Christianity and the fall of Jerusalem, the rivalry between priests, Pharisees and Christians for control of the media of redemption within Judaism involved bitter economic, social and political competition over the related questions of (*a*) how the community would pay its debts and (*b*) who would control the procedure. Each group sought the monopoly for itself. Here again, we find the strongest possible contrast between the actualities of religion at the moment in history which witnessed the birth of both the Christian church and the rabbinic tradition on the one hand, and Buber's distinctive interpretation of the nature of authentic faith on the other. For example, the conflict between the largely Galilean Christian movement and the priestly aristocrats of Jerusalem can be seen as a center-periphery conflict. It can also be seen as a conflict between the urban metropolis and the agrarian hinterland. The priestly monopoly of the nation's central religious institutions carried with it considerable financial, political and social advantage. By the same token, there were very serious disabilities, then as now, for those who were cut off from access to leadership of the metropolitan institutions, as were the Galileans. It is not at all surprising that more than one religious rebellion against the metropolis began in peripheral Galilee.[18] Similarly, there was bound to be violent hostility between a scribal class such as the Pharisees, whose status was acquired through the diligent and arduous pursuit of religious learning, and a priestly aristocracy whose advantageous status was inherited through no distinctive personal merit.[19]

Nor was it surprising that the scribal class insisted that the ways in which it excelled, namely, learning and meticulous ritual discipline, were uniquely prized by God, or that the Galileans were hostile to both the inherited sacerdotal status of the priests and the scribal learning and ritual discipline of the Pharisees. Nor, in contrast to Buber's negative views on ritual and religious law, was there anything dead, ossified, or devoid of spirit in the bitter quarrels between the rival groups over such questions as tithing, taxing, ritual purity and impurity, sabbath observance, sacrifice, and sacerdotal authority. On the contrary, the questions at issue constituted the language in which was expressed the highly complicated social and economic relationships between the warring groups within the household of Israel.

As we have said, until the Judaeo-Roman War, these rivalries were intramural. When the parting of the ways between Church and Synagogue finally came, it was as much due to the way the two groups were compelled to deal with the political consequences of the fall of Jerusalem as to any strictly religious conflict. Regrettably, nowhere in Buber's analysis of Jesus and Paul in *Two Types of Faith,* which Gershom

Scholem has called Buber's weakest book, do we find any consideration of these salient historical issues.[20]

Because of the limited scope of this essay, we cannot consider the response of the Christian Church to the fall of Jerusalem. Let us, however, consider briefly the way the Pharisees responded. Immediately before the Judaeo-Roman War, the Pharisees seem to have been a relatively small table fellowship group with little political power within the Jewish community. Afterwards, the Pharisees undertook the work of religious and communal reconstruction which permitted the stricken community to survive the loss of the Temple and to find in the synagogue and school adequate surrogates for the vanquished Temple cult. Nevertheless, without the active political backing of Roman Imperial authorities, it would have been impossible for the Pharisees and the rabbinic party to have assumed religious and political leadership of the Jewish community. Moreover, there was a heavy political and psychological price to be paid for Roman backing of the Pharisees.

In the aftermath of 70 the Romans sought loyal and dependable agents who could govern the volatile Jewish community on their behalf. Of the competing Jewish groups, only the pacifist wing of the Pharisees met the Roman political requirements. The Zealots had fought a war to the death against Rome and had been forced to leave the scene; the priestly aristocrats had lost their central institution and had been compromised as collaborationists. Only the Pharisees were prepared to take the lead and to train their community to live within the confines of Roman domination. In return for their submission the Pharisees sought and received imperial assurance of Jewish religious and cultural autonomy. Once this issue was settled, the Pharisees, together with some former scribes, shaped the distinctive institutions and literature that were to characterize the diaspora for the next two thousand years. The arrangement first made by the Pharisees under Yohanan ben Zakkai and the Romans under Vespasian endured until the time of the Nazis.[21]

Every aspect of diaspora Judaism for the next two thousand years was decisively affected by the political bargain made by the Romans and the Pharisees in the aftermath of 70. Implicit in the rise of the Pharisees to dominance was the enforced renunciation of resort to force and power as an option available to Jews in achieving their ends. Without an independent political entity it is in any event impossible to wage war effectively. The Zealots at Masada preferred to die rather than live in a world where their dignity and their security were entirely depend upon the power of strangers. By contrast, under Yohanan ben Zakkai, the Pharisees were not only prepared to accept the risks of total powerlessness; they were also prepared to create a religious culture predicated upon that powerlessness and to train two thousand years of Jews to eschew force and aggression in their relations with their neighbors and their hosts. This was a calculated risk. It entailed the very real possibility that at regular intervals Jews might become the impotent objects of violent aggression.

It is my conviction that no other realistic course was available to the Jews at the time or thereafter in the European diaspora. Hence, I find absolutely no fault in Yohanan and his peers for having accepted Roman domination. Nevertheless, it must be acknowledged that every single indignity visited upon the Jews of the diaspora during the next two thousand years, including the horrors of the Holocaust, was an absolutely predictable consequence of the conditions accepted by their classic religious leaders. The Pharisees consented to lead a community whose dignity and security rested upon the power, the interests, and the whim of strangers, who more often than not regarded the Jews as enemies. The Pharisees took the daring risk that Caesar would be a trustworthy master. Unfortunately, they could not guarantee that *every* heir to the power and authority of Caesar would also refrain from abusing his unlimited power over the Jews.

It must be remembered that Adolf Hitler was the legitimate head of the German Reich and, as such, an heir to the power and authority of the Caesars. It was he who finally utilized the power renounced by the Pharisees to bring about the degradation and annihilation of every single Jew within his grasp. The extermination of the Jews of Europe during World War II must be seen as part of the total price, albeit long delayed, which was exacted from the Jewish community for its defeat in 70.

When seen in this light, the Holocaust raises some exceedingly urgent questions about the relationship between power and dignity. The Holocaust reminds us that he who lacks the power to defend himself, yet is unprepared to choose death, must be prepared for the possibility that an adversary may inflict upon him and his family any obscenity whatsoever, as indeed was the lot of the Jews during World War II. This sad fact about the human condition was clearly understood by the Zealots at Masada. They chose death rather than to endure the predictable consequences of impotent servility.[22]

I regret to report that I find no discussion of the relationship between power and dignity in Buber's presentation of the dynamics of
interpersonal encounter in *I and Thou,* in spite of the fact that no people
was ever compelled to endure a more total assault on its very being than
the community of which he was so important a figure. Instead, Buber
presents us with descriptions of encounters between abstract personal
pronouns, without taking cognizance of the inherent absence of individual specificity of all such forms of speech.[23] Buber presents us with
images of totally unspecified I's and Thou's relating to each other in
openness and mutuality, as if mutual acceptance in the real world can
ever ignore the claims of class, caste, status, and power. Nor is it
sufficient to dismiss the issue of the abuse of the powerless by the powerful as yet another instance of I-It. The world is the arena in which men
and women of unequal power confront each other. Openness, mutuality, and acceptance are only possible between those who are more or less
equal in station, actually only between those possessed of relatively equal
power. When one thinks of those Jews who were compelled to strip
naked and lie down sardine-fashion in mass graves to await their death
at the hands of *SS Einsatzkommandoes,* those camp-inmates who were
compelled to submit to the mutilation of their sex organs in SS medical
experiments, and those women who were compelled to serve as military
Feldhüre, we have an image of the extent to which dignity is always
dependent upon power. Yet, *nowhere in Buber's description of the world of
human mutuality or in his descriptions of the need to meet and redeem those
committed to the path of evil do we find the issue of power seriously raised.*
Instead, we find such utopian admonitions as that Buber offered in 1919
to his German fellow-citizens at the moment their country was being
lacerated by the postwar problems of defeat, revolution and civic disor-
der:

> You, imprisoned in shells in which society, state, church, school,
> economy, public opinion, and your own pride have stuck you,
> indirect ones among direct ones break through shells, become di-
> rect; man have contact with man! . . . You shall not withhold your-
> selves![24]

Perhaps impressive as rhetoric, one wonders to what avail such counsel
could be in solving the problems Germans had to contend with at the
time.

Nor does the counsel he offered his own Jewish community at the time of the Nazi seizure of power ring less hollow despite its characteristically utopian rhetoric. In 1933 he admonished German Jewry:

> If we would turn to Him, abandon the false freedom with all its deceptive assurances, turn to God's freedom which is binding to God, then this reeling through the dark mountain pass will reveal itself as a way, our way to the light.[25]

Again one wonders of what avail was Buber's counsel when his people were confronting their most dangerous hour.

Could it be that Buber was incapable of dealing responsibly with the problem of power, a problem which is never irrelevant to interpersonal encounter, because he came from a community of people whose political perspectives had been distorted by the fact that for two thousand years they had experienced power primarily as its objects? Could it have been that Buber was more the heir of the traditions of the Pharisees and their bargain with Caesar, with all of the Caesars, than his heterodoxy might initially indicate? Could it have been that nothing in his background, training or social milieu prepared him to face the issue of power realistically in his life, his thought, or his career as a Jewish leader?

One also wonders to what extent this unfamiliarity with the inner workings of political power was operative in the intense distrust of the state and its institutions that characterized both Buber's Zionism and his socialism. Buber's inability to deal realistically with the world of politics was noted by his admirer Paul Tillich. Tillich observed that in his distrust of politics, Buber relegated the state "almost completely to the 'demons' and to the absolutized I-It relationship." It was for that reason, according to Tillich, that Buber affirmed the Zionist movement as a *messianic* attempt to create a *Gemeinschaft* while negating it "as a political attempt to create a state." Tillich maintained that Buber was profoundly mistaken, for "history . . . seems to show that without the shell of a state, a community cannot exist. . . . "[26] Unlike Buber, Tillich apparently understood why political Zionism had arisen.

Buber's unrealism in dealing with the world of actuality can be documented from many sources, but his position on the trial and execution of Adolf Eichmann is particularly instructive.[27] Let it be said at the outset that I agree with Buber that the State of Israel was in error in executing Eichmann and that it would have been a far more appropriate punishment for Eichmann to have lived out his natural life as a prisoner of the very people he did so much to destroy. What I find problematic are the reasons Buber offered for the stand he took.

In the first place, Buber questioned the legitimacy of a Jewish court sitting in judgment over Eichmann. Instead, he favored the convening of an international court in Jerusalem. Among his reasons were: (*a*) he did not believe that the victims should be the judges; (*b*) he maintained that Eichmann's crimes against humanity were no less monstrous than his crimes against the Jews; and (*c*) he opposed the death sentence because he did not believe that the state has the right to take a man's life. But, if victims are to be excluded from executing judgment upon those that have assaulted them, who is to assume that responsibility? Where can we find a disinterested agency of justice belonging to no state yet possessing a state's power both to pass and to render justice? Does not the sad history of the United Nations indicate the impossibility of finding such a disinterested agency?

Moreover, Buber was profoundly mistaken in regarding the State of Israel as a victim of Eichmann or any other Nazi. The state was founded largely because of the terrible lessons to be drawn from the experience of Eichmann's victims, but it itself was no victim. On the contrary, the purpose of the state was to offer the hope that the successor Jewish community would no longer be the gathering place of future defenseless victims. This meant that the State of Israel not only had the right but was compelled to acquire and, at times, to employ instruments of coercion against both internal and external adversaries. Regrettably, human nature is such that this may at times involve war and capital punishment. To assert, as did Buber, that the state has no right to take human life is to betray a fundamental ignorance of the nature of political sovereignty as well as the imperatives confronting a sovereign state. A state founded on law has no right *capriciously* to take human life, but to ask that the state unconditionally forgo that right is tantamount to asking for its ultimate dissolution.

Here again we see Buber's consistent failure to deal seriously and responsibly with the life and death problems which confronted his own people at a time in their history when their survival was called radically into question both in Europe and in the Middle East. Buber's failure to take the Holocaust seriously as a theological problem was in fact a reflection of a larger inability to deal realistically with the world of concrete actuality.

As is well known, Buber used his enormous international prestige publicly to advocate the establishment of a bi-national Arab-Jewish state. Buber made his views known in 1946 before the ovens had cooled, when Great Britain was attempting to resolve the question of the postwar future of Palestine.[28] In any multi-national state composed of rival communities, the crucial question is often, which community shall possess a monopoly of the means of coercion? A bi-national state was impossible in Palestine because neither the Jews nor the Arabs could trust the other community with control over the state's instruments of coercion. In spite of the Holocaust's bitter lessons, this issue was characteristically ignored by Buber.

Finally, Buber's assertion that Eichmann's crimes were as much "crimes against humanity" as they were against the Jews reveals once again Buber's consistent evasion of the concrete and the specific, whether he was employing ambiguous personal pronouns totally devoid of identifiable content such as "I" and "Thou" to describe interpersonal encounter, whether he was holding forth on an ineffable divine-human encounter which eluded all of the verifications of ordinary discourse, or whether he was dealing with the historical agonies of his own people.

Let us remember who Eichmann was. He was a middle-level SS officer who was specifically charged with important responsibilities in the so-called Final Solution of the Jewish problem. He was at no time charged with responsibility in the annihilation of an abstraction, "humanity"; he did have a leading role in the physical destruction of Europe's Jews. Upon first hearing, Buber's phrase "crimes against humanity" does seem to be an appropriate description of the Holocaust. Upon reflection, it is apparent that humanity is a term of such broad generality as to be without meaningful content. In the Final Solution it was not humanity but a very specific community that suffered.

Regrettably, there is an overload of evidence that the Final Solution was in fact welcomed by a goodly portion of "humanity," as long as the Germans did the dirty work. In the summer of 1939, the Polish government informed the world that Poland's number one problem was to get rid of its Jewish population;[29] nor was the Final Solution unwelcome to the wartime British government which was concerned lest hordes of Jews survive and seek to enter Palestine, thereby destabilizing England's "lifeline to India;"[30] even highly influential members of the wartime Roosevelt administration regarded the Final Solution as a convenient means of eliminating an unwelcome population that might otherwise have sought to enter the United States.[31]

The more one studies the Holocaust, the more apparent it becomes that, far from being a crime against humanity, a very significant proportion of the political and the religious leaders of the Western world regarded it as a convenient operation so long as their police and armed forces were not directly involved.[32] When Buber asserted that Eichmann's crimes against humanity were at least as great as his crimes against the Jewish people, he was in effect diminishing the significance of the real violence done to real people by likening it to an empty and misleading abstraction. Here again we find a strange inability on Buber's part to take seriously concrete instances of evil, suffering, and tragedy.

It is sometimes said that Buber was a poet and that we must not expect his thought to have much relevance in the domain of practical affairs, but it was Buber himself who taught us that the fundamental reality of human existence is to be found not in conceptual abstractions, but in concrete human relationships. In examining his life and thought in the light of the agony of his time and community, we do no more than take his own teachings seriously. When measured by such a standard, it is difficult to avoid the conclusion that a man whose thought had so little relevance to the concrete experience of his own time and people is hardly likely to be of much relevance to ours. When we compare Buber's life and thought with that of Rabbi Yohanan ben Zakkai in ancient times, or Karl Barth and Paul Tillich in modern times, we note that all these men lived through overwhelmingly important historical crises. However, unlike Buber, their teachings were directly relevant to their times and each contributed in his own way to the work of reconstruction which followed the misfortunes of their era. We look in vain for such relevance in Buber.

Perhaps the real question we must ask is why Buber achieved the worldwide eminence he did. Perhaps Buber's eminence reveals more about us than it does about him. There were other great Jewish teachers in our terrible century. Why did all of us bestow our laurels upon him? When Buber's life and thought is viewed in the light of the Holocaust, I must confess that I have no answer to that question. Of one thing, however, I am certain. We needed him. Why, I do not know.

NOTES

1. Some of the representative writings in the field of contemporary Jewish Holocaust theology include: Emil Fackenheim, *God's Presence in History* (New

York: New York University Press, 1970); Irving Greenberg, "Cloud of Smoke, Pillar of Fire: Judaism, Christianity and Modernity After the Holocaust," in *Auschwitz: Beginning of a New Era? Reflections on the Holocaust,* ed. Eva Fleischner (New York: Ktav, 1977), 26–55; Jacob Neusner, "The Implications of the Holocaust," *The Journal of Religion* 53, no. 3 (July 1973); Elie Wiesel, "Jewish Values in the Post-Holocaust Future: A Symposium," *Judaism* 16 (Summer 1967): 298ff.; Richard L. Rubenstein, *After Auschwitz* (Indianapolis: Bobbs-Merrill, 1966); Richard L. Rubenstein, *The Religious Imagination* (Indianapolis: Bobbs-Merrill, 1968).

2. See Michael Berenbaum, "Elie Wiesel and Contemporary Jewish Theology," *Conservative Judaism* 30, no. 3 (Spring 1976): 19–39.

3. G. W. F. Hegel, *The Philosophy of Right,* trans. T. M. Knox (Oxford: Oxford University Press), 12–13.

4. Martin Buber, *Pointing the Way,* ed. and trans. Maurice S. Friedman (New York: Harper Torchbooks, 1957), 238.

5. Martin Buber, *Eclipse of God: Studies in the Relation Between Philosophy and Religion* (New York: Harper and Row, 1952).

6. Buber, *Eclipse of God,* 129–30.

7. Martin Buber, *I and Thou,* trans. Walter Kaufmann (New York: Charles Scribner's Sons, 1970), 158. This edition hereafter referred to as *I and Thou.*

8. Buber, *I and Thou,* 127.

9. See Gunther Bornkamm, *Jesus of Nazareth,* trans. Irene and Fraser McLuskey with James M. Robinson (London: Hodder and Stoughton, 1960), 124–29. Regrettably, Bornkamm's excellent description of Jesus' sense of trust and intimacy in his relationship with God as Father is marred by Bornkamm's insistence on dichotomizing Jesus' experience and that of his predecessors.

10. Buber, *I and Thou,* 68. I have, however, used "Thou" where Kaufmann uses "You" in his translation.

11. On Buber's rejection of Jewish religious law, see Chaim Potok, "Martin Buber and the Jews," *Commentary,* March 1965, 43–49.

12. This is clearly seen in the explicit rejection of Auschwitz as divine punishment in the writings of the Orthodox Jewish scholar Irving Greenberg. See his article, "Cloud of Smoke, Pillar of Fire: Judaism, Christianity and Modernity," cited above in note 1.

13. "The destruction of Jerusalem and the Temple by the Gentiles sent a shock wave through the Jewish-Christian world whose importance it is impossible to exaggerate. Indeed, much of the subsequent literature of both Judaism and Christianity took the form it did precisely in an attempt to come to terms with the catastrophe of A.D. 70." Norman Perrin, *The New Testament: An Introduction* (New York: Harcourt, Brace and Jovanovich, 1974), 40–41; see S. G .F. Brandon, *The Fall of Jerusalem and the Christian Church* (London: S.P.C.K., 1968), 154–66 and 185–205; Jacob Neusner, *From Politics to Piety: The Emergence of Pharissaic Judaism* (Englewood Cliffs, N.J.: Prentice-Hall, 1973), 143–54.

14. On the concept of redemptive media, see Kenelm Burridge, *New Heaven New Earth: A Study of Millennarian Activities* (New York: Schocken, 1969), 6–7. I am indebted to Sheldon Isenberg for its application to the interpretation of first-century Judaism and Christianity. See his "Power Through Temple and

Torah in Greco-Roman Palestine," in *Morton Smith Festschrift,* ed. Jacob Neusner (Leiden: Brill, 1975), 24–52.

15. See Richard L. Rubenstein, *My Brother Paul* (New York: Harper and Row, 1972), 144–73.

16. Martin Buber, *Two Types of Faith,* trans. Norman P. Goldhawk (London: Routledge and Kegan Paul, 1951), 43–50.

17. Both Paul and his Pharisaic contemporaries held that death came into the world as a result of Adam's sin. Both believed that a person wholly without sin could live forever. The rabbis believed that there was as yet no such person. The connection between sin and death is succinctly stated by Paul: "It was through one man that sin entered the world and through sin death. . . . " Romans 4:12. For a summary of comparable rabbinic views, see Richard L. Rubenstein, *The Religious Imagination: A Study in Psychoanalysis and Jewish Theology* (Indianapolis: Bobbs-Merrill, 1968), 43ff.

18. See S. G. F. Brandon, *Jesus and the Zealots: A Study in the Political Factor in Primitive Christianity* (New York: Charles Scribner's Sons, 1967), 54ff. Also Martin Hengel, *Die Zeloten* (Leiden: Brill, 1961), 57ff.

19. See Jacob Neusner, *First Century Judaism in Crisis* (Nashville: Abingdon, 1975), 34–37.

20. Gershom Scholem, *On Jews and Judaism in Crisis* (New York: Schocken, 1976), 164.

21. Neusner, *From Politics to Piety,* 153ff.

22. This was clearly understood by Josephus in his version of Eleazar ben Yair's speech to the men and women defending Masada in which Eleazar counsels his followers to choose death rather than surrender to the Romans. Flavius Josephus, *The Jewish War,* trans. H. St. John Thackeray (Cambridge: Harvard University Press, 1968), 7:320–88.

23. This point is made in an unpublished paper by Professor Steven Katz of Dartmouth, "A Critical Review of Martin Buber's Epistemology of I-Thou." The abstract character of personal pronouns is a crucial issue in Hegel's philosophy. Regrettably, I know of no discussion of this issue by Buber although it is highly relevant to his fundamental categories of I-Thou and I-It. See G. W. F. Hegel, *Phänomenologie des Geistes* (Hamburg: Felix Meiner, 1952), 78–79.

24. Buber, "What is to be Done" (1919), in *Pointing the Way,* ed. and trans. Maurice Friedman (New York: Harper and Row, 1963), 109.

25. This statement is cited by Greta Schaeder, *The Hebrew Humanism of Martin Buber,* trans. Noah J. Jacobs (Detroit: Wayne State University Press, 1973), 197.

26. Paul Tillich, "Martin Buber and Christian Thought," *Commentary* 5, no. 6 (June 1948): 521.

27. Buber's views on the Eichmann trial are sympathetically interpreted by Aubrey Hodes, *Martin Buber: An Intimate Portrait* (New York: Viking, 1971), 111–16.

28. Proceedings of the Anglo-American Commission on Palestine, 1946, cited in Hodes. For a sympathetic view of Buber's political stand on Zionism, see Hodes, 90–104.

29. See Celia S. Heller, *On the Edge of Destruction: Jews of Poland between Two World Wars* (New York: Columbia University Press, 1977), 138–39.

30. See Martin Gilbert, "Britain, Palestine and the Jews: The Evolution of the 1939 Palestine White Paper" (Oxford: Centre for Postgraduate Hebrew Studies, 1977). This is available in pamphlet form and was originally given at Oxford as a lecture.

31. For a full discussion of this bitter issue, see Henry Feingold, *The Politics of Rescue: The Roosevelt Administration and the Holocaust, 1938–1945* (New Brunswick: Rutgers University Press, 1970).

32. Full discussion of this issue would require an examination of the response of the western governments and the Christian Church to *what they knew* about the extermination process as well as an inquiry concerning whether they perceived the extermination process to be serving their interests. The recent release by the CIA of aerial photographs of Auschwitz taken by the United States Army Air Force in which lines of victims are clearly visible, waiting their turn for the gas chambers, demonstrates that, in addition to verbal reports by survivors and others, the American government had photographic corroboration of the testimony. Although installations were bombed by the western powers five miles from Auschwitz, no attempt was made to disrupt the killing operation by the British or American air forces, in spite of the fact that they had complete control of the air in the region. On December 12, 1942, Josef Goebbels wrote in his diary, "At bottom, I believe that both the English and the Americans are happy that we are exterminating the Jewish riffraff." Goebbels may not have been entirely wrong in his perception. See Richard L. Rubenstein, *The Cunning of History: Mass Death and the American Future* (New York: Harper and Row, 1975), 18ff., for a discussion of this painful issue.

The Uses of Diversity

Clifford Geertz

1

Anthropology, my *fröhliche Wissenschaft,* has been fatally involved over the whole course of its history (a long one, if you start it with Herodotus; rather short, if you start it with Tylor) with the vast variety of ways in which men and women have tried to live their lives. At some points, it has sought to deal with that variety by capturing it in some universalizing net of theory: evolutionary stages, pan-human ideas or practices, or transcendental forms (structures, archetypes, subterranean grammars). At others, it has stressed particularity, idiosyncrasy, incommensurability—cabbages and kings. But recently it has found itself faced with something new: the possibility that the variety is rapidly softening into a paler, and narrower, spectrum. We may be faced with a world in which there simply aren't any more headhunters, matrilinealists, or people who predict the weather from the entrails of a pig. Difference will doubtless remain—the French will never eat salted butter. But the good old days of widow burning and cannibalism are gone forever.

In itself, as a professional issue, this process of the softening of cultural contrast (assuming it is real) is perhaps not so disturbing. Anthropologists will simply have to learn to make something of subtler differences, and their writings may grow more shrewd if less spectacular. But it raises a broader issue, moral, aesthetic and cognitive at once, that is much more troubling, and which lies at the center of much current discussion about how it is that values are to be justified: what I will call, just to have something that sticks in the mind, The Future of Ethnocentrism.

I shall come back to some of those more general discussions after a bit, for it is toward them that my overall concern is directed; but as a way into the problem I want to begin with the presentation of an argument, unusual I think and more than a little disconcerting, which the

French anthropologist Claude Lévi-Strauss develops at the beginning of his collection of essays contentiously entitled (contentiously, at least for an anthropologist) *The View from Afar—Le regard éloigné.*

2

Lévi-Strauss's argument arose in the first place in response to a UN-ESCO invitation to deliver a public lecture to open The International Year to Combat Racism and Racial Discrimination, which, in case you missed it, was 1971. "I was chosen," he writes,

> . . . because twenty years earlier I had written [a pamphlet called] "Race and History" for UNESCO [in which] I had stated a few basic truths. . . . [In] 1971, I soon realized that UNESCO expected me [simply] to repeat them. But twenty years earlier, in order to serve the international institutions, which I felt I had to support more than I do today, I had somewhat overstated my point in the conclusion to "Race and History." Because of my age perhaps, and certainly because of reflections inspired by the present state of the world, I was now disgusted by this obligingness and was convinced that, if I was to be useful to UNESCO and fulfill my commitment honestly, I should have to speak in complete frankness.

As usual, that turned out not to be altogether a good idea, and something of a farce followed. Members of the UNESCO staff were dismayed that "I had challenged a catechism [the acceptance of which] had allowed them to move from modest jobs in developing countries to sanctified positions as executives in an international institution." The then Director General of UNESCO, another determined Frenchman, unexpectedly took the floor so as to reduce Lévi-Strauss's time to speak and thus force him to make the "improving" excisions that had been suggested to him. Lévi-Strauss, *incorrigible,* read his entire text, apparently at high speed, in the time left.

All that aside, a normal day at the UN, the problem with Lévi-Strauss's talk was that in it "I rebelled against the abuse of language by which people tend more and more to confuse racism . . . with attitudes that are normal, even legitimate, and in any case, unavoidable"—that is, though he does not call it that, ethnocentrism.

Ethnocentrism, Lévi-Strauss argues in that piece, "Race and Culture," and somewhat more technically in another, "The Anthropologist and the Human Condition," written about a decade further on, is not only not in itself a bad thing, but, at least so long as it does not get out of hand, rather a good one. Loyalty to a certain set of values inevitably makes people "partially or totally insensitive to other values" to which other people, equally parochial, are equally loyal. "It is not at all invidious to place one way of life or thought above all others or to feel little drawn to other values." Such "relative incommunicability" does not authorize anyone to oppress or destroy the values rejected or those who carry them. But, absent that, "it is not at all repugnant":

> It may even be the price to be paid so that the systems of values of each spiritual family or each community are preserved and find within themselves the resources necessary for their renewal. If . . . human societies exhibit a certain optimal diversity beyond which they cannot go, but below which they can no longer descend without danger, we must recognize that, to a large extent, this diversity results from the desire of each culture to resist the cultures surrounding it, to distinguish itself from them—in short to be itself. Cultures are not unaware of one another, they even borrow from one another on occasion; but, in order not to perish, they must in other connections remain somewhat impermeable toward one another.

It is thus not only an illusion that humanity can wholly free itself from ethnocentrism, "or even that it will care to do so"; it would not be a good thing if it did do so. Such a "freedom" would lead to a world "whose cultures, all passionately fond of one another, would aspire only to celebrate one another, in such confusion that each would lose any attraction it could have for the others and its own reason for existing."

Distance lends, if not enchantment, anyway indifference, and thus integrity. In the past, when so-called primitive cultures were only very marginally involved with one another—referring to themselves as "The True Ones," "The Good Ones," or just "The Human Beings," and dismissing those across the river or over the ridge as "earth monkeys" or "louse eggs," that is, not, or not fully, human—cultural integrity was readily maintained. A "profound indifference to other cultures was . . . a guarantee that they could exist in their own manner and on their own terms." Now, when such a situation clearly no longer obtains, and everyone, increasingly crowded on a small planet, is deeply interested in everyone else, and in everyone else's business, the possibility of the loss of such integrity, because of the loss of such indifference, looms. Ethnocentrism can perhaps never entirely disappear, being "consubstantial with our species," but it can grow dangerously weak, leaving us prey to a sort of moral entropy:

> We are doubtless deluding ourselves with a dream when we think that equality and fraternity will some day reign among human beings without compromising their diversity. However, if humanity is not resigned to becoming the sterile consumer of values that it managed to create in the past... capable only of giving birth to bastard works, to gross and puerile inventions, [then] it must learn once again that all true creation implies a certain deafness to the appeal of other values, even going so far as to reject them if not denying them altogether. For one cannot fully enjoy the other, identify with him, and yet at the same time remain different. When integral communication with the other is achieved completely, it sooner or later spells doom for both his and my creativity. The great creative eras were those in which communication had become adequate for mutual stimulation by remote partners, yet was not so frequent or so rapid as to endanger the indispensable obstacles between individuals and groups or to reduce them to the point where overly facile exchanges might equalize and nullify their diversity.

Whatever one thinks of all this, or however surprised one is to hear it coming from an anthropologist, it certainly strikes a contemporary chord. The attractions of "deafness to the appeal of other values" and of a relax-and-enjoy-it approach to one's imprisonment in one's own cultural tradition are increasingly celebrated in recent social thought. Unable to embrace either relativism or absolutism, the first because it disables judgment, the second because it removes it from history, our philosophers, historians, and social scientists turn toward the sort of we-are-we and they-are-they *imperméabilité* Lévi-Strauss recommends. Whether one regards this as arrogance made easy, prejudice justified, or as the splendid, here-stand-I honesty of Flannery O'Connor's "when in Rome do as you done in Milledgeville," it clearly puts the question of The Future of Ethnocentrism—and of cultural diversity—in rather a new light. Is drawing back, distancing elsewhere, The View from Afar, really the way to escape the desperate tolerance of UNESCO cosmopolitan-ism? Is the alternative to moral entropy moral narcissism?

3

The forces making for a warmer view of cultural self-centeredness over the last twenty-five or thirty years are multiple. There are those "state of the world" matters to which Lévi-Strauss alludes, and most especially the failure of most Third World countries to live up to the thousand-flowers hopes for them current just before and just after their independence struggles. Amin, Bokassa, Pol Pot, Khomeini at the extremes, Marcos, Mobuto, Sukarno, and Mrs. Gandhi less extravagantly, have put something of a chill on the notion that there are worlds elsewhere to which our own compares clearly ill. There is the successive unmask-ing of the Marxist utopias—the Soviet Union, China, Cuba, Vietnam. And there is the weakening of the Decline of the West pessimism in-duced by world war, world depression, and the loss of empire. But there is also, and I think not least important, the rise in awareness that universal consensus—trans-national, trans-cultural, even trans-class—on norma-tive matters is not in the offing. Everyone—Sikhs, Socialists, Positivists, Irishmen—is not going to come around to a common opinion con-cerning what is decent and what is not, what is just and what is not, what is beautiful and what is not, what is reasonable and what is not; not soon, perhaps not ever.

If one abandons (and of course not everyone, perhaps not even most everyone, has) the idea that the world is moving toward essential agreement on fundamental matters, or even, as with Lévi-Strauss, that it should, then the appeal of relax-and-enjoy-it ethnocentrism naturally grows. If our values cannot be disentangled from our history and our institutions and nobody else's can be disentangled from theirs, then there would seem to be nothing for it but to follow Emerson and stand on our own feet and speak with our own voice. "I hope to suggest," Richard Rorty writes in a recent piece, marvelously entitled "Postmodernist Bourgeois Liberalism," "how [we postmodernist bourgeois liberals] might convince our society that loyalty to itself is loyalty enough . . . that it need be responsible only to its own traditions. . . . "[1] What an anthro-pologist in search of "the consistent laws underlying the observable di-versity of beliefs and institutions" (Lévi-Strauss) arrives at from the side of rationalism and high science, a philosopher, persuaded that "there is no 'ground' for [our] loyalties and convictions save the fact that the beliefs and desires and emotions which buttress them overlap those of lots of other members of the group with which we identify for purposes of moral and political deliberation . . . " arrives at from the side of pragmatism and prudential ethics.

The similarity is even greater despite the very different starting points from which these two savants depart (Kantianism without a transcendental subject, Hegelianism without an absolute spirit), and the even more different ends toward which they tend (a trim world of transposable forms, a disheveled one of coincident discourses), because Rorty, too, regards invidious distinctions between groups as not only natural but essential to moral reasoning.

> [The] naturalized Hegelian analogue of [Kantian] "intrinsic human dignity" is the comparative dignity of a group with which a person identifies herself. Nations or churches or movements are, on this view, shining historical examples not because they reflect rays emanating from a higher source, but because of contrast-effects—comparison with worse communities. Persons have dignity not as an interior luminescence, but because they share in such contrast-effects. It is a corollary of this view that the moral justification of the institutions and practices of one's group—e.g., of the contemporary bourgeoisie—is mostly a matter of historical narratives (including scenarios about what is likely to happen in certain future contingencies), rather than of philosophical meta-narratives. The principal backup for historiography is not philosophy but the arts, which serve to develop and modify a group's self-image by, for example, apotheosizing its heroes, diabolizing its enemies, mounting dialogues among its members, and refocusing its attention.

Now, as a member of both these intellectual traditions myself, of the scientific study of cultural diversity by profession and of postmodern bourgeois liberalism by general persuasion, my own view, to get round now to that, is that an easy surrender to the comforts of merely being ourselves, cultivating deafness and maximizing gratitude for not having been born a Vandal or an Ik, will be fatal to both. An anthropology so afraid of destroying cultural integrity and creativity, our own and everyone else's, by drawing near to other people, engaging them, seeking to grasp them in their immediacy and their difference, is destined to perish of an inanition no manipulations of objectivized data sets can compensate. Any moral philosophy so afraid of becoming entangled in witless relativism or transcendental dogmatism that it can think of nothing better to do with other ways of going at life than make them look worse than our own is destined merely to conduce (as someone has said of the writings of V. S. Naipaul, perhaps our leading adept at constructing such "contrast effects") toward making the world safe for condescension. Trying to save two disciplines from themselves at once may seem like hubris. But when one has double citizenships one has double obligations.

4

Their different demeanors and their different hobby horses notwithstanding (and I confess myself very much closer to Rorty's messy populism than to Lévi-Strauss's fastidious mandarinism—in itself, perhaps, but a cultural bias of my own), these two versions of to-each-his-own morality rest, in part anyway, on a common view of cultural diversity: namely, that its main importance is that it provides us with, to use a formula of Bernard Williams's, alternatives to us as opposed to alternatives for us. Other beliefs, values, ways of going on, are seen as beliefs we would have believed, values we would have held, ways we would have gone on, had we been born in some other place or some other time than that in which we actually were.

So, indeed, we would have. But such a view seems to make both rather more and rather less of the fact of cultural diversity than it should. Rather more, because it suggests that to have had a different life than one has in fact had is a practical option one has somehow to make one's mind up about (should I have been a Bororo? am I not fortunate not to have been a Hittite?); rather less, because it obscures the power of such diversity, when personally addressed, to transform our sense of what it *is* for a human being, Bororo, Hittite, Structuralist, or Postmodern Bourgeois Liberal, to believe, to value, or to go on: what it is like, as Arthur Danto has remarked, echoing Thomas Nagel's famous question about the bat, "to think the world is flat, that I look irresistible in my Poiret frocks, that the Reverend Jim Jones would have saved me through his love, that animals have no feeling or that flowers do—or that punk is where it's at."[2] The trouble with ethnocentrism is not that it commits us to our own commitments. We are, by definition, so committed, as we are to having our own headaches. The trouble with ethnocentrism is that it impedes us from discovering at what sort of angle, like Forster's Cavafy, we stand to the world; what sort of bat we really are.

This view—that the puzzles raised by the fact of cultural diversity have more to do with our capacity to feel our way into alien sensibilities, modes of thought (punk rock and Poiret frocks) we do not possess, and are not likely to, than they do with whether we can escape preferring our own preferences—has a number of implications which bode ill for a we-are-we and they-are-they approach to things cultural. The first of these, and possibly the most important, is that those puzzles arise not merely at the boundaries of our society, where we would expect them under such an approach, but, so to speak, at the boundaries of ourselves. Foreignness does not start at the water's edge but at the skin's. The sort of idea that both anthropologists since Malinowski and philosophers since Wittgenstein are likely to entertain that, say, Shi'is, being other, present a problem, but, say, soccer fans, being part of us, do not, or at least not of the same sort, is merely wrong. The social world does not divide at its joints into perspicuous we-s with whom we can empathize, however much we differ *with* them, and enigmatical they-s, with whom we cannot, however much we defend to the death their right to differ *from* us. The wogs begin long before Calais.

Both recent anthropology of the From the Native's Point of View sort (which I practice) and recent philosophy of the Forms of Life sort (to which I adhere) have been made to conspire, or seem to conspire, in obscuring this fact by a chronic misapplication of their most powerful and most important idea: the idea that meaning is socially constructed.

The perception that meaning, in the form of interpretable signs—sounds, images, feelings, artifacts, gestures—comes to exist only within language games, communities of discourse, intersubjective systems of reference, ways of worldmaking; that it arises within the frame of concrete social interaction in which something is a something for a you and a me, and not in some secret grotto in the head; and that it is through and through historical, hammered out in the flow of events, is read to imply (as, in my opinion, neither Malinowski nor Wittgenstein—nor for that matter Kuhn or Foucault—meant it to imply) that human communities are, or should be semantic monads, nearly windowless. We are, says Lévi-Strauss, passengers in the trains which are our cultures, each moving on its own track, at its own speed, and in its own direction. The trains rolling alongside, going in similar directions and at speeds not too different from our own are at least reasonably visible to us as we look out from our compartments. But trains on an oblique or parallel track which are going in an opposed direction are not. "[We] perceive only a vague, fleeting, barely identifiable image, usually just a momentary blur in our visual field, supplying no information about itself and merely irritating us because it interrupts our placid contemplation of the landscape which serves as the backdrop to our daydreaming." Rorty is more cautious and less poetic, and I sense less interested in other people's trains, so concerned is he where his own is going, but he speaks of a more or less accidental "overlap" of belief systems between "rich North American bourgeois" communities and others that "[we] need to talk with" as enabling "whatever conversation between nations may still be possible." The grounding of feeling, thought, and judgment in a form of life, which indeed is the only place, in my view, as it is in Rorty's, that they can be grounded, is taken to mean that the limits of my world are the limits of my language, which is not exactly what the man said.

What he said, of course, was that the limits of my language are the limits of my world, which implies not that the reach of our minds, of what we can say, think, appreciate, and judge, is trapped within the borders of our society, our country, our class, or our time, but that the reach of our minds, the range of signs we can manage somehow to interpret, is what defines the intellectual, emotional and moral space within which we live. The greater that is, the greater we can make it become by trying to understand what flat earthers or the Reverend Jim Jones (or Iks or Vandals) are all about, what it is like to be them, the clearer we become to ourselves, both in terms of what we see in others that seems remote and what we see that seems reminiscent, what attractive and what repellent, what sensible and what quite mad; oppositions that do not align in any simple way, for there are some things quite appealing about bats, some quite repugnant about ethnographers.

It is, Danto says in that same article I quoted a moment ago, "the gaps between me and those who think differently that I—which is to say everyone, and not simply those segregated by differences in generations, sex, nationality, sect, and even race—[that] define the real boundaries of the self." It is the asymmetries, as he also says, or nearly, between what we believe or feel and what others do, that makes it possible to locate where we now are in the world, how it feels to be there, and where we might or might not want to go. To obscure those gaps and those asymmetries by relegating them to a realm of repressible or ignorable difference, mere unlikeness, which is what ethnocentrism does and is designed to do (UNESCO universalism obscures them—Lévi-Strauss is quite right about that—by denying their reality altogether), is to cut us off from such knowledge and such possibility: the possibility of quite literally, and quite thoroughly, changing our minds.

5

The history of any people separately and all peoples together, and indeed of each person individually, has been a history of such a changing of minds, usually slowly, sometimes more rapidly; or if the idealist sound of that disturbs you (it ought not, it is not idealist, and it denies neither the natural pressures of fact nor the material limits of will), of sign systems, symbolic forms, cultural traditions. Such changes have not necessarily been for the better, perhaps not even normally. Nor have they led to a convergence of views, but rather to a mingling of them. What, back in his blessed Neolithic, was indeed once something at least rather like Lévi-Strauss's world of integral societies in distant communication has turned into something rather more like Danto's postmodern one of clashing sensibilities in inevadable contact. Like nostalgia, diversity is not what it used to be; and the sealing of lives into separate railway carriages to produce cultural renewal or the spacing of them out with contrast-effects to free up moral energies are romantical dreams, not undangerous.

The general tendency that I remarked in opening for the cultural spectrum to become paler and more continuous without becoming less discriminate (indeed, it is probably becoming more discriminate as symbolic forms split and proliferate), alters not just its bearing on moral argument but the character of such argument itself. We have become used to the idea that scientific concepts change with changes in the sort of concerns to which scientists address themselves—that one does not need the calculus to determine the velocity of a chariot or quantal energies to explain the swing of a pendulum. But we are rather less aware that the same thing is true of the speculative instruments (to borrow an old term of I. A. Richards's, which deserves to be resuscitated) of moral reasoning. Ideas which suffice for Lévi-Strauss's magnificent differences do not for Danto's troubling asymmetries; and it is the latter with which we find ourselves increasingly faced.

More concretely, moral issues stemming from cultural diversity (which are, of course, far from being all the moral issues there are) that used to arise, when they arose at all, mainly between societies—the "customs contrary to reason and morals" sort of thing on which imperialism fed—now increasingly arise within them. Social and cultural boundaries coincide less and less closely—there are Japanese in Brazil, Turks on the Main, and West Indian meets East in the streets of Birmingham—a shuffling process which has of course been going on for quite some time (Belgium, Canada, Lebanon, South Africa—and the Caesars' Rome was not all that homogeneous), but which is, by now, approaching extreme and near universal proportions. The day when the American city was the main model of cultural fragmentation and ethnic tumbling is quite gone; the Paris of *nos ancêtres les gaulois* is getting to be about as polyglot, and as polychrome, as Manhattan, and may yet have an Asian mayor (or so, anyway, many of *les gaulois* fear) before New York has a Hispanic one.

This rising within the body of a society, inside the boundaries of a "we," of wrenching moral issues centered around cultural diversity, and the implications that has for our general problem, "the future of ethnocentrism," can perhaps be made rather more vivid with an example; not a made up, science-fiction one about water on anti-worlds or people whose memories interchange while they are asleep, of which philosophers have recently grown rather too fond, in my opinion, but a real one, or at least one represented to me as real by the anthropologist who told it to me: The Case of The Drunken Indian and The Kidney Machine.

The case is simple, however knotted its resolution. The extreme shortage, due to their great expense, of artificial kidney machines led, naturally enough, to the establishment a few years ago of a queuing process for access to them by patients needing dialysis in a government medical program in the southwestern United States directed, also naturally enough, by young, idealistic doctors from major medical schools, largely northeastern. For the treatment to be effective, at least over an extended period of time, strict discipline as to diet and other matters is necessary on the part of the patients. As a public enterprise, governed by antidiscrimination codes, and anyway, as I say, morally motivated, queuing was organized not in terms of the power to pay but simply severity of need and order of application, a policy which led, with the usual twists of practical logic, to the problem of the drunken Indian.

The Indian, after gaining access to the scarce machine refused, to the great consternation of the doctors, to stop, or even control, his drinking, which was prodigious. His position, under some sort of principle like that of Flannery O'Connor's I mentioned earlier of remaining oneself whatever others might wish to make of you, was: I am indeed a drunken Indian, I have been one for quite some time, and I intend to go on being one for as long as you can keep me alive by hooking me up to this damn machine of yours. The doctors, whose values were rather different, regarded the Indian as blocking access to the machine by others on the queue, in no less desperate straits, who could, as they saw it, make better use of its benefits—a young, middle-class type, say, rather like themselves, destined for college and, who knows, medical school. As the Indian was already on the machine by the time the problem became visible they could not quite bring themselves (nor, I suppose, would they have been permitted) to take him off it; but they were very deeply upset—at least as upset as the Indian, who was disciplined enough to show up promptly for all his appointments, was resolute—and surely would have devised some reason, ostensibly medical, to displace him from his position in the queue had they seen in time what was coming. He continued on the machine, and they continued distraught, for several years until, proud, as I imagine him, grateful (though not to the doctors) to have had a somewhat extended life in which to drink, and quite unapologetic, he died.

Now, the point of this little fable in real time is not that it shows how insensitive doctors can be (they were not insensitive, and they had a case), or how adrift Indians have become (he was not adrift, he knew exactly where he was); nor to suggest that either the doctors' values (that is, approximately, ours), the Indian's (that is, approximately, not-ours), or some trans-parte judgment drawn from philosophy or anthropology and issued forth by one of Ronald Dworkin's herculean judges, should have prevailed. It was a hard case and it ended in a hard way; but I cannot see that either more ethnocentrism, more relativism, or more neutrality would have made things any better (though more imagination might have). The point of the fable—I'm not sure it properly has a moral—is that it is this sort of thing, not the distant tribe, enfolded upon itself in coherent difference (the Azande or the Ik that fascinate philosophers only slightly less than science fiction fantasies do, perhaps because they can be made into sublunary Martians and regarded accordingly) that best represents, if somewhat melodramatically, the general form that value conflict rising out of cultural diversity takes nowadays.

The antagonists here, if that's what they were, were not representatives of turned-in social totalities meeting haphazardly along the edges of their beliefs. Indians holding fate at bay with alcohol are as much a part of contemporary America as are doctors correcting it with machines. (If you want to see just how, at least so far as the Indians are concerned—I assume you know about doctors—you can read James Welch's shaking novel, *Winter in the Blood,* where the contrast effects come out rather oddly.) If there was any failure here, and, to be fair, it is difficult at a distance to tell precisely how much there was, it was a failure to grasp, on either side, what it was to be on the other, and thus what it was to be on one's own. No one, at least so it seems, learned very much in this episode about either themselves or about anyone else, and nothing at all, beyond the banalities of disgust and bitterness, about the character of their encounter. It is not the inability of those involved to abandon their convictions and adopt the views of others that makes this little tale seem so utterly depressing. Nor is it their lack of a disincorporated moral rule—The Greatest Good or The Difference Principle (which would seem as a matter of fact, to give different results here)—to which to appeal. It is their inability even to conceive, amid the mystery of difference, how one might get round an all-too-genuine moral asymmetry. The whole thing took place in the dark.

6

What tends to take place in the dark—the only things of which "a certain deafness to the appeal of other values" or a "comparison with worse communities" conception of human dignity would seem to allow—is either the application of force to secure conformity to the values of those who possess the force; a vacuous tolerance that, engaging nothing, changes nothing; or, as here, where the force is unavailable and the tolerance unnecessary, a dribbling out to an ambiguous end.

It is surely the case that there are instances where these are, in fact, the practical alternatives. There doesn't seem much to do about the Reverend Jones, once he is in full cry, but physically to stop him before he hands out the Kool-Aid. If people think punk rock is where it's at, then, at least so long as they don't play it in the subway, it's their ears and their funeral. And it *is* difficult (some bats are battier than others) to know just how one ought to proceed with someone who holds that flowers have feelings and that animals do not. Paternalism, indifference, even superciliousness, are not always unuseful attitudes to take to value differences, even to ones more consequential than these. The problem is to know when they are useful and diversity can safely be left to its connoisseurs, and when, as I think is more often the case, and increasingly so, they are not and it cannot, and something more is needed: an imaginative entry into (and admittance of) an alien turn of mind.

In our society, the connoisseur *par excellence* of alien turns of mind has been the ethnographer (the historian too, to a degree, and in a different way the novelist, but I want to get back on my own reservation), dramatizing oddness, extolling diversity, and breathing broad-mindedness. Whatever differences in method or theory have separated us, we have been alike in that: professionally obsessed with worlds elsewhere and with making them comprehensible first to ourselves and then, through conceptual devices not so different from those of historians and literary ones not so different from those of novelists, to our readers. And so long as those worlds really were elsewhere, where Malinowski found them and Lévi-Strauss remembers them, this was, though difficult enough as a practical task, relatively unproblematical as an analytical one. We could think about "primitives" ("savages," "natives,"...) as we thought about Martians—as possible ways of feeling, reasoning, judging and behaving, of going on, discontinuous with our own, alternatives to us. Now that those worlds and those alien turns of mind are mostly not really elsewhere, but, alternatives for us, hard nearby, instant "gaps between me and those who think differently than I," a certain readjustment in both our rhetorical habits and our sense of mission would seem to be called for.

The uses of cultural diversity, of its study, its description, its analysis, and its comprehension, lie less along the lines of sorting ourselves out from others and others from ourselves so as to defend group integrity and sustain group loyalty than to define the terrain reason must cross if its modest rewards are to be reached and realized. This terrain is uneven, full of sudden faults and dangerous passages where accidents can and do happen, and crossing it, or trying to, does little or nothing to smooth it out to a level, safe, unbroken plain, but simply makes visible its clefts and contours. If our peremptory doctors and our intransigent Indian (or Rorty's "rich North American[s]" and "[those we] need to talk with") are to confront one another in a less destructive way (and it is far from certain—the clefts are real—that they actually can) they must explore the character of the space between them.

It is they themselves who must finally do this; there is no substitute for local knowledge here, nor for courage either. But maps and charts may still be useful, and tables, tales, pictures, and descriptions, even theories, if they attend to the actual, as well. The uses of ethnography are mainly ancillary, but they are nonetheless real; like the compiling of dictionaries or the grinding of lenses, it is, or would be, an enabling discipline. And what it enables, when it does so, is a working contact with a variant subjectivity. It places particular we-s among particular they-s, and they-s among we-s, where all, as I have been saying, already are, however uneasily. It is the great enemy of ethnocentrism, of confining people to cultural planets where the only ideas they need to conjure with are "those around here," not because it assumes people are all alike, but because it knows how profoundly they are not and how unable yet to disregard one another. Whatever once was possible and whatever may now be longed for, the sovereignty of the familiar impoverishes everyone; to the degree it has a future, ours is dark. It is not that we must love one another or die (if that is the case—Blacks and Afrikaners, Arabs and Jews, Tamils and Sinhalese—we are I think doomed). It is that we must know one another, and live with that knowledge, or end marooned in a Beckett-world of colliding soliloquy.

The job of ethnography, or one of them anyway, is indeed to provide, like the arts and history, narratives and scenarios to refocus our attention; not, however, ones that render us acceptable to ourselves by representing others as gathered into worlds we don't want and can't arrive at, but ones which make us visible to ourselves by representing us and everyone else as cast into the midst of a world full of irremovable strangenesses we can't keep clear of.

Until fairly recently (the matter now is changing, in part at least because of ethnography's impact, but mostly because the world is changing) ethnography was fairly well alone in this, for history did in fact spend much of its time comforting our self-esteem and supporting our sense that we were getting somewhere by apotheosizing our heroes and diabolizing our enemies, or with keening over vanished greatness; the social comment of novelists was for the most part internal—one part of Western consciousness holding a mirror, Trollope-flat or Dostoevski-curved, up to another; and even travel writing, which at least attended to exotic surfaces (jungles, camels, bazaars, temples) mostly employed them to demonstrate the resilience of received virtues in trying circumstances—the Englishman remaining calm, the Frenchman rational, the

American innocent. Now, when it is not so alone and the strangenesses it has to deal with are growing more oblique and more shaded, less easily set off as wild anomalies—men who think themselves descended from wallabies or who are convinced they can be murdered with a sidelong glance—its task, locating those strangenesses and describing their shapes, may be in some ways more difficult; but it is hardly less necessary. Imagining difference (which of course does not mean making it up, but making it evident) remains a science of which we all have need.

7

But my purpose here is not to defend the prerogatives of a homespun *Wissenschaft* whose patent on the study of cultural diversity, if it ever had one, has long since expired. My purpose is to suggest that we have come to such a point in the moral history of the world (a history itself of course anything but moral) that we are obliged to think about such diversity rather differently than we have been used to thinking about it. If it is in fact getting to be the case that rather than being sorted into framed units, social spaces with definite edges to them, seriously disparate approaches to life are becoming scrambled together in ill-defined expanses, social spaces whose edges are unfixed, irregular, and difficult to locate, the question of how to deal with the puzzles of judgment to which such disparities give rise takes on a rather different aspect. Confronting landscapes and still lifes is one thing; panoramas and collages quite another.

That it is the latter we these days confront, that we are living more and more in the midst of an enormous collage, seems everywhere apparent. It is not just the evening news where assassinations in India, bombings in Lebanon, coups in Africa, and shootings in Central America are set amid local disasters hardly more legible and followed by grave discussions of Japanese ways of business, Persian forms of passion, or Arab styles of negotiation. It is also an enormous explosion of translation, good, bad, and indifferent, from and to languages—Tamil, Indonesian, Hebrew, and Urdu—previously regarded as marginal and recondite; the migration of cuisines, costumes, furnishings, and decor (caftans in San Francisco, Colonel Sanders in Jogjakarta, bar stools in Kyoto); the appearance of *gamelan* themes in *avant-garde* jazz, Indio myths in Latino novels, magazine images in African painting. But most of all, it is that the person we encounter in the grocery store is as likely, or nearly, to come from Korea as from Iowa, in the post office from Algeria as from the Auvergne, in the bank from Bombay as from Liverpool. Even rural settings, where alikeness is likely to be more entrenched, are not immune: Mexican farmers in the Southwest, Vietnamese fishermen along the Gulf Coast, Iranian physicians in the Midwest.

I need not go on multiplying examples. You can all think of ones of your own out of your own traffickings with your own surroundings. Not all this diversity is equally consequential (Jogja cooking will survive finger-lickin'-good); equally immediate (you don't need to grasp the religious beliefs of the man who sells you postage stamps); nor does it all stem from cultural contrast of a clear-cut sort. But that the world is coming at each of its local points to look more like a Kuwaiti bazaar than like an English gentlemen's club (to instance what, to my mind—perhaps because I have never been in either one of them—are the polar cases) seems shatteringly clear. Ethnocentrism of either the louse eggs or of the there-but-for-the-grace-of-culture sort may or may not be coincident with the human species; but it is now quite difficult for most of us to know just where, in the grand assemblage of juxtaposed difference, to center it. *Les Milieux* are all *mixtes*. They don't make *Umwelte* like they used to do.

Our response to this, so it seems to me, commanding fact, is, so it also seems to me, one of the major moral challenges we these days face, ingredient in virtually all the others we face, from nuclear disarmament to the equitable distribution of the world's resources, and in facing it counsels of indiscriminate tolerance, which are anyway not genuinely meant, and, my target here, of surrender, proud, cheerful, defensive, or resigned, to the pleasures of invidious comparison, serve us equally badly; though the latter is perhaps the more dangerous because the more likely to be followed. The image of a world full of people so passionately fond of each other's cultures that they aspire only to celebrate one another does not seem to me a clear and present danger; the image of one full of people happily apotheosizing their heroes and diabolizing their enemies alas does. It is not necessary to choose, indeed it is necessary not to choose, between cosmopolitanism without content and parochialism without tears. Neither is of use for living in a collage.

To live in a collage one must in the first place render oneself capable of sorting out its elements, determining what they are (which usually involves determining where they come from and what they amounted to when they were there) and how, practically, they relate to one another, without at the same time blurring one's own sense of one's own location and one's own identity within it. Less figuratively, "understanding" in the sense of comprehension, perception, and insight needs to be distinguished from "understanding" in the sense of agreement of opinion, union of sentiment, or commonality of commitment; the *je vous ai compris* that De Gaulle uttered from the *je vous ai compris* the *pieds noirs* heard. We must learn to grasp what we cannot embrace.

The difficulty in this is enormous, as it has always been. Comprehending that which is, in some manner of form, alien to us and likely to remain so, without either smoothing it over with vacant murmurs of common humanity, disarming it with to-each-his-own indifferentism, or dismissing it as charming, lovely even, but inconsequent, is a skill we have arduously to learn, and having learnt it, always very imperfectly, work continuously to keep alive; it is not a connatural capacity, like depth perception or the sense of balance, upon which we can complacently rely.

It is in this, strengthening the power of our imaginations to grasp what is in front of us, that the uses of diversity, and of the study of diversity, lie. If we have (as I admit I have) more than a sentimental sympathy with that refractory American Indian, it is not because we hold his views. Alcoholism is indeed an evil, and kidney machines are ill-applied to its victims. Our sympathy derives from our knowledge of the degree to which he has earned his views and the bitter sense that is therefore in them, our comprehension of the terrible road over which he has had to travel to arrive at them and of what it is—ethnocentrism and the crimes it legitimates—that has made it so terrible. If we wish to be able capaciously to judge, as of course we must, we need to make ourselves able capaciously to see. And for that, what we have already seen—the insides of our railway compartments; the shining historical examples of our nations, our churches, and our movements—is, as engrossing as the one may be and as dazzling as the other, simply not enough.

NOTES

1. *Journal of Philosophy*, 1983, 583–89.
2. "Mind as Feeling; Form as Presence; Langer as Philosopher," *Journal of Philosophy*, 1984, 641–47.

On Ethnocentrism: A Reply to Clifford Geertz

Richard Rorty

In his provocative paper on "The Uses of Diversity," Professor Geertz asserts that ethnocentrism relegates gaps and asymmetries between individuals or groups to "a realm of repressible or ignorable difference, mere unlikeness." This is a good description of how we treat people whom we think not worth understanding: those whom we regard as irredeemably crazy, stupid, base, or sinful. Such people are not viewed as possible conversational partners, but, at most, as means to ends. We think we have nothing to learn from such people, for we would rather die than share the beliefs which we assume are central to their self-identities. Some people think of Jews and atheists in these terms. Others think this way about Nazis and religious fundamentalists.

When we bourgeois liberals find ourselves thinking of people in this way—when, for example, we find ourselves reacting to the Nazis and the fundamentalists with indignation and contempt—we have to think twice. For we are exemplifying the attitude we claim to despise. We would rather die than be ethnocentric, but ethnocentrism is precisely the conviction that one would rather die than share certain beliefs. We then find ourselves wondering whether our own bourgeois liberalism is not just one more example of cultural bias.

This bemusement makes us susceptible to the suggestion that the culture of Western liberal democracy is somehow "on a par" with that of the Vandals and the Ik. So we begin to wonder whether our attempts to get other parts of the world to adopt our culture are different in kind from the efforts of fundamentalist missionaries. If we continue this line of thought too long we become what are sometimes called "wet" liberals. We begin to lose any capacity for moral indignation, any capacity to feel contempt. Our sense of selfhood dissolves. We can no longer feel pride in being bourgeois liberals, in being part of a great tradition, a citizen of no mean culture. We have become so open-minded that our brains have fallen out.

This collapse of moral self-confidence, what Geertz calls "the desperate tolerance of UNESCO cosmopolitanism," provokes a reaction in the direction of anti-anti-ethnocentrism—the direction exemplified by the passages from Lévi-Strauss and myself which Geertz cites. This in turn provokes Geertz's counter-reaction. He says, for example: "Any moral philosophy so afraid of becoming entangled in witless relativism or transcendental dogmatism that it can think of nothing better to do with other ways of going at life than make them look worse than our own is destined merely toward making the world safe for condescension." Geertz fears that if the anti-anti-ethnocentrist reaction goes too far we shall become content to think of human communities as "semantic monads, nearly windowless."

Some human communities are such monads, some not. Our bourgeois liberal culture is not. On the contrary, it is a culture which prides itself on constantly adding on more windows, constantly enlarging its sympathies. It is a form of life which is constantly extending pseudopods and adapting itself to what it encounters. Its sense of its own moral worth is founded on its tolerance of diversity. The heroes it apotheosizes include those who have enlarged its capacity for sympathy and tolerance. Among the enemies it diabolizes are the people who attempt to diminish this capacity, the vicious ethnocentrists. Anti-anti-ethnocentrism is not an attempt to change the habits of our culture, to block the windows up again. Rather, it is an attempt to cope with the phenomenon of wet liberalism by correcting our culture's habit of giving its desire for windows a philosophical foundation. Anti-anti-ethnocentrism does not say that we are trapped within our monad or our language, but merely that the well-windowed monad we live in is no more closely linked to the nature of humanity or the demands of rationality than the relatively windowless monads which surround us.

I shall enlarge on this latter point later, but first I should like to comment on Geertz's Case of the Drunken Indian and the Kidney Machine. This case looks different to me than it does to Geertz. So I shall begin by saying how I see it, and then comment on the way Geertz sees it.

My own reaction to the case as Geertz presents it is that it is not particularly depressing, but rather cheering. It shows our liberal institutions functioning well and smoothly. Geertz says that "queuing [for the kidney machine] was organized in terms of severity of need and order of application." So it should have been. Since, as he says, "the Indian was already on the machine by the time the problem became visible," the doctors "could not quite bring themselves" to take him off. He then adds, in parentheses, "Nor, I suppose, would they have been permitted." Indeed they would not, and this is what I find cheering. If they had tried to take him off the machine, the media and the malpractice lawyers would have been all over them the next day. The whole apparatus of the liberal democratic state, an apparatus to which the press is as central as are the officers of the court, insured that once that Indian had the sense to get into the queue early, he was going to have more years in which to drink than he would otherwise have had.

Geertz says that this was "a hard case and it ended in a hard way." From the legal point of view, surely, it was not a hard case. Procedural justice was visibly done. Nor does it seem hard from a moral point of view. It is morally satisfying to think that life-or-death decisions are made on the basis of "severity of need and priority of application"— rather than, say, on the basis of political or financial clout, family membership, or the sympathies of those present. We take moral pride in the fact that our society hands such decisions over to the mechanisms of procedural justice.

Geertz goes on to say that he "cannot see that either more ethnocentrism, more relativism, or more neutrality would have made things any better (though more imagination might have)." I agree that no philosophical position or strategy could have made things any better, but I am not sure what he thinks imagination could have made better, because I am not sure what needed improvement. I take it that Geertz means that the doctors might have been less upset by the Indian's failure to be a good patient if they had been able to put themselves in the Indian's shoes. But it is not clear that they had any business being so distraught in the first place. We do not really want doctors to differentiate between the values of the lives they are saving, any more than we want defense lawyers to worry too much about the innocence of their clients, or teachers to worry about which students will make the best use of the education they are offering. A society built around procedural justice needs agents who do not look too closely at such matters.

Geertz says that "nobody in this episode learned very much about either themselves or about anyone else," that "the whole thing took place in the dark." At the end of his paper he suggests that what the doctors lacked was "knowledge of the degree to which he [the Indian] has earned his views and the bitter sense that is therefore in them," and "comprehension of the terrible road over which he has had to travel to arrive at them and of what it is—ethnocentrism and the crimes it legitimates—that has made it so terrible." What Geertz has and the doctors presumably didn't have is some knowledge of what it was like to be a member of that Indian's tribe before, during, and after the conquest of that tribe by the whites.

I want to make two points about this difference between Geertz and the doctors. First, the fact that lots of doctors, lawyers, and teachers are unable to imagine themselves in the shoes of lots of their patients, clients, and students does not show that anything is taking place in the dark. There is light enough for them to get their job done, and to do it right. The only sense in which something took place in the dark is the sense in which *all* human relations untouched by love take place in the dark. This is an extended sense of "in the dark" analogous to the extended sense of "alone" in which we mortal millions live alone. When we gun down the psychopath, or send the war criminal to the gallows, we *are*, in this extended sense, acting in the dark. For if we had watched the war criminal grow up, had traveled the road he had traveled, we might have had difficulty reconciling the demands of love and of justice. But it is well for society that in most cases our ignorance permits us to avoid this dilemma. Most of the time, justice has to be enough.

The second and more important point I want to make about Geertz and the doctors is that it is the signal glory of our liberal society that it entrusts power to people like Geertz and his fellow anthropologists as well as to people like the doctors. Anthropologists, and Geertz's other connoisseurs of diversity, are the people who are expected and empowered to extend the range of society's imagination, thereby opening the doors of procedural justice to people on whom they had been closed. Why is it, after all, that the Indian was ever allowed into the clinic? Why are drunken Indians, in Geertz's words, "as much a part of contemporary America" as yuppie doctors? Roughly, because anthropologists have made them so. Drunken Indians were more common in America a hundred years ago than now, but anthropologists less common. Because of the absence of sympathetic interpreters who could place their behavior in the context of an unfamiliar set of beliefs and desires, drunken Indians were not part of nineteenth-century America: that is, the vast majority of nineteenth-century Americans took no more notice of them than they did of criminal psychopaths or village idiots. The Indians, whether drunk or sober, were nonpersons, without human dignity, means to our grandparents' ends. The anthropologists made it hard for us to continue thinking of them that way, and thereby made them into "part of contemporary America." To be part of a society is, in the relevant sense, to be taken as a possible conversational partner by those who shape that society's self-image. The media, prodded by the intellectuals in general and the anthropologists in particular, have been making such partners of the Indians. But if the anthropologists had not sympathized with, learned from, even sometimes loved, the Indians, Indians would have remained invisible to the agents of social justice. They would never have gotten into the queue in the first place.

Now let me draw some conclusions from what I have been saying about Geertz's case. The principal one is that the moral tasks of a liberal democracy are divided between the agents of love and the agents of justice. In other words, such a democracy employs and empowers both connoisseurs of diversity and guardians of universality. The former insist that there are people out there whom society has failed to notice. They make these candidates for admission visible by showing how to explain their odd behavior in terms of a coherent, if unfamiliar, set of beliefs and desires—as opposed to explaining this behavior with terms like stupidity, madness, baseness, or sin. The latter, the guardians of universality, make sure that once these people are admitted as citizens, once they have been shepherded into the light by the connoisseurs of diversity, they are treated just like all the rest of us.

Our society's device for resolving what Geertz calls "wrenching social issues centered around cultural diversity" is simply to keep lots of agents of love, lots of connoisseurs of diversity, on hand. Our society has, tacitly, given up on the idea that theology or philosophy will supply general rules for resolving such issues. It recognizes that moral progress has, in recent centuries, owed more to the specialists in particularity—historians, novelists, ethnographers, and muckraking journalists, for example—than to such specialists in universality as theologians and philosophers. The formulation of general moral principles has been less useful to the development of liberal institutions than has the gradual expansion of the imagination of those in power, their gradual willingness to use the term "we" to include more and more different sorts of people. Engels's *Condition of the Working Class in England* and the writings of people like Harriet Beecher Stowe, Fenellosa, and Malinowski, did more than Engels's *Dialectics of Nature,* or the writings of Mill and Dewey, to justify the existence of the weak outsiders to the powerful insiders.

So I am inclined to set aside the questions Geertz poses about the resolution of social issues created by cultural diversity by saying that we should simply keep doing what our liberal society is already in the habit of doing: lending an ear to the specialists in particularity, permitting them to fulfill their function as agents of love, and hoping that they will continue to expand our moral imagination. There is nothing incompatible with this hope in the sort of anti-anti-ethnocentrism Geertz describes.

Let me now return to an explicit defense of the anti-anti-ethnocentrism which I sketched earlier. This mini-movement should be seen neither as putting forward a large philosophical view about the nature of culture nor as recommending a social policy. Rather, it should be seen as an attempt to resolve a small, local, psychological problem. This psychological problem is found only within the souls of bourgeois liberals who have not yet gone postmodern, the ones who are still using the rationalist rhetoric of the Enlightenment to back up their liberal ideals. These liberals hold on to the Enlightenment notion that there is something called a common human nature, a metaphysical substrate in which things called "rights" are embedded, and that this substrate takes moral precedence over all merely "cultural" superstructures. Preserving this idea produces self-referential paradox as soon as liberals begin to ask themselves whether their belief in such a substrate is itself a cultural bias. Liberals who are both connoisseurs of diversity and Enlightenment rationalists cannot get out of this bind. Their rationalism commits them to making sense of the distinction between rational judgment and cultural bias. Their liberalism forces them to call any *doubts* about human equality a result of such irrational bias. Yet their connoisseurship forces them to realize that most of the globe's inhabitants simply do not believe in human equality, that such a belief is a Western eccentricity. Since they think it would be shockingly ethnocentric to say "So what? We Western liberals *do* believe in it, and so much the better for us," they are stuck.

Anti-anti-ethnocentrists suggest that liberals should say exactly that, and that they should simply drop the distinction between rational judgment and cultural bias. The Enlightenment had hoped that philosophy would both justify liberal ideals and specify limits to liberal tolerance by an appeal to transcultural criteria of rationality. But our philosophers no longer attempt this. They tell us that we are going to have to work out the limits case by case, by hunch or by conversational compromise, rather than by reference to stable criteria. So we postmodernist bour-geois liberals no longer tag our central beliefs and desires as "necessary" or "natural" and our peripheral ones as "contingent" or "cultural." This is partly because the anthropologists, novelists, and historians have done such a good job of exhibiting the contingency of various putative neces-sities. In part it is because philosophers like Quine, Wittgenstein and Derrida have made us wary of the very idea of a necessary-contingent distinction.

These philosophers describe human life by the metaphor of a con-tinual reweaving of a web of beliefs and desires. Insofar as we adopt this metaphor, we shall regard the web as seamless, in the sense that we shall no longer use epistemological distinctions to divide it. So we no longer think of ourselves as having reliable "sources" of knowledge called "rea-son" or "sensation," nor unreliable ones called "tradition" or "common opinion." We put aside such distinctions as "scientific knowledge vs. cultural bias," and "question of fact vs. question of value."

The latter distinctions were once used to mark off the beliefs that appeared notably clear and distinct from those that seemed relatively debatable, those about which we self-consciously tried to keep an open mind. But in their absence it is natural for us to look about for other terms which will serve to mark off—if only temporarily and for certain purposes—the center of our self from its perpiphery. Typically, the terms we fall back on are self-consciously ethnocentric: being a Chris-tian, or an American, or a Marxist, or a philosopher, or an anthropolo-gist, or a postmodernist bourgeois liberal. In adopting these self-charac-terizations we announce to our audience "where we are coming from," our contingent spatio-temporal affiliations.

To sum up, anti-anti-ethnocentrism should be seen as a protest against the persistence of Enlightenment rhetoric in an era in which our connois-seurship of diversity has made this rhetoric seem self-deceptive and ster-ile. It is not a reaction against love, or against justice, or against liberal institutions. It is just a bit of *ad hoc* philosophical therapy, an attempt to cure the cramps caused in liberals by what Bernard Williams calls "the rationalist theory of rationality"—the idea that you are being irrational, and probably viciously ethnocentric, whenever you cannot appeal to neutral criteria. It urges liberals to take with full seriousness the fact that the ideals of procedural justice and human equality are parochial, recent, eccentric, cultural developments, and then to recognize that this does not mean they are any the less worth fighting for. It urges that ideals may be local and culture-bound, and nevertheless be the best hope of the species.

I shall conclude these comments by turning to Geertz's claim that "we have come to such a point in the moral history of the world that we are obliged to think about [cultural] diversity rather differently than we have been used to thinking about it." He develops this point by saying that "we are living more and more in the midst of an enormous collage," that "the world is coming at each of its local points to look more like a Kuwaiti bazaar than like an English gentlemen's club." These latter descriptions seem right to me, but I do not see why Geertz thinks that we bourgeois liberals need to change our thinking about cultural diversity in order to deal with this situation. For this is just the sort of situation that the Western liberal ideal of procedural justice was *designed* to deal with. John Rawls has remarked that "the historical circumstances of the emergence of the Western liberal notion of justice" include "the development of the principle of [religious] toleration" and "the institutions of large market economies." Both sources, he says, "spring from and encourage the diversity of doctrines and the plurality of conflicting and indeed incommensurable conceptions of the good affirmed by the members of existing democratic societies."

The relevant point is that one does not have to accept much *else* from Western culture to find the Western liberal ideal of procedural justice attractive. The advantage of postmodernist liberalism is that it recognizes that in recommending that ideal one is not recommending a philosophical outlook, a conception of human nature or of the meaning of human life, to representatives of other cultures. All we should do is point out the practical advantages of liberal institutions in allowing individuals and cultures to get along together without intruding on each other's privacy, without meddling with each other's conceptions of the good. We can suggest that UNESCO think about cultural diversity on a world scale in the way our ancestors in the seventeenth and eighteenth centuries thought about religious diversity on an Atlantic scale: as something to be simply *ignored* for purposes of designing political institutions. We can urge the construction of a world order whose model is a bazaar surrounded by lots and lots of exclusive private clubs.

Like Geertz, I have never been in a Kuwaiti bazaar (nor in an English gentleman's club). So I can give free rein to my fantasies. I picture many of the people in such a bazaar as preferring to die rather than share the beliefs of many of those with whom they are haggling, yet as haggling profitably away nevertheless. Such a bazaar is, obviously, not a community, in the strong approbative sense of "community" used by critics of liberalism like Alasdair MacIntyre and Robert Bellah. You cannot have an old-timey *Gemeinschaft* unless everybody pretty well agrees on who counts as a decent human being and who does not. But you *can* have a civil society of the bourgeois democratic sort. All you need is the ability to control your feelings when people who strike you as irredeemably different show up at the *Hotel de Ville,* or the greengrocers', or the bazaar. When this happens, you smile a lot, make the best deals you can, and, after a hard day's haggling, retreat to your club. There you will be comforted by the companionship of your moral equals.

Wet liberals will be repelled by this suggestion that the exclusivity of the private club might be a *crucial* feature of an ideal world order. It will seem a betrayal of the Enlightenment to imagine us as winding up with a world of moral narcissists, congratulating themselves on neither knowing nor caring what the people in the club over on the other side of the bazaar are like. But if we forget about the Enlightenment ideal of the self-realization of humanity as such, we can disassociate liberty and equality from fraternity. If we attend rather to the reports of our agents of love, our connoisseurs of diversity, we may agree with Lévi-Strauss that such exclusivity is a necessary and proper condition of selfhood. By attending to the reports of our agents of justice, we can see how such strong, ethnocentric, exclusivist selves might cooperate in keeping the bazaar open, in keeping the institutions of procedural justice functioning. Putting the two sets of reports together, we realize that the Enlightenment should not have yearned for a world polity whose citizens share common aspirations and a common culture. Then we will not try for a society which makes assent to beliefs about the meaning of human life or certain moral ideals a requirement for citizenship. We will aim at nothing stronger than a commitment to Rawlsian procedural justice—a moral commitment when made by members of some clubs (e.g., ours) but a matter of expediency when made by members of others. The ultimate political synthesis of love and justice may thus turn out to be an intricately-textured collage of private narcissism and public pragmatism.

On the Contemporary Hunger
for Wonders

Theodore Roszak

There is a moment in Hermann Hesse's *Steppenwolf* when the hero is ushered down a dark alley into a "magic theater" where he will witness an esoteric ritual. Above the door through which he enters a sign reads:

NOT FOR EVERYBODY

But the novel which offers us this tantalizing glimpse of a forbidden rite is (as Hesse would never have guessed) a paperback bestseller available in drugstores and supermarkets across America, an assigned text for many thousands of college students each year.

The mysteries of redemption, the secrets of initiation: "not for everybody," but on display in every shop, for sale on every street corner. It is an apt and ironic summary of the strange cultural condition in which this generation finds itself as the public fascination with transcendent experience intensifies on all sides.

Until the end of the Second World War, even a passing acquaintance with the spiritual crisis of modern Western society might have been labeled "not for everybody." The age of longing was not presumed to be a democratic fact. The stuff of high art and difficult literature, it was the elite concern of tormented poets, anguished philosophers: the soulful few sensitive enough to suffer the pangs of metaphysical dislocation. The philistine bourgeoisie—what more could one expect them to have on their shallow minds except money and new clothes? Their religious attention was wholly invested in the gospel of wealth. As for the woebegone masses at the bottom of the social order . . . their heads were filled to distraction with hunger and hard times. If they were also in search of a soul, surely the effort would lead them no further than Dostoyevsky's Grand Inquisitor or various ideologies of social revolution.

But by the time I reached college—in the mid-fifties—the death of

God had become the stuff of undergraduate survey courses, even in a state university like UCLA vastly enrolled with middle- and working-class students. The standard reading list must be familiar to all of us: Kafka's *Trial,* Eliot's *Waste Land,* Auden's *Age of Anxiety,* Russell's *Free Man's Worship,* Mann's *Magic Mountain,* Camus's *Stranger,* Colin Wilson's *Outsider,* Beckett's *Waiting for Godot,* a dash of Kierkegaard and Heidegger, snippets of Nietzsche and Sartre. The elite concern had become three units of freshman humanities. We learned the existential abyss, the cosmic abandonment of man, like so many data points in the history of the modern world; we took essay exams on "contrasting concepts of the absurd in human existence—time limit 30 minutes."

Perhaps these grave matters are still handled in the same pedantic way in the universities. But something has clearly shifted in the surrounding society. The longing has gotten around; the sense of absurdity and alienation, now widely publicized, has invaded the popular culture of our day, suddenly and massively. Weekly news magazines run slick features on crisis theology and the death of God; a clever comic like Woody Allen confabulates with existentialist clichés, finessing the heavy angst into successful film satire. But as the experience of spiritual crisis enters the popular mind, it is significantly transformed. The tragic sense of life becomes a temporary discomfort; the dilemma becomes a problem. And like all problems that appear in the public realm, this too is presumed to have a solution . . . somewhere, somehow. A technique, a medicine, a cure-all that will bring fast relief.

Does such vulgar optimism cheapen the experience? Or does it introduce a certain brash and healthy resiliency into what too often becomes, in more complex minds, a morbid fascination with despair? It may, after all, be the bad habit of creative talents to invest themselves in pathological extremes that yield remarkable insights, but no durable way of life for those who cannot translate their psychic wounds into significant art or thought.

Over the past several years, in the opportunities I have had to travel and speak, I have become acutely aware of this restless spiritual need in the audiences I meet. They wonder: Have I a vision, an epiphany, an uncanny tale to relate? A moment of illlumination or unearthly dread, a close encounter with arcane powers . . . ? It is a need, I hasten to add, which I have never sought to or been able to gratify. This hunger for wonders powerfully engages my sympathetic concern, but utterly outruns my knowledge and skill. I have, however, seen it fasten upon others about me in ways that often leave me sad or fearful. Because the appetite can be so indiscriminately eager, so mindlessly willing to be fed on banalities and poor improvisations—on anything that purports to be an experience of the extraordinary. And at that point, I realize that the eclipse of God in our time has never been the exclusive anguish of an intellectual and artistic few, except in its more articulate forms. As a nameless moral anxiety, a quiet desperation, it has been festering in the deep consciousness of people everywhere, and at last it has erupted into the totalitarian mass movements of our century. Self-enslavement to easy absolutes and mad political messiahs: that is the poison tree which flourishes peculiarly in the Waste Land.

Mercifully, the metaphysical insecurity of our time does not always reach out toward such vicious manifestations. Currently, its foremost expression in the industrial societies is the rapid spread of evangelical and charismatic forms of Christianity, faiths that teach the immediate inspiration of the Holy Spirit. These highly personal, emotionally electrifying versions of Christianity are now the most burgeoning congregations of our day and growing apace. In America they are fast developing an alternative educational establishment and their own mass media, which now rival the outreach of the major broadcasting networks.

Beyond such formal, religous affiliations, the hunger for wonders expresses itself in countless forms of pop psychiatry and lumpen occultism which thinly disguise the same impetuous quest for personal salvation. The most widely read newspapers in the United States—weekly gossip and scandal sheets like *The National Enquirer* which sell at supermarket checkout stands everywhere—carry steady coverage of UFO cults and ESP, spiritualism, reincarnation, and faith cures. Esoteric forms of oriental meditation have been opened to the public by university extensions and the YMCA; they have even been organized into successful franchise businesses that promise tranquility and enlightenment to anyone who can spare twenty minutes a day. At the other extreme from transcendental calm, there is the undiminished popular fascination with Gothic horror which makes Satanism, demonic possession, supernatural thrills and chills one of the film industry's most reliable attractions. Very likely a reader of this journal would never guess that there exists a busy trade in mystical comic books in our society: *Dr Strange, The Eternals, The New Gods, The First Kingdom,* a pulp-paper folklore of sorcery and psychic phenomena whose avid readership is by no means restricted to mindless adolescents.

One might conclude that at the popular cultural level such preternatural curiosities have always been incorrigibly and insatiably with us, from the mystery cults of the ancient world to the table-tilting spiritualism of the late nineteenth century. That would be true, and all the more to be pondered that they should survive and even flourish as a feature of modern industrial life. But more significant is the fact that the allure of psychic and spiritual prodigies has lately traveled well up the cultural scale, and not only, as at the turn of the century, in the form of clandestine fraternities like the Order of the Golden Dawn. We might say it has "come out of the closet" among academics and professionals who have been touched by the same metaphysical yearnings as the public at large, and who have simply stopped defending against them as if they were some form of unmentionable sexual perversion. They make up the principal audience for the human potential therapies, the main membership of the Associations of Humanistic and Transpersonal Psychology, organizations which offer a professional shelter where psychiatry, Eastern religions, etherealized healing, and the exploration of altered states of consciousness may freely cohabit. Far and away the largest number of students who have gravitated to Zen and Tibetan Buddhism, and to spiritual masters like Swami Muktananda, Bhagwan Shree Rajneesh, and the lama Chögyam Trungpa are maverick or dropped-out academics. Intellectuals constitute the largest public for such developments as Elisabeth Kubler-Ross's investigations of immortality, and the remarkably successful Course on Miracles (a new Christian mystical discipline revealed by way of "channeled messages" to a New York University clinical psychologist). There are also the many study centers—the Institute for Noetic Sciences, the Parapsychology Department at the University of Virginia Medical School, the Kundalini Research Foundation—which serve to draw academic talent into the realm of the extraordinary.

I cannot vouch for the depth or quality of these efforts; what I do know is that more and more frequently I find myself at conferences and gatherings in the company of learned and professional people who are deliberately and unabashedly dabbling in a sort of higher gullibility, an assertive readiness to give all things astonishing, mind-boggling, and outrageous the chance to prove themselves true . . . or true enough. Among these academic colleagues, as among my undergraduate students, the most prominent laudatory expletives of the day are "Incredible!" "Fantastic!" "O, wow!"

Let me mention only a few of the "incredible" breakthroughs and "fantastic" possibilities that have come my way lately.

A prominent psychotherapist remarks to me over lunch that people sleep and die only because they have been mistakenly "programmed" to believe they have to . . . and goes on to suggest how this erroneous programming might be therapeutically undone. A neurophysiologist tells me of her research in liberating latent mental controls over pain, infection, and aging. A psychologist shows me photos of himself being operated on by Philippine psychic surgeons whom he has seen penetrate his body with their bare hands to remove cartilage and tissue. I attend a lecture where another psychologist tells of his promising experimentation with out-of-the-body phenomena. I come upon a physicist writing in *Physics Today* about "imaginary energy" and the supposedly proven possibilities of telepathic communication and precognition. I find myself in a discussion with a group of academics who are deeply involved in Edgar Cayce's trance explorations of past and future, which they accept as indisputably valid. A historian tells me of his belief that we can, by altering consciousness, plug into the power points of the Earth's etheric field and by so doing move matter and control evolution. An engineer I meet at a party explains how we might influence the Earth's geomantic centers and telluric currents by mental manipulations, which he believes to be the technology that built Stonehenge and the pyramids.

In the presence of such dazzling speculation, I find myself of two minds. These are hardly such things as I would believe at second or third hand; and in so far as they involve physical or historical events, I am inclined to hold that standard rules of verification should apply in distinguishing fact from fallacy. I tend to welcome the clarity that a decent respect for logic and evidence brings to such matters.

On the other hand, I can so clearly hear the restless spiritual longings behind the reports, the urgent need to free the fettered imagination from a Reality Principle that brings no grace or enchantment to one's life, that I usually listen sympathetically, unresistingly . . . though seldom credulously. This is not the course I would follow, but perhaps these unauthorized speculations can also lead to a Renaissance of wonder. In any case, I am dealing here with people who learned all the objections I might raise—as I did—in their undergraduate years. This is clearly a post-skeptical intellectual exercise for them, requiring a critical response that is more than simple doubt and denial.

What impresses me especially about these strange metaphysical fevers is the way they blithely appropriate the authority of the hard sciences. In these circles, far from being rejected, science enjoys (or suffers) a smothering embrace. There is a certain broad license that has been borrowed from theoretical physics—especially by nonphysicists in the academic world—which leads even well-educated minds to believe that, since the fifth Solvay Conference a half-century ago, all standards of verification and falsification have been indefinitely suspended in the scientific community, and anything goes. For, after all, if matter is energy and time is space, then all things are one, as the Upanishads taught. And if the observer jostles the infinitesimal observed, then the world is our will and idea, and one paradigm is as good as the next. Accordingly, the revolution in modern physics is freely interpreted as having abolished the objective reality of nature and sanctioned all forms of paranormal and mystical experience. Einstein is understood to have established that "everything is relative"; Bell's theorem and the uncertainty principle are invoked as a defense of unrestrained subjectivity; split-brain research is said to validate the status of metaphysical intuition; Kirlian photography is cited as evidence of auras and astral bodies; holograms are construed as proof of extrasensory perception, synchronicity, and transcendental realities. In recent days, I have had students spin me tales about "charmed quarks" rather as if these might be characters invented by Tolkien.

Robert Walgate, discussing books like Lyall Watson's *Supernature,* John Gribbin's *Timewarps,* Gary Zukav's *The Dancing Wu Li Masters,* and the science fact and fiction magazine *Omni,* has made an interesting distinction. Such literature, he suggests, is not "popularized science, but a truly *popular* science, transformed by the interests of the readers it serves. . . . Like science fiction, it is much better supplied with speculation and myth than the dry, exclusive world of science that feeds it."

Popular science in this vein is not much to my taste. I sometimes enjoy its freewheeling and fanciful brainstorming, but I back off rapidly as it approaches a scientized mysticism. By my lights at least, that is a fruitless confusion of categories. Still, it is hardly within my province to censor these rhapsodic variations on scientific, or quasi-scientific themes. The positivists among us, however, would seem to have a tricky new problem on their hands: *scientific superstitions,* the loose use of scientific ideas to appease an essentially religious appetite.

What I offer here is only a brief sketch of a post-Christian, post-industrial society in search of the miraculous. I believe that search could be documented at great length and at many social levels—from teenage acid rock to the painstaking labors of scholars and philosophers to salvage the teachings of the world's endangered spiritual traditions. But even this impressionistic survey points to a significant conclusion. If we can agree that Western society's most distinctive cultural project over the last three centuries has been to win the world over to an exclusively science-based Reality Principle, then we have good reason to believe that, for better or worse, the campaign has stalled and may even be losing ground in the urban-industrial heartland. Though it continues to dominate our economic and political life, in the deep allegiance of people, in the secret crises of decision and commitment, the scientific worldview simply has not taken. Our culture remains as divided as ever—top from bottom—in its metaphysical convictions. Now, as at the dawn of the Age of Reason, the commanding intellectual heights are held by a secular humanist establishment devoted to the skeptical, the empirical, the scientifically demonstrable. That viewpoint may admit a sizeable range of subtle variations; but, taken as a whole, as a matter of stubborn ethical principle, it refuses rational status to religious experience, it withholds moral sanction from the transcendent needs.

But meanwhile, in the plains a thousand miles below that austere high ground, there sprawls a vast popular culture that is still deeply entangled with piety, mystery, miracle, the search for personal salvation—as much so today as the pious many were when the Cartesian chasm between mind and matter was first opened out by the scientific revolution. If anything has changed about this cultural dichotomy, it would be, as I have suggested, that the membership of the humanist elite has lately been suffering a significant and open defection as academics, intellectuals, and artists take off in pursuit of various strange visionary and therapeutic adventures. It would be my conclusion that the great cultural synthesis of the Enlightenment—Reason, Science, Progress—is much less securely positioned today than in the heyday of crusading positivism . . . say, in the time of Darwin and Marx, Freud and Comte. (On the other hand, as I have indicated, the democratic values of that synthesis are very much with us now as a brash demand for access to the mysteries and wonders.) It may be that the only substantial popular support the ideals of the Enlightenment and the scientific revolution still enjoy stems from their lingering promise of material abundance . . . and how heavily will we be able to lean on that expectation in the years ahead?

Now, what is one to make of this schizoid state of affairs? There are two major interpretations open to us.

The first—I would call it the secular humanist orthodoxy—would be to regard the hunger for wonders as a continuing symptom of incurable human frailty, an incapacity to grow up and grow rational that is as much with us today as in the Stone Age past. Sadly, one would have to conclude that the masses have not yet matured enough to give up their infantile fantasies, which are, as Freud once designated religion, illusions that have no future. As for the intellectuals who surrender to that illusion, their choice would have to be regarded as a lamentable failure of nerve. They betray the defense of reason, the cause of progress.

One memorable example of this position: at the end of his highly successful television series *The Ascent of Man,* Jacob Bronowski—who had laboriously defined that ascent as man's struggle toward scientific knowledge—deplored the new climate of irrationality he saw growing up around him. He offered a short bill of particulars: "ESP, mystery, Zen Buddhism."

It is important to recognize that this interpretation of religious need as neurosis or moral weakness is deeply rooted in humanitarian values. Any criticism it may merit must begin by acknowledging its essential ethical nobility, or we will fail to do justice to a central truth of contemporary history: namely, that the rejection of religion in modern society is an act of conscience and has functioned as a liberating force in a world long darkened by superstition and ecclesiastical oppression. There should be no question but that the service done by secular humanism in this regard is to be respected and preserved.

Then, there is the second interpretation of our society's undiminished transcendent longings. It accepts that need as a constant of the human condition inseparably entwined with our creative and moral powers: a guiding vision of the Good that may often be blurred, but which is as real as the perception of light when it first pierced the primordial blindness of our evolutionary ancestors. In this interpretation, it is not transcendent aspiration that needs critical attention, but the repressive role of secular humanism in modern culture, which may be seen as a tragic overreaction to the obscurantism and corruption of the European ecclesiastical establishment: a justified anticlericalism which has hardened into a fanatical, antireligious crusade.

In following out this second line of interpretation, I have found the work of William Blake especially valuable. Because he was gifted with an extraordinary visionary power, Blake was among the first to perceive clearly the way in which a psychology of willful alienation had fastened itself upon the ideals of the Enlightenment and the worldview of science. Hence his prayer:

May God us keep
From single vision and Newton's sleep.

"Single vision" would be Blake's term for secular humanism in its alienative mode. In his prophetic epics, he embodies this sensibility in the mythic figure of Urizen, an awesome and dynamic titan who turns against the other energies of the personality—the "Zoas," as Blake called them: the sensuous, the compassionate, the visionary. The result is a cruel censorship of human experience in body, emotion, and mind. Urizen is "Your Reason," acting as a repressive power in the personality, tyrannically closing the doors of perception until only a narrow range of scientifically productive objectivity is left to occupy the mind—and carrying out this psychic mutilation as the agent of high moral duty. Curious, is it not, that in modern Western society alone "Enlightenment" with a capital E came to mean the repression of transcendent aspiration, the destruction of religious experience.

Here we have the secret psychological warfare that has underlain the tumultuous history of industrial society since the advent of the "dark satanic mills." In the depths of the psyche, a brutal politics of consciousness has been played out which pits critical intellect against the innate human need for transcendence. Because both parties to the struggle are welded into the foundations of our full humanity, neither can finally be cast out. But the personality—torn between them—can be disfigured to the point of insanity and self-destruction. Steadily, as the best minds of our society have been drawn into the service of Urizen's withering skepticism, the human will to transcendence, especially at the popular level, has been left without counsel or guidance. Untutored, it runs off into many dead ends and detours. It easily mistakes the sensational for the spiritual, the merely obscure for the authentically mysterious. Dominated by the technological ethos of single vision, it strives to outdo the technicians at their own game by identifying psychic stunts (ESP, levitation, spirit readings, etc.) with enlightenment. It may reach out toward emotionally charged, born-again religions that generally weaken toward smugness, intolerance, and reactionary politics. It may blunder into occult follies and sheer gullibility, discrediting itself at every step. At last, it falls into the vicious circle: as spiritual need becomes more desperate for gratification, it rebels against intellect and moral discernment, losing all clear distinction between the demonic and the transcendent. Accordingly, the secular humanist establishment is confirmed in its hostility and proceeds to scorn and scold, debunk and denigrate more fiercely. But, indeed, this is like scolding starving people for eating out of garbage cans, while providing them with no more wholesome food. Of course, they will finally refuse to listen and become more rebellious. Under severe critical pressure, the transcendent energies may be bent, twisted, distorted; but Blake's dictum finally holds true: "Man must and will have some religion," even if it has to be "the Religion of Satan."

The wisdom of Blake's diagnosis lies in its honest attempt to integrate the splintered faculties of the psyche. He recognized that the "mental fight" within the self cannot be brought to peace by choosing sides between the antagonists. To choose sides is not to win, but to repress—and only for the time being. Our course is not to strengthen half the dichotomy against the other, because *the dichotomy is the problem*. It must be healed, made whole.

In the most general terms, what we face in the tragic stand-off between single vision and spiritual need is the place of experience in the life of the mind—a problem that has not been adequately addressed by the religion, philosophy, or science of Western society.

"Experience" is not an easy word to use here; I take it up for lack of any better term, recognizing that it sprawls troublesomely toward ubiquity. What *isn't* an experience, after all? In a sense, *everything* is an experience of some order. We experience words and ideas as meanings that stir the mind to thought. We experience another's report of experience. Let me, arbitrarily then, delimit experience here to that which is *not* a report, but knowledge before it is reflected in words or ideas: immediate contact, direct impact, knowledge at its most personal level as it is lived.

In the growing popular hunger for wonders, what we confront is an effort to experience the transcendent energies of the mind as directly as possible, to find one's way back through other people's reports to the source and bedrock of conviction. Charismatic faith, mystical religion, oriental meditation, humanistic and transpersonal psychotherapy, altered states of consciousness . . . there are obviously many differences between these varied routes. Yet, I would argue that they point in a common direction—toward a passionate desire to break through the barriers of single vision into the personal knowledge of the extraordinary. At one extreme, this surely accounts for the obsession with psychedelic drugs that has gripped our society during the past generation. That fascination arises from a craving for transcendent experience, a willingness to try anything that might jar, jolt, shock, batter, blast the benumbed mind into some heightened state of awareness resembling the reported ecstasies of the saints and sages. It is a risky form of neurophysical alchemy.

All this must be seen against the background of an extraordinary historical fact: that ours is a society which has been peculiarly starved for experience as I speak of it here. It is the uncanny characteristic of Western society that so much of our high culture—religion, philosophy, science—has been based on what contemporary therapists would call "head trips": that is, on reports, deductions, book learning, argument, verbal manipulations, intellectual authority. The religous life of the Christian world has always had a fanatical investment in belief and doctrine: in creeds, dogmas, articles of faith, theological disputation, catechism lessons . . . the Word that too often becomes mere words. In contrast to pagan and primitive societies with their participative rituals, and to the oriental cultures which possess a rich repertory of contemplative techniques, getting saved in the Christian churches has always been understood to be a matter of learning correct beliefs as handed down by authorities in the interpretation of scripture.

Philosophy has shared this same literal bias. True, Descartes, at the outset of the modern period, developed his influential method by way of attentive introspection. Even so, his approach is a set of logical deductions intended for publication. Philosophy has not gone on from there to create systematic disciplines that seek to lead the student through a similar process. Instead, one works logically and critically from Descartes's argument, or from that of other philosphers, writing books out of other books. As philosophy flows into its modern mainstream, it invests its attention more and more exclusively in language: in the minute analysis of reports, concepts, definitions, arguments. The English positivist Michael Dummett, in a recent work, offers the following revealing definition of philosophy:

> The goal of philosophy is the analysis of the structure of thought which is to be sharply distinguished from the study of the psycho-

logical process of *thinking*. And the only proper method for analyzing thought consists in the analysis of language.

I do not question the value of such a project. I only observe that it is, like the theological approach to religion, a "head trip." Its virtue may be the utmost critical clarity, but, as the literature of linguistic and logical analysis grows, we are left to wonder: is there anybody out there still experiencing anything besides somebody else's book commenting on somebody else's book? Where do we turn to find the experience—preverbal, nonverbal, subverbal, transverbal—on which the books and reports must finally be based? If we follow Dummett's program, such "psychological processes" are driven out of philosophy. Where? Presumably, into psychiatry, psychotherapy, meditation—which is exactly where we find so many people in our day turning to have their untapped capacity for experience authorized and explored.

If Existentialist philosophy has found its way to a larger public in our day than the various linguistic and analytical schools, it is doubtlessly because the Existentialists ground their thought in vivid, even anguished experience: moral crisis, dread, the fear of death, even the nausea of hopeless despair. There is the high drama here of "real life," the urgent vitality that allows philosophy to flow into art and so reach a wide audience. But there are strict limits to what Existentialism can contribute to the transcendent need of our society. Excepting the Christian Existentialists, the range of experience that dominates the movement is restricted almost dogmatically to the dark and terrible end of the psychological spectrum. The terrors of alienation we find there are posited as the defining qualities of the human condition. This is, in fact, the bleak underside of single vision employed rather like a scriptural text for endless, painstaking exegesis. Paradoxically, we are offered a minute examination of such experience as is left over for us after the experience of transcendence has been exiled from our lives. We are left to explore a psychological Inferno, with no Purgatory or Paradise in sight beyond.

It may seem strange to include science among the nonexperiential head trips of our culture. Isn't science grounded in physical experimentation and empirical method? Yes, it is. But as science has matured across the centuries, its experiments and methods have become ever more subtle and technical, ever more mediated by ingenious instruments whose readings must be filtered through intricate theories and mathematical formulations. As scientific techniques of observation grow steadily more remote from the naked senses, they require the intervention of more intricate apparatus between knower and known. Whoever may be doing the "experiencing" in modern science, it is not the untutored public. Here, indeed, is a body of knowledge, supposedly our only valid knowledge of the universe, which is "not for everybody"—except by way of secondhand accounts. We are a long way off from the day of the gentleman scientists, figures like Benjamin Franklin and Thomas Young, who might keep up with the professional literature and even make significant contributions to basic research in their spare time.

There is a special irony to this development in the history of science. As the field has moved toward professionalization, it has become more and more involved with subliminal realities, entities, or theoretical structures which, while understood to be in some sense "physical" (surely the word has been strained to its limit) are yet "occult" in much the same sense in which Newton understood the force of gravitation to be occult: known only by the mathematical expression of its visible effects. Particle physics is obviously such a science of the subliminal; microbiology is only a shade less so in its dependence on techniques like x-ray crystallography. Astronomy, in its use of radio wave, x-ray, and gamma ray observation, in its reliance on advanced physical theory, becomes ever more preoccupied with bodies, vibrations, processes beyond the range of direct visibility. These are no longer fields of study that can be explored by those lacking special training and elaborate apparatus; often even ordinary language will not cope with their subtleties.

For that matter, much the same tendency toward the subliminal can be seen in psychology and the newer human sciences like semiotics, or structural linguistics and anthropology, or highly statistical forms of sociology. These too tend to locate their realities in exotic theoretical realms that defy common sense and the evidence of ordinary experience. In search of the foundations of human conduct, they burrow into unconscious instincts, into hidden structures of language and the brain. Currently, the sociobiologists are busy tracing human motivations to the subliminal influence of as yet undiscovered (and perhaps undiscoverable) behavioral genes. In all these cases, the surface of life is understood to be underlain by deep structures which cannot be fathomed by untrained minds and which are envisaged as being of a wholly different order from surface phenomena. I grant that all these entities and forces are still dealt with by scientists as objective and physical; but from the view of the unschooled public, nature—including human nature—seems to recede into a phantom province that is nothing like the everyday world of appearances. The visible and tangible stuff around us becomes a Maya-like shadow-show; nothing that happens there is the "real" nature of things. Only trained minds can penetrate this veil of illusions to grasp the occult realities beyond.

And here is the irony of the matter. Psychologically speaking, the relationship this creates between scientists and public cannot be widely different from that between priesthood and believers in more traditional societies. It might even be seen as a secularized transformation of the age-old religious distinction between the esoteric and the exoteric. And in modern science as in religion, much that crosses the line between the priestly and public realms becomes garbled in the mind of the laity. Hence, the "scientific superstitions" I alluded to earlier—essentially attempts, as in all religious superstitions, to wring some hint of the extraordinary from reports and verbal formulations imperfectly understood.

If I interpret the contemporary hunger for wonders correctly, it is at once a profoundly religious and a profoundly democratic movement. Its rejection of single vision is a rejection of the peculiar literalism of Western culture, and of the elitism that has dominated almost every culture of the past. It is a demand for mass access to sacramental experiences that have traditionally been the province of a select spiritual minority, and which have been "retailed" to the populace by way of prescribed rites under priestly guidance. I will not presume to judge every culture of the past that dealt with the mysteries in this way; perhaps not all were plagued with corrupted mystagoguery and caste privilege. But most were, surely within the civilized period, where, again and again, we find priest and king, church and state interlocked as an exploitative power elite grounded in obfuscation and brutal dominion. They betrayed and discredited the natural authority that may properly belong to spiritual instruction. So today we are faced with an unprecedented demand for popular access to the temple, a demand that could arise only in a society deeply imbued with democratic values. That, in turn, could happen only in a society that had passed through a secular humanist phase in which all hierarchical structures had been called into question.

We might see this as a dialectical process which progresses by way of contradiction. The theological literalism of Western religion makes its doctrines vulnerable to the skeptical thrust of single vision. Thus, single vision undercuts the religious establishment of its society and projects a revolutionary, humanitarian ethic into the world. In its turn, single vision produces a new scientific and technocratic elite that betrays its democratic commitment; at the same time, it inflicts an even more oppressive, because wholly secularized, literalism upon its culture. As a result, it leaves the transcendent longings of the populace unsatisfied. So we have the insurgent contemporary demand that sacramental experience cease to be labeled "not for everybody," that the esoteric be demystified and democratized.

Perhaps that is an impossible demand . . . perhaps. If that is so, then we may see our society settle for a dismal and degrading compromise. The familiar pattern of priestly authority will regenerate itself, only now it would most likely organize itself around the sort of ersatz religion that Nazism and Bolshevism have represented, with priestly authority vested in the state, the party, the leader; and the mass rituals of the totalitarian cult would be vicious celebrations of collective power. So our industrial culture in its time of troubles might lurch from one "Religion of Satan" to another. We have had more than enough signs to warn us that such forms of self-enslavement remain an ever-present temptation for desperate people.

But there is a happier possibility: that we will indeed find ways to democratize the esoteric that are morally becoming and life-enhancing. And here philosophy might find a guiding ideal in its own history: the image of Socrates in the marketplace, among the populace, practicing his vocation as an act of citizenship.

We know that Socrates went among the ordinary people—tradesmen, merchants, athletes, politicians—and brought into their lives a critical clarity that only a persistent gadfly might achieve. It is this element of intellectual rigor that distinguishes Socrates from prophet, messiah, mystagogue. There is the willingness to put the uncomfortable question—to oneself and others—which separates philosophy from faith. But why was the populace willing to come to Socrates? Why were these ordinary citizens willing to face his hard critical edge? I suggest it was because this gadfly was also something of a guru: both at once at the expense of neither. Socrates placed personal experience at the center of philosophy; he used deep introspection as his primary tool of inquiry. There was that quality of personal attention, even loving concern, about his work that we might today associate with psychotherapy or spiritual counseling.

More than this, Socrates himself embodied the promise of transcendence at the end of the dialogue. For him, criticism and analysis were not ends in themselves; there was something beyond the head trip, a realm of redeeming silence where the mysteries held sway. Socrates had been there and returned many times. So he was often found by his students standing entranced, caught up in his private vision. He had escaped from the cave of shadows; he had seen the Good. Something of the old Orphic mysteries clung to this philosopher and saved his critical powers from skeptical sterility. I suspect it was because he offered this affirmative spiritual dimension that Socrates found affectionate and attentive company in the agora—though, of course, finally martyrdom as well.

Just as he had borrowed his fragile balance of intellect and vision from Pythagoras, so Socrates bequeathed it to his pupil Plato. But neither Pythagoras nor Plato was daring enough (or mad enough) to follow Socrates into the streets in search of wisdom. Instead, the one sequestered philosophy in a secret fraternity; the other retreated to the academy. As these two options come down to us today, they have fallen disastrously out of touch with one another. The academy has come to specialize in a sheerly critical function; the spiritual fraternity—any that su rive—has concentrated upon techniques and disciplines of illumination that are no longer on speaking terms with critical intellect.

Can these two be brought together once again in their proper Socratic unity as an ideal of rhapsodic intellect: the critical mind open to transcendent energy? More challenging still, can that balance of intellect and vision once more be taken into the public realm, to meet the spiritual need that has arisen there? Or will philosophy shrink back from the importunate vulgarity, the citizenly burden of the task?

This much is certain: we will not find what we refuse to seek; we will not do what we refuse to dare.

Two: The Mediations of Art

Television: The Medium in the Mass Age

Sven Birkerts

No one who has walked through the excavations at Herculaneum and Pompeii is likely to forget the oppressiveness of the experience, far outweighing its historical fascination or its cachet as future table talk. The dreariness of a George Segal sculpture has been multiplied a thousandfold: the heavy seal of Time has been impressed upon the ordinariness of daily life. We are suddenly able to imagine our lives embalmed at a casual moment. Indeed, I sometimes wonder what hypothetical aliens might find if our planet were surprised by an avalanche of ash—especially if their craft landed, years hence, somewhere on our shores. I try to imagine their exclamations, their cries of puzzlement, as they go from house to house. I envision through their eyes the petrified, whitewashed figures, their arrangement—singly, in groups—some four to eight feet from a prominent up-ended box. There would be boxes with horns, boxes without. Gender markings? The more enlightened among them would shake their heads. "These are clearly religious objects, domestic shrines. We have found the remains of a very spiritual race."

Television. The truth of it is too much to grasp, too various. Seen synoptically, from an imagined altitude, all these blue lights look like a radiant roe, or a swarm of cells in a tissue culture. But from another place, from the ease of a chair in a room, they seem like nothing much, a breather from the assaults of the day, a few laughs, a shine of fantasy. Both views are true; neither view is true. Who is going to say? And how? Stalk it with language and it cackles at you, formulate a concept and it sprays you with dots. It is as tricky as mercury. You shiver it to pieces and it hugs itself back together. Mercury is apt. If you could do the impossible, if you could contrive some kind of barometric instrument for which television and its contents would be a mercury, you would be able to read the spiritual air-pressure of a time and place. But in fact you can do little more than play, break it into blobs, stare at their sheen, watch as they hurry back into a single imponderable lump.

At one time, twenty years ago, say, to write about television was a more feasible undertaking. Twenty years ago television had not yet seeped as deeply into the culture; it was not so coextensive with the social fabric. There were still free zones, places to stand, Archimedean points from which to work the lever. This is no longer the case. Where television could once be considered apart from reality, as a toy, an "entertainment," it has now greatly expanded its reach and impact: it has become, by way of massive social participation, a significant portion of the reality itself. So much so, in fact, that the interface between society and television can no longer be clearly described. Television programs increasingly comprise the content of private lives; shows and situations are discussed as if the personalities and events were real and in the world; the information and opinion purveyed determine, to a large extent, the public perception of historical and political events. To discuss the phenomenon, therefore, with some hope of grasping its essential nature, its *quidditas*, is to embark on one of those classic fool's errands—to quest for fleece. Though in this case the fleece takes the form, in Norman Mailer's words, of "a pullulation of electrons."[1]

Tele-vision. Quite literally "vision at a distance" or "over a distance"; also, the instrument or appliance whereby this is accomplished. When not in use it is a strange enough object, an opaque window fronting a box, the box studded with dials and connected, by way of wire and plug, to the sorcery of an electrical system. Its function, by all accounts, is to provide entertainment and information. Like the automobile and the telephone, it has become nearly indispensable. Like the automobile and the telephone, it is one of our guarantors of equality: anyone can drive anywhere, call anywhere—any American can watch any show.

Television watching, this vast and ramified ritual, this mass phenomenon, is scarcely served by the word "entertainment." It wears the guise of being a relaxant—like softball, dancing or drinking—but it is so much more, or less, than that. If it were simply entertainment or relaxation that people sought, they would soon be driven to other expedients: the fare is passing poor. No, there is very little correlation between the available entertainment content and the 800 or so million man-hours that are put in—every day—in front of 200 million television sets.

Television represents the "outside world" to the individual. This is one of its services. To own a television is to have a seat in the arena where the world is visually presented. Of course, television is by no means co-extensive with the world, nor do its visual contents in any way encompass the world; but it is part of the nature of the medium to convey this impression subliminally. By simply pressing a button, the viewer makes contact with what is, in his imagination, an international information empire. The assurance is patent that if anything of urgent importance happens anywhere in the world, the information will be promptly conveyed. In this one sense television is no different from the radio. The fact that it is a visual medium, however, greatly magnifies the unconscious impact of this function.

But this is basic, obvious. There is another function that is far more important and worrisome: television acts upon the unconscious of the viewer not as an appliance or a plaything, but as a consciousness. It fosters and encourages the most bizarre sort of identification. The implications are staggering. But before we consider them we must question some of the mechanics of this phenomenon.

The identification is not really attributable to the fact that the medium delivers human voices and images. Those are contents. Prior to contents are the impacts of the form itself, the medium. Consider, first of all, the seamlessness: the impression derived from the absence of holes and gaps, coupled with its electronic nature, coupled further with its insistent uniformity. The visual possibilities of the medium are, potentially speaking, inexhaustible. But what has in fact happened is that the corporation-owned networks have narrowed the range and content of presentation to such an extent that it is impossible to distinguish one channel from another. The idea of channels as separate bands is further negated by constant switching. Not only is the medium seamless, its contents are as well. The result is that the images, sequences and structures are so much alike that they become, for the viewer, different simultaneous utterances by the same entity, and, in the last analysis, one utterance. And this entity, television, thereby takes on the lineaments of consciousness.

This ersatz consciousness is, so far as its contents are concerned, rudimentary enough. It scarcely reflects the complexities of the human mental operation. Its form, however, is unconsciously most persuasive. It depends upon—and itself creates—lack of resistance. There are no obstacles. The

visual and audial materials are ingested directly with no need for translation. They are calculated thus: to resemble reality while being simpler
than reality. The fluidity of the medium conditions us to passive absorp-
tion. There is nothing to engage the conscious faculty. A broad, one-way
"channel" is opened between the medium and the unconscious. As we
suspend our supervisory powers, the medium sets itself up as a surrogate. It is with our consent that a generally flat, banal configuration of
materials is alchemized into a ghostly dimensionality.

What is the nature of the medium that can effect so subtle an interchange? Norman Mailer, in his essay "Of a Small and Modest Malignancy, Wicked and Bristling with Dots," writes:

> Often, when the stations would go off the air and no programs
> were left to watch, he would still leave the set on. The audio would
> hum in a tuneless pullulation, and the dots would hiss in an agitation
> of what forces he did not know. This hiss and the hum would fill
> the room and then his ears. There was, of course, no clamor—it
> was nearer to anti-noise dancing in eternity with noise. And watch-
> ing the empty video, he would recognize it was hardly empty.
> Bands of grey and lighter grey swam across the set, rollovers swept
> away the dots, and something like sunspots crackled forth.

The primeval echo of the passage is not fortuitous—the grey, tuneless
hum represents nothing so much as our idea of undifferentiated consciousness. We know these sputtering voids because we produce something very like them in ourselves. Eyes closed, emptied of thought,
hovering near sleep, we fill up with a similar pullulation. This is the
primary level of identification: that our consciousness generates images
and thoughts—contents—out of an agitated void just as television does.
The medium has a psychic likeness. And we project upon that likeness
something of our own sense of psychic dimension. It is this dimensionality—which does not actually exist—which welds into a disquieting
unity the various differentiated emanations.

Identification and projection, both subliminal, secure a reality status for
what is, in essence, a play of illusion. It could even be argued that we
attribute a higher reality status to television than we do to life itself. I say
this only half in jest. I suspect that there is a certain by no means small
percentage of chronic viewers in whom the organized materials of televi-

sion programming have effectively replaced any active, discriminating consciousness they might have once possessed. But can it be that the two—consciousness and television—are similar enough to be inter-changeable? Or, to put the question differently, can it be that life as seen on television is effectively interchangeable with life as the individual experiences it? These are by no means idle questions.

It is not television that is conforming to modern life so much as it is modern life that is taking on the hues of the medium. The processes that strip modern experience of uniqueness and resonance, that make possible the shopping mall, the housing project, the uniformity of the suburb, the bland interiors of the workplace—the list could go on and on—these prepare us for television. Since televison cannot transmit uniqueness or resonance by its very nature (I will discuss this later with reference to the concept of "aura"), it is admirably suited to mirror modern experience. To television belongs all the persuasiveness of the ordinary. Its flatness, banality, the ambient feel it confers to time, all conform closely to our experience. What is more, it presents us with that experience in distilled and organized shape. We experience ordinariness in condensation; it is more real to us than the ordinariness of our lives. The fact that it is electronically "bedded" impresses upon it the stamp of authority.

Television as consciousness. This impression comes, in part, from a simple, potent illusion: that we perceive the medium as layered, and therefore deep. The illusion is created by constant alternation of con-tents. The hero is, say, trapped inside a burning building; a sudden—but expected—elision brings us the imagery of a tropic isle, a voice enticing us to sample something unique; another elision brings us the face of our local news anchorman, the pulsing sound of a ticker, a quickly-pitched summary of the hour's headlines. And then we are back in the burning building. The impression is not one of segmentation, but of layering. With our partial suspension of disbelief, we imagine that our hero was battling flames while we were hearing the latest on the border war. The illusion reinforces in yet another way the idea that we are in contact with a complex, superintendent, perhaps even profound, entity.

Walter Benjamin was one of the first thinkers to investigate seriously the impacts of technology upon the sphere of art. He did not live to see the invention of television, but the structure of his analysis is such that the subsequent technological advance has not altered it significantly. The ideas about "aura" which he articulated and elaborated in his essay "The Work of Art in the Age of Mechanical Reproduction" are perfectly applicable to the problem of television.[2]

Briefly, aura can be conceived as the invisible envelope of presence or context that surrounds and, in effect, guarantees the uniqueness and reality of a work of art. It is by nature impenetrable and intransmissible. Though Benjamin defines the concept primarily with reference to art, he recognizes its generality. Aura is the essential attribute of any individual, location, situation or object that has not been compromised by displacement or reproduction. He writes:

> We define the aura . . . as the unique phenomenon of a distance, however close it [the object] may be. If, while resting on a summer afternoon, you follow with your eyes a mountain range on the horizon or a branch which casts its shadow over you, you experience the aura of those mountains, of that branch.

Aura forms, in other words, the basis of subjective experience; it cannot be objectively isolated. To take anything from its natural context is to destroy its aura. Anything stripped of its aura is no longer that thing—its certificate of uniqueness is gone. Insofar as it then presents itself in the guise of the original, it is false.

This fairly simple recognition—though, of course, much ramified by Benjamin's prismatic intelligence—was one of the bases for his critique of modern life, a critique which centered itself upon the disintegration of meaning and the radical disharmony between the individual and his world.

A few sentences later, Benjamin claims:

> Every day the urge grows stronger to get hold of an object at very close range by way of its likeness, its reproduction. Unmistakably, reproduction as offered by picture magazines and newsreels differs from the image as seen by the unarmed eye. Uniqueness and permanence are as closely linked in the latter as are transitoriness and reproducibility in the former. To pry an object from its shell, to destroy its aura, is a mark of a perception whose "sense of the universal equality of things" has increased to such a degree that it extracts it even from a unique object by means of reproduction.

If we consider not just objects, but the fragile, context-bound webbing of all human interchange—which television undertakes to mimic and reproduce—then the concept of aura is immensely useful.

We must take care, however, to avoid the direct substitution of terms. The situation is somewhat more complicated. For television does not set out to reproduce the actual world. Nor, with few exceptions, does it pretend to transmit genuine human interaction in context. No, what television does is to manufacture situations and interactions among created, scripted personalities. What it delivers, therefore, is essentially a caricature of social reality, the simulacra of human exchange. There is no question of aura being destroyed—what is captured by the television cameras has no aura to begin with. Instead, subtly and insidiously, reality, the genuine human interaction, is being steadily sponged, divested of authority. The aura is robbed, not directly, but by proxy. All human exchange—travestied, replicated, absorbed by 200 million watchers—is progressively, and perhaps permanently, diminished.

Television and aura are incompatible. Anything filmed directly—an animal, a landscape, an embrace—is promptly dispossessed of presence. The image preserves certain accuracies while the essence is flattened out and caricatured. What we receive through the picture tube has the outer lineaments of the actual with none of the pith or savor. The viewer, of course, is not unaware of this. The problem is that after a while—after sufficient exposure—he starts to forget. The more he watches, the more the tension between the thing and its image is vitiated.

Television, I have said, provides a psychic likeness and is received by the unconscious as a consciousness. But it is not a consciousness. It is a hybrid, a collage possessing some of the rudimentary attributes of consciousness. It is utterly bereft of aura. And consciousness without aura, without context or uniqueness, is a monstrosity, a no-presence that matches up with nothing in the natural world. It is something that is not alive that is trying to impersonate life: it is travesty. Possibly Mailer has something like this in mind when he writes:

> So, in those early mornings when television was his only friend, he knew already that he detested his habit. There was not enough to learn from watching TV. Some indispensable pieces of experience were missing. Except it was worse than that. Something not in

existence was also present, some malignancy to burn against his own malignancy, some onslaught of dots into the full pressure of his own strangled vision.

That "something not in existence" is the Frankenstein of a consciousness pieced together like a quilt from a thousand heteroclite fragments.

To turn on the television set is to make the flight from three dimensions into two. It is an escape, an effort to kill self-reflective consciousness, at least for a time. Two dimensions are easier to reconnoiter in than three. But it is not only while watching that one participates in two-dimensionality. After enough exposure to the medium, the world itself—which we may here define as everything that is *not* television—loses some of its thickness and complexity. The eye of the beholder is altered. Television has the same power of alteration as art, except that it works in the opposite direction. The reality content of the world is diminished rather than augmented. But why? That is, why would consciousness, the supreme distinguishing feature of the species, its evolutionary trademark, wish to obliterate itself? It must, to some extent, be due to the quality of life available to the individual. That life consists, for too many people, of meaningless work and prolonged exposure to the concentrated ordinariness of television. A self-perpetuating tautology sits near the heart of the issue.

Television watching also represents a diffusely-enacted participation in ritual. The viewer is, to a certain extent, looking past the content, engaging the form itself, the sentient global mesh which gives the medium much of its authority. This participation is passive and abstract. The viewer interacts with the medium; the medium, in turn, interacts with the whole world of viewers. One makes oneself a part of the circuitry and thereby extends and deepens the circuitry. It is participation in the life of the times—insofar as television watching is itself a significant part of the life of our times. Another tautology. The same impulses that were once discharged actively—in public assembly—are now expressed from the armchair. The medium thus becomes the abstraction of community itself. It is a touchstone, a point of reference. A common mental property attains a powerful pseudo-reality through cross-referencing. The coffee-break ritual—"Did you see 'Dynasty' last night?"—is not so much an expression of interest in the show as it is an act of self-substantiation.

Most discussions and analyses of the effects of television occupy themselves with the contents of programming. I would contend that the effects of the medium itself, the fact of it, its form, the structure through which the contents are presented, is of far greater importance. It is the medium that forges the connection with the unconscious, enables the contents to pass directly by all conscious monitoring. It is the form that gradually conditions the psyche of the viewer.

Television establishes a path of least resistance—visually, psychologically—indeed, it *is* that path. It is a prism that refracts the rays of attentiveness. The attention faculty itself is gradually altered. For one thing, new time-expectancies are created. The viewer becomes accustomed not only to 30- and 60-minute units, but to mini-units as well, two- and three-minute blocks of commercial interruption coming every five to seven minutes. The effects of this are not easily gauged, except in the realm of television viewing. Here we find that people come to expect—and need—side-tracking every few minutes. Uninterrupted programming generates anxiety and boredom. The fact is that the commercial interruptions are a welcome distraction from the banality of most programming. Night after night, month after month, the mind is made to be a shuttlecock. How can we believe that this leaves its focus and tenacity unimpaired?

In the same way, the structure of programming promotes the idea of resolvability. The container shapes the content, and not vice-versa. Thus, every thirty minutes there has to be a wrap-up, a conclusion. Can it be that the constant repetition of this expectation does not begin to affect the viewer's psyche? That it cannot be proven to do so is no assurance. There are other questions. For example: if television does function as a surrogate consciousness, does this in any way undermine the viewer's existential base, his awareness of himself as a creature suffering time? No one will disagree with the assertion that televison makes time more palatable. But what does it mean that time is made more palatable? What painful encounters with the voids in the self are thereby short-circuited?

We cannot very well pursue these questions without bringing will into the discussion. Will, the capacity or power whereby the self consciously acts upon itself. It is will that we call upon in order to persevere in an action, to endure difficulty without relinquishing our intention. Any movement against the natural grain of a situation requires some amount of will. But what are the effects upon the will of prolonged passivity, of putting the self repeatedly into a state of suspended animation, of replacing obstacles by a path of least resistance? Is the faculty of will analogous to a muscle—does it atrophy from lack of use? If it is, then the whole issue of television is tremendously important. For the world will not change its nature to conform to the laws of television. If the will is indeed eroded by television watching, then what is affected is the public as well as private domain. The obvious consequence is political passivity, a passivity that readily translates into susceptibility to power. Nature abhors a vacuum; so does the social sphere. Where there is passivity there will flourish, in some form, the will to power. This is not to say that watching television is paving the way for the demagogue. It is to say, however, that the arena of impact may be larger then we at first imagine.

I have avoided almost entirely the discussion of the contents of television. This is not to say that the contents are negligible. They are not. But I don't believe that their effects can be properly taken into account until certain features of the medium have been examined. Secondly—and this is a more elusive reason—I believe that the contents cannot be discussed independently. They are too much influenced and shaped by the nature of the medium. For this reason a substantial amount of what is "on" television exists below the threshold of language. It is too diffuse, too ambient, too random. It generates a liquid near-emptiness that defies words or concepts.

This randomness is an attribute of the medium more than of the contents. It is a direct consequence of the inability of the electron tube to transmit aura. There is a permanent shortage of legitimate material, of visual elements that will effectively "play." The contents, therefore, are always inadequate to the container; they cannot fill it up enough. What happens as a result is that there are, cumulatively speaking, long minutes of visual vacuum—eternal-seeming car-chase sequences, desolate facial pans, etc. Visual Muzak. A network must fill up all of its allotted time, daily, weekly, yearly. There is not enough quality to go around. What little there is must be diluted into the solution of available time. Television maneuvers, therefore, in a field of extremely narrow options. And the options grow fewer as repetition exhausts the basic repertoire of scenarios. Networks are forced to use the same formulaic high-tension sequences over and over. The stock sit-com imbroglio has not changed from the times of Terence. There is no possibility for visual beauty—nothing beautiful has ever survived passage through the electron tube. For beauty is the apotheosis of aura—it dies running the electronic gauntlet. Instead, there is ambience—not "ambiance"—deadtime in which the viewer is brought face to face with the medium itself, its gray, crackling, fundamentally alien presentness.

The case of John Hinckley, Jr., invites a few observations on television content. We are informed that the would-be assassin was a misfit and a loner—the usual epithets—and that prior to his attempt on President Reagan, he put in hundreds of hours in motels across the country watching game shows, soap operas, and crime shows. Now, I would not dare to be so simplistic as to assert any actual causal connection. Hinckley did not become the kind of person he was by watching television—if he had there would be fifty million Hinckleys in the streets. No, he watched as much television as he did because he was the kind of person he was. The question that emerges is whether or not there was some small but vital area of overlap, some way in which watching exacerbated something in his psyche and rendered certain previously passive traits volatile.

In any case, the issue raised—as murky as it is important—is that of the impact of television, form and content, upon the unconscious. Not just the unconscious of John Hinckley, Jr., but of millions of children and adolescents who have not yet integrated their unconscious into their ego structure. The more hours put in before the pullulating tube, the fewer are the hours spent in contact with the stubborn grain of the world. In other words, the materials absorbed into the unconscious include proportionately more illusion. The unformed, atomized ego structure absorbs the form, the violence, the caricature of relations, and shapes itself to those in the way that it should be shaping itself to actual experience. Again, consider the extreme case—Hinckley. He turned to fantasies of violence, I would argue, not because he had been made violent, but because he did not comprehend what violence really is. Shooting the president was a garish fantasy that took up obvious, available imagery without any understanding of its real nature. Not only is the will subject to erosion; the reality sense is as well.

It has been argued that television, along with certain other developments in modern technology—computerization, information processing—is opening the way for a new social evolution, that the time-honored view of the self—as a solitary, suffering being—is giving way to another. Maybe there is a new socially-integrated species of "mass man" waiting in the wings. If so, this passive acceptance of circuitry, this collective participation in suspended animation, is to be regarded as highly advantageous.

If this turns out to be the case, I, for one, would surround the word "evolution" with a thicket of quotation marks.

I don't believe that transformations like this take place without profound upheaval. I hold with the Freudian model enough to think that repressed instincts return in altered form. The species is not yet at a point where the instincts have atrophied entirely. I pray that it is not one of the secret offices of television to insure that atrophy.

I come back, finally, to my epiphanic moments on neighborhood streets, to my shock at seeing so many separate patches of blue light. I cannot shake the feeling that these form in their aggregate some new terrestrial constellation. Like all constellations, this one will have to be named and charted. And we will have to determine whether its occult influences are finally benign or not. I would be surprised if they were.

NOTES

1. All Norman Mailer quotations are taken from the essay "Of A Small and Modest Malignancy, Wicked and Bristling with Dots," in *Pieces and Pontifications* (Boston: Little, Brown Co., 1982).

2. All Walter Benjamin quotations are taken from the essay "The Work of Art in the Age of Mechanical Reproduction," in *Illuminations,* translated by Harry Zohn (New York: Harcourt Brace, 1968).

The Beatles as Artists: A Meditation for December Ninth

James Anderson Winn

The stark white graphics on the television screen were terrible in both their symmetry and their finality: John Lennon: 1940–1980. If you had thought of him as permanently twenty-five, the knowledge that Lennon had reached age forty became a part of the larger, more horrifying news that he was dead. For even in separation and disarray, the Beatles served several generations as symbols on which to hang fantasies, aspirations, and not-yet-formed identities. And as they came to realize, first from the physically dangerous way their young fans pelted them with jelly beans and grabbed at their clothing, then from the grinding daily impossibility of achieving privacy, their status as symbols was a heavy burden indeed. Typically, it was John who found a way of expressing their plight, with a metaphor many found scandalous; in a song complaining about the way the press hounded him on his honeymoon ("Ballad of John and Yoko," 1969), he predicted with wry and eerie accuracy the final bloody cost of his notoriety:

> Christ! You know it ain't easy,
> you know how hard it can be.
> The way things are going
> they're going to crucify me.

Predictably, the first eulogies in the press concentrated on the public aspects of Lennon's career: the mass hysteria called Beatlemania, the admissions of drug use, the flirtation with Eastern religions, the naive but touching billboard campaign for world peace. But I shall be arguing here that the lasting accomplishment of Lennon and his mates, their emergence as self-consciously artistic makers of songs, was itself a response to and attempted escape from the burdens of public notoriety. The Beatles gave their last public concert on 29 August 1966; in that same month, they issued the ironically-titled *Revolver,* an album that signaled a new introspection and a greater willingness to test and tease the hearer. Freed from the exhausting and demeaning business of touring, they were able to sustain their growing complexity and creativity for four highly productive years, during which they produced *Sergeant Pepper's Lonely Hearts Club Band* (1967), *Magical Mystery Tour* (1967), the double album called *The Beatles* (1968), *Abbey Road* (1969), and *Let It Be* (1970)—albums that expanded and apparently exhausted the possibilities of the rock song.

The fruitful withdrawal from public performance necessarily followed at least a decade of frequent performance; indeed, in the early years of the group's development, the Beatles sought every opportunity to perform, presumably because they craved money, success, and notoriety—not because they wished to make an artistic statement. John's wacky and deliberately inaccurate account of their early history, written in 1961, dismisses the motives for their trip to Hamburg as purely monetary: "And then a man with a beard cut off said—will you go to Germany and play mighty rock for the peasants for money? And we said we would play mighty anything for money." One thinks of Dr. Johnson's equally proud and practical statements: "Sir, I could write a preface upon a broomstick" or (even closer) "No man but a blockhead ever wrote, except for money." In both cases, the claim to be motivated by money is at once a declaration of professional pride and a rejection of more Romantic notions of the reasons for creativity. By declaring that one plays concerts or writes prefaces for money, one emphasizes the work involved and casts doubt on the notion that the making of music or literature is a mysterious, metaphysical, quasi-religious calling. By 1968, when "interpretations" of Beatles lyrics were a constant topic of journalism and party conversation, John would debunk the idea of his work as "art" in an even more savage way: "It's nice when people like it, but when they start 'appreciating' it, getting great deep things out of it, making a thing of it, then it's a lot of shit. It proves what we've always thought about most sorts of so-called art. It's all a lot of shit. It is depressing to realize we were right in what we always thought, all those years ago. Beethoven is a con, just like we are now. He was just knocking out a bit of work, that was all." For the young Beatles, playing concerts was basically "knocking out a bit of work," and getting paid meant being able to keep playing, avoiding the duller jobs as deliverymen and factory workers they had briefly held as teenagers. Thus money, as a way to escape the grim Liverpool life of their parents, was a motive they could acknowledge; the notion of making "so-called art," by contrast, was a ludicrous idea they actively rejected.

Fame fell somewhere in between. According to George Harrison, "we used to send up the idea of getting to the top. When things were a real drag and nothing happening, we used to go through this routine: John would shout, 'Where are we going, fellas?' We'd shout back, 'To the Top, Johnny!' Then he would shout, 'What Top?' 'To the Toppermost of the Poppermost, Johnny!'" But was this routine a "send-up," a completely ironic gesture of disdain, or was it a therapeutic way of pretending, as record company after record company turned them down, that getting to the top didn't matter, and thus ultimately a ritual of morale-boosting? If, as I suspect, the young Beatles desperately wanted to achieve fame, but had a concurrent need to pretend to disdain it, would it not be possible to extend that argument to cover their attitude toward "so-called art" as well? To be sure, they did not want to be thought of as pale aesthetes; John's remarks about Beethoven make that clear enough. But it was the same John Lennon who described his song "Because" (1969) as "the *Moonlight* Sonata backwards," and the introduction to that song does strongly suggest the harmonic motion of Beethoven's piece. So despite John's warnings against commentary couched in artistic language, and despite what must always have been their own powerful ambivalence about their status as "artists," the Beatles' tireless work at the making and recording of songs after their withdrawal from public performance was ultimately motivated by a quite subtle and impressive aesthetic sense, and by a driving need to create that they shared with many poets and composers. As John himself once said, "I can't retire. I've got these bloody songs to write."

This remark suggests not only a need to write songs but a sense of that writing as work; like the early story of the morale-boosting routine, it underscores the Beatles' determination and persistence, qualities that would serve them well when their musical ideas became so complex as to require hours of overdubbing and mixing. Even George Martin, the producer whose technical expertise had so much to do with the excellence of the later albums, has spoken admiringly of the Beatles' patient perfectionism, their capacity for hard work. The Beatles themselves, while sometimes disparaging their group as "an average band," were nonetheless careful to give themselves credit for putting out effort. Speaking of the pressure under which he and John often produced the last few songs to fill out an album, Paul McCartney once referred to such songs, written by "pure slog," as "not necessarily worse than ones done out of imagination," indeed "often better," and John extended this principle to a definition of "talent" as "believing you can do something." This notion of talent as confidence and effort, a curiously overlooked consequence of the Beatles' working-class origins, freed them from the crippling Romantic notion of "originality" as "inspiration." Without knowing it, the Beatles were recovering a philosophy of art frequently encountered in the Renaissance and the eighteenth century, the simpler idea of the artist as artisan. Paul used to write proudly at the top of each of the hundreds of unrecorded songs they wrote as teenagers, "Another Original by Lennon and McCartney," but the songs were actually highly derivative, drawing on Elvis Presley, Chuck Berry, and the English music hall, among other sources. By turning out these imitative exercises, and by striving in their singing for flawless imitations of Elvis or Little Richard, the Beatles were putting themselves through an apprenticeship of the kind thought normal for poets and composers before the triumph of Romanticism: one thinks of Shakespeare's Plautine plays, or of Pope's derivative *Pastorals,* or of Beethoven's early exercises in a style overtly dependent on Haydn and Mozart. For these artists as for the Beatles, creation was hard work, and apprenticeship involved the mastering of idioms learned from earlier artists. At the level of vocal style, those imitated idioms remained with the Beatles as *personae:* as late as *Abbey Road* Paul was using his "Little Richard" voice for "Oh Darling," and his "Elvis" voice for the barrel-house bridge of "You Never Give Me Your Money" ("Out of college, money spent . . . ").

Beyond providing a poet or composer with a sense of what style *is* or a *persona* he may later employ with ironic effect, imitation may also be a way of developing the habit of making; having written their hundreds of teenage "originals," John and Paul were ready to flex those muscles in more personal ways when their chance came. In their very first English recording, made in November 1962, they display, at least in embryo, a distinct idiom as composers and singers, though their lyrics remain shamelessly conventional. They knew that the path "to the Toppermost of the Poppermost" would lead through the recording studios, and that their material for records would have to be different or arresting in some way besides the sheer volume on which they had relied in Hamburg. They also had the good fortune to begin recording at a moment when seeming new or different was not terribly difficult; American and English popular music were both in a period of stagnation. After a great burst of energy in the middle 1950s, largely the result of Elvis Presley's popularizing of a previously black "rhythm and blues" idiom, American "Top 40" hits had settled into a predictable pattern: chord changes were restricted to primary triads (usually I-VI-IV-V, in that order); guitar playing was almost always a mindless banging out of those chords, with very little linear interest; vocal harmony rarely involved anything more complex than the smooth thirds of the Everly Brothers; lyrics, rhythms, and melodies were equally dull. Only the Beach Boys, still at a very early stage, promised any development beyond this pattern. In England, where the top group was Cliff Richard and the Shadows, the situation was no better, indeed, as the antiseptic primness of that group's style suggested, probably worse.

The Beatles' first single ("Love Me Do" and "PS I Love You") was palpably different. Their teenage fans, when referring to the "new sound" they heard in these songs, were probably responding first of all to the strong two-part singing of John and Paul, the most immediately obvious of a number of principles of contrast that would make their maturer work so musically interesting. Paul, a natural tenor with unusually clear, well-produced high notes, sounded quite unlike John, a natural baritone singing with obvious but expressive strain when reaching for his high notes. (Later, the Beatles would find uses for John's low range: he sings a low G in "I'm a Loser" and a low A in "Happiness is a Warm Gun.") The frequent open fifths between the voices in "Love Me Do" emphasize this difference in vocal quality; unlike the Everly Brothers and others who sought an anonymously smooth blend, the Beatles had to be heard as individuals working together. Even in "Love Me Do," first composed in their skiffle-group days, John and Paul constantly vary the vocal texture: they sing separately, in unison, in octaves, in fifths, in thirds, and even in contrary motion. This variety of texture, together with George's tight, witty guitar work and John's bluesy harmonica, gives a basically primitive song enough musical content to sustain our interest.

The desire for variety was a compositional principle, not merely a matter of performance. Remembering how they decided to proceed after their highly successful second single ("Please Please Me"), Paul says: "we decided we must do something different for the next song. We'd put on one funny hat, so we took it off and looked for another one to put on." Other groups were content to grind out follow-up songs in the mold of the last hit, but the Beatles had an almost obsessive need to "change hats"; it came to characterize their approach to composition, instrumental texture, electronic production, and form (both the form of individual songs and the larger forms they learned to construct on whole album sides). Groups with immediately identifiable but unchanging "sounds" (the Supremes, for example) had little difficulty producing individual hits, but their albums, which made the similarities between those hits painfully obvious, seemed pointless. The Beatles, with their rhetorical, hat-changing theory of style, were ideally suited to the album format. The strong contrasts between John and Paul, which extended well beyond mere vocal quality, helped them achieve continual variety. Paul began as a facile composer of melodies and bass lines, John as a writer of clever nonsense words, but even as teenagers theirs was no simple collaboration between tune man and word man. By their own account, John began writing tunes to keep up with Paul, and Paul would eventually be encouraged to improve his lyrics by his contact with John. By not rigorously dividing the tasks, one taking responsibility for words, the other for tunes, as other songwriting teams had done, they gained a much richer and more complex kind of collaboration. As they worked together, each constantly adding to, improving, and developing what the other had done, they achieved not one composite style but a kaleidoscopic series of styles. John even thought of the composing process, verbal and musical, as a matter of linking up "bits"—the more different the "bits," the better, as in "I Am the Walrus" or "Happiness is a Warm Gun."

Another kind of variety important to the Beatles' later work, its rich harmonic language, is hardly apparent in "Love Me Do," which uses only three chords. But following the principle of contrast, the other side, "PS I Love You," employs augmented dominants and a deceptive cadence on the flatted sixth. Remembering their earliest days together, John once remarked that he and Paul took George into the group "because he knew more chords, a lot more than we knew. So we got a lot from him. Every time we learned a new chord, we'd write a song around it." This reminiscence provides another valuable glimpse into the Beatles' apprenticeship; their willingness to write songs *around* each new chord would prove more important than the chords themselves, which were complex only by comparison with the dull triads of American groups. By writing songs around chords, not merely using chords as ornamental flourishes, the Beatles gained a new principle of variety.

Some of the earliest analytical pieces on their music noticed the frequency of major chords built on the flat sixth and the flat third; my point is that phrases moving through such harmonies may be effectively contrasted with phrases moving through more conventional "changes," as in "It Won't Be Long Now" (November 1963), a song in C major which juxtaposes a refrain moving through A minor against a verse moving through A-flat major. The Beatles were learning to use chord changes not only for variety but for wit, and even as expressive devices. "If I Fell" (August 1964), perhaps the most beautiful of the early songs, gains some of its tenderness by beginning in E-flat minor, with an uncertain and unsettled series of harmonies, while the speaker asks, "If I fell in love with you, would you promise to be true, and help me understand?" With his assertion that "love is more than just holding hands," the song finds D major, its true key; the modulation underscores the text, an early example of something the Beatles did continually in their mature period.

During the three years between their first single and the album called *Rubber Soul* (December 1965), despite a hectic schedule of tours and appearances, the Beatles managed to make steady progress as composers and musicians. They relied less and less on the conventional 32-bar AABA form in which pop songs had most often been written in previous decades, increasingly inventing new, less symmetrical forms; "Another Girl" (August 1965), in which a shortened chorus used as an introduction enjambs into the verse, provides one striking example. They also escaped the rock convention of the "fade out" ending; the endings of "A Hard Day's Night," "And I Love Her," and "We Can Work it Out," each of which restates some harmonic or rhythmic motif of the song in a fresh and conclusive way, justify Leonard Bernstein's famous remark that the Beatles were "the greatest composers of codas since Beethoven." But as they improved and developed, they naturally began to seek effects in the studio which they could not reproduce in performance: the string quartet accompaniment to Paul's "Yesterday," for example, or the technically difficult piano solo George Martin plays on "In My Life." As George Harrison later put it, "we were held back in our development by having to go onstage all the time and do it, with the same old guitars, drums, and bass."

"Having to go onstage and do it" held the Beatles' development back in ways less obvious and more important than mere instrumentation. The chaotic conditions under which they performed made them understandably reluctant to try complex rhythms: a concert in a stadium, where the performers often had trouble hearing each other, was hardly the place to experiment with tricky rhythms, nor would such rhythms have been appreciated by fans who expected such concerts to provide a heavy "beat" as an aid to ritual hypnosis. Significantly, the first Beatles song involving a change of meter, John's "She Said She Said," in which $\frac{4}{4}$ slides into $\frac{3}{4}$ in the third bar of the bridge, was first recorded on *Revolver,* at the point of the withdrawal from public concerts. Once that breakthrough had occurred, effective metric changes were frequent: the energetic $\frac{5}{4}$ bars in "Good Morning, Good Morning" account for some of that song's electricity, while the stumbling alternation of $\frac{4}{4}$ and $\frac{3}{4}$ in "All You Need Is Love" keeps the hearer off balance. Such innovations, while certainly less complex than the rhythms of modern serious music or those of the Indian music that came to fascinate George Harrison, were previously unheard of in rock and roll, in which one unbreakable rule had been regular dance rhythm. ("It's got a good beat, Murray. You could dance to it. I'd give it about 85.") And by breaking free of that rule, the Beatles gained not only a new kind of variety, but the ability to use regular rhythm ironically, again as a *persona*. In John's "Happiness is a Warm Gun," for example, the words of the title are sung to a slow, mindlessly regular $\frac{4}{4}$ beat, while the harmonies move through the I-VI-IV-V triadic pattern of the early 1960s, but that obviously parodic section is preceded by an irregularly accented section in triple time ("Mother Superior, jump the gun"), in which the cross-rhythms suggest African drumming, not "American Bandstand." The juxtaposition enriches both segments, and the implication is that the kind of listener who would require that all music have a beat "you could dance to" is the kind likely to respond to the American hunting magazine ad from which John lifted the title. "Mother Superior" is John's wife Yoko Ono, the Oriental who "jumps the gun" by running traffic signals, so of course her music is irregular, non-Western, and vigorous.

This kind of rhythmic complexity, especially when rendered mimetic by a careful matching to words, requires a listener of a far different kind than the listener addressed by "She Loves You." If the early songs were designed to be heard over a public address system, the later songs were produced to be heard through headphones. Despite the melodic and harmonic and formal progress the Beatles were making during their lucrative years as the "Fab Four," the conditions under which they performed virtually arrested their development as lyricists. John could hardly have projected the punning ambiguities of his later style when singing over the din of thousands of prepubescent girls who had come to hear such unambiguous messages as "I wanna hold your hand." But as the recording studio rather than the public stage became their arena, the Beatles' approach to lyrics began to change. An honest appraisal will have to admit that "Drive My Car," "Norwegian Wood," and "Nowhere Man," all first recorded on the British version of *Rubber Soul,* are the first Beatles songs that can claim to have interesting lyrics; the contrast between these witty, fully shaped lyrics and those of the vapid early love songs is instructive.

In the early songs, the first-person speaker is usually a teenage lover: most often he talks to his girl ("Please please me oh yeh, like I please you"); sometimes he talks about her ("Well, she was just seventeen, /And you know what I mean"); if he complains about her ("Well I gave you everything I had, / But you left me sitting on my own"), it is only as part of a plea for reconciliation ("I beg you on my bended knees"). The situations dramatized by the songs were simple plots into which a teenage girl could project herself, casting her favorite Beatle as the devoted lover; this ploy was probably as important a cause of Beatlemania as Brian Epstein's aggressive press-agentry. But these songs merely set up situations; they never resolve them, leaving what happens *after* the speaker delivers his message to our imagination. Some of the songs on the album *Help!* (August 1965) have a little more bite: now the speaker responds to mistreatment with more resentment ("For I have got another girl, another girl who will love me to the end") and even addresses another male with a threat ("You're going to lose that girl"). But these situations were still simple; the fourteen-year-old girl apparently as msumed as the listener needed only to cast herself as the "other girl" or the mistreated girl whose boyfriend would soon be replaced by a Beatle.

The more complicated songs on *Rubber Soul* make this kind of identification impossible by completing their stories, and by creating characters with whom no teenager would readily identify. In "Drive My Car," for example, we meet a girl who is so confident that she is going to be "famous, a star of the screen" that she offers the speaker a job as her chauffeur:

> "Baby, you can drive my car,
> Yes I'm gonna be a star.
> Baby, you can drive my car,
> and maybe I'll love you."

The speaker is attracted but wary:

> I told that girl that my prospects were good,
> She said, "Baby, it's understood.
> Working for peanuts is all very fine,
> But I can show you a better time."
> "Baby, you can drive my car, . . . " (*etc.*).

So the speaker takes the bait, only to discover that a crucial element is missing:

> I told that girl I could start right away,
> She said, "Baby I've got something to say.
> I got no car and it's breaking my heart,
> But I've found a driver, that's a start."
> "Baby, you can drive my car, . . . " (*etc.*).

Unlike the early songs, this one does not seem designed to arouse sympathy or affection, nor is it simply a complaint, like "Day Tripper." Both the girl, with her delusions of Hollywood, and the speaker, whose good "prospects" yield to a willingness to "start right away," are satirized, and "Drive My Car" marks the first time in the Beatles' development that a speaker is an object of satire. Indeed, he sounds like the kind of marginally employed Liverpool character the Beatles themselves might have been had they not become "stars of the screen," and the girl sounds suspiciously like someone eager to reach "the Toppermost of the Poppermost." By declaring that she wants to be famous, she is able (for one brief moment) to enjoy one of the fruits of fame, an amorous chauffeur. If talent is "believing you can do something," she has it. She cannot create a car out of thin air, but the Beatles do it for her in the exuberant "Beep Beep" refrain that ends the song. If the song satirizes the longings for fame and comfort of both its characters, it does so from the vantage point of people already ambivalent about fame, though doubtless enjoying its comforts. And it cannot be heard in the way audiences presumably heard the early love songs. No teenage girl would identify with the girl in the song, whose fantasies are exposed as illusory; no teenage boy would identify with the speaker, who is foolish enough to believe her. Nor does the song encourage adulation of its makers as sex objects. If we admire them, we must now admire them as we admire the writers of stories, for the amusing shape they have given their little tale and perhaps for the wry and indirect way it dramatizes something about their own lives, in this case their bemusement about their status as "stars."

"Norwegian Wood," another story about a failed encounter with a woman, features a series of absurdities and ambiguities. In the very first line ("I once had a girl, or should I say, she once had me"), a cliché is redefined in a way that makes it ambiguous: in which of its many senses, we wonder, is the word "had" being used? Like the girl in "Drive My Car" this one is associated with a physical object, apparently real this time, but never defined: "She showed me her room, isn't it good Norwegian wood." If we think that the Norwegian wood is her expensive modern furniture, we soon learn otherwise:

> She asked me to stay and she told me to sit anywhere,
> So I looked around and I noticed there wasn't a chair.

We never learn just what the wood is (paneling?), nor do we learn why, after the speaker has "sat on a rug, biding my time, drinking her wine," the girl apparently rejects him:

> She told me she worked in the morning and started to laugh,
> I told her I didn't and crawled off to sleep in the bath.

Most mysterious of all, we are left to puzzle about what really happens the next morning, when our hero wakes up, finds himself alone, and lights a fire, adding the inevitable refrain, "Isn't it good, Norwegian wood." Perhaps he burns her precious wood in the fireplace; perhaps he merely has a smoke. But the song itself is the real act of arson; its hint of destructiveness at the end dramatizes the resentment a working-class youth (say, a singer from Liverpool) might feel after an awkward social failure in an upper-class *milieu*. Still, just as in "Drive My Car," both figures are satirized; if we sympathize with the speaker, we surely also chuckle as he crawls off to sleep in the bath, and John's ability to include himself in the satire saves the song from being merely destructive. Perhaps it is even another song about the limits of fame, if we may credit John's claim that its story is autobiographical; perhaps he learned from the real encounter here turned into fiction that his fame and money were still insufficient to gain him entry into the upper-class world, the world here symbolized by a woman more interested in wood than in sex.

Similar class or political concerns do figure in the lyrics of the

Beatles' maturity (John's "Revolution" and George's "Taxman" and "Piggies" come immediately to mind), but social commentary is finally less important than the basic theme of failed communication established in "Norwegian Wood." As in many later songs, the withholding of information and uncertainty of reference allow "Norwegian Wood" to enact its theme: our confusion about the meaning of the refrain makes us like the speaker, who must also wonder why the girl keeps talking about wood. "Nowhere Man," the third striking lyric on *Rubber Soul,* develops this theme of isolation without recourse to a story; here John invents a mythic figure, significantly described in the third person before being compared to both listener and speaker:

> He's a real Nowhere Man,
> Sitting in his Nowhere Land,
> Making all his nowhere plans for nobody.
> Doesn't have a point of view,
> Knows not where he's going to,
> Isn't he a bit like you and me?

After describing Nowhere Man in that verse, the speaker addresses him directly in the bridge:

> Nowhere Man, please listen,
> You don't know what you're missing,
> Nowhere Man, the world is at your command.

Then the alternation of description and address is recapitulated in even briefer compass:

> He's as blind as he can be,
> Just sees what he wants to see,
> Nowhere Man, can you see me at all?

By talking *about* Nowhere Man and then immediately talking *to* him, John gives the song's point of view a rich confusion. How can we project ourselves into this song? "Please listen, / You don't know what you're missing" sounds like a message to us about the growing complexity of Beatles music, but if we accept that identification of ourselves as Nowhere Man, the song is accusing us of blindness. John's account of the making of the song suggests an alternate possibility: "I was just sitting, trying to think of a song, and I thought of myself sitting there, doing nothing and getting nowhere . . . . Nothing would come. I was cheesed off and went for a lie down, having given up. Then I thought of myself as Nowhere Man—sitting in his nowhere land." But if John is Nowhere Man, then he is talking to himself in this song. By having it both ways ("Isn't he a bit like you *and* me"), the song ultimately shows us how uncertainty about identity and point of view leads to failed communication.

The complexity of these lyrics suggests a more intimate relationship between singer and hearer, and musically these songs are ill-suited to public performance: "Norwegian Wood" employs a sitar and quiet acoustic guitars, while "Nowhere Man" begins with four-part *a capella* singing (a chancy procedure in concert for singers used to instruments— especially Ringo). Musically and lyrically, these are "studio" songs, relying on us to listen carefully and repeatedly to their subtle effects; they are harbingers of the more sweeping changes coming on *Revolver*. On the one single issued between the two albums ("Paperback Writer," June 1966), the Beatles seem to be musing about the meaning of those changes; Paul was the main composer, though the lyrics confirm John's remark that he "helped out." It is hard to escape the conclusion that beneath its satire, this song concerns the new relationship in which the Beatles were beginning to engage the public. This time the story takes the form of a letter:

> Dear Sir or Madam will you read my book?
> It took me years to write, will you take a look?
> Based on a novel by a man named Lear
> And I need a job, so I want to be a paperback writer, paperback writer.

Here we have another satirized speaker, again in part a projection of John, whose own books (*In His Own Write* and *A Spaniard in the Works*) are indeed heavily influenced by the nonsense verse of Edward Lear. But the circles of self-consciousness are just beginning to spin; now the writer summarizes his plot:

> It's the dirty story of a dirty man,
> And his clinging wife doesn't understand.
> His son is working for the Daily Mail;
> It's a steady job, but he wants to be a paperback writer, paperback writer.

Formally, this is a comic use of refrain, a trick as old as the medieval French *rondeau,* enforced by the high seventh chord on the second "paperback writer." Considered as narrative, the song constitutes a tiny example of the Quaker Oats box effect, since the characters in the proffered manuscript are little versions of its maker. But since that maker, the author of the manuscript and the letter, is in turn a version of John, what we finally have here is another consideration of the complex relationship between fame and communication. "Dear Sir or Madam will you read my book" is in many ways the same plea as "Nowhere Man, please listen," but the speaker's need for fame, his hope to be a "paperback writer" (or a "star of the screen" or a Beatle) makes him all too eager to alter his art to gain popularity and money. In the last verse, he is quick to assure the editor that he can write to order: "I can make it longer if you like the style, / I can change it 'round, and I want to be a paperback writer." The main reason why he urges acceptance of his manuscript is its sales potential: "It could make a million for you overnight."

Properly understood, the paperback writer is an even more complex *persona* than the Nowhere Man; he captures the Beatles' ambivalence about fame and communication at the very moment when they made their brave decision to withdraw from that public ritual of fame, the rock concert, a ritual they had come to see as an inferior form of communication—sexual, perhaps political, certainly dramatic, but not finally musical. Leaving the hot, physical communication of such concerts to the Rolling Stones and The Who, they deliberately chose the cooler, more writerly, ultimately more musical medium of the long-playing album, and from *Revolver* on, they made the goal of their work the production of albums: not performances or even individual songs, but whole, structured artifacts with cunning musical and lyrical relations between their parts. Conceived on this larger scale, the later albums demand of the hearer the kind of repeated, serious, analytical attention we normally reserve for high art. Like high art they are impossible to paraphrase: even the published music, roughly accurate as to melodies and chord changes, is hopelessly inadequate as a transcription of *Sergeant Pepper* or *Abbey Road.* The album itself is the text, the finished product, the authority.

The songs on these later albums return to the theme of isolation, questioning whether meaningful communication can ever be achieved, but the albums themselves offer the best answer to that repeated question: they achieve a kind of communication not previously even attempted in popular music, a kind best understood by those fortunate enough to have been part of a successful musical ensemble. Nobody understands how a string quartet achieves perfect attacks and well-tuned chords, but everyone agrees that much of what is involved cannot be discussed verbally. The Beatles in 1966 had already experienced a decade of such privileged musical communication, and their ensemble in the studio years became even tighter. The film *Let It Be,* which preserves some moments from their last recording sessions, offers tantalizing glimpses of this musical communication even though the cohesiveness of the group is already suffering from the strains that would lead to their breakup. Still, we see Paul and Ringo communicating entirely with their eyes as they work out a coherent pattern for bass and drums, John adjusting the tempo of one of Paul's tunes, George working out guitar lines that reveal new features of melodies by the others. And in the case of John and Paul, musical communication was not merely a matter of tight performing ensemble; it extended to composition as well. One example of this uncanny rapport will have to suffice, John's account of the way a tune originally conceived by Paul alone ("Woke up, fell out of bed, dragged a comb across my head"), turned out to be exactly what was needed for the bridge of John's "A Day in the Life." Increasingly aware of the special qualities of this rapport, its superiority as communication to small talk, newspaper interviews, *and concerts,* the Beatles became unable to go through the motions of writing teenage love songs and performing them on stage. That decision doubtless lost them that portion of their audience for whom they were only sex objects or symbols of youthful rebellion, but it gained them the continuing respect of musicians of all kinds.

As John explained in 1968, "We talk in code to each other as Beatles. We always did that, when we had so many strangers round us on tours. We never really communicated with other people. . . . Talking is the slowest form of communicating anyway. Music is much better. We're communicating to the outside world through our music." Indeed they were, and the careful listener to the later albums is not part of a mass audience, but a fortunate eavesdropper, allowed to witness the Beatles' own private kind of communication, and trusted to respond to it; that, I take it, is one meaning of the lines on *Sergeant Pepper* that say "You're such a lovely audience, / We'd like to take you home with us." I have been arguing that collaboration was the crucial factor for the Beatles from the beginning, that by finding ways to bring their disparate voices and contrasting musical personalities together, they achieved a richer and more satisfying art than other groups. My point here is that their abandoning of the concert stage enriched their collaboration and extended it, that their communication with the listener, now more intimate and complex, became more like their communication with each other, and that the primary mode of communication, in both cases, was music.

Once we understand this fact, we can abandon the hopeless process of trying to understand the lyrics of John's most complex later songs as if they had exact, referential meaning. Some commentators imagine that it is sufficient to explain such songs as "Tomorrow Never Knows," "Lucy in the Sky with Diamonds," "I Am the Walrus," "Strawberry Fields," "Glass Onion," and "Happiness is a Warm Gun" by making the obvious point that they seem connected to drug experiences. But even if drugs were a part of the genesis of some of the imagery in these songs, they cannot account for the way that imagery communicates to its hearers. A more serious approach might consider the ways these lyrics achieve the goal of French Symbolist poetry, the way they attain what Pater called "the condition of music." For even if the opaque and nonsensical phrases in these songs originally had some private meaning for the Beatles, we often cannot recover that original reference, so that a phrase like "a soap impression of his wife which he ate and donated to the National Trust" must communicate to us in the way that music *always* communicates to us: not as a series of sounds with precise, lexical meaning, but as a series of sounds rich with suggestion, pregnant with possibilities, resistant to paraphrase. Of the many ways poets have tried to attain "the condition of music," nonsense verse, which prefers rhyming to syntax, sound to logic, is one of the closest approaches. To be sure, part of the fun of nonsense—in Lear, Ionesco, or Lennon—comes from the way it frustrates our instinctive urge to make sense of it; our example is amusing because carving one's wife in soap is absurd, eating the soap carving is more absurd, and donating something one has already eaten is impossible. But pure sound plays a vital role as well; the internal chime of "*ate* and don*ated*" produces what W. K. Wimsatt, in his seminal essay on rhyme, called "an alogical pattern of implication." Because rhyming and punning depend on accidental rather than grammatical resemblances between sounds, they produce kinds of meaning which are purely contextual, unique to the phrase, poem, or song in which they occur. And *all* musical meaning is like that: the note G means nothing by itself, but in a given context, it may be a tonic, a leading tone, or (most like a pun) the pivot note for a modulation. The prevalence of punning on the later Beatle albums is another indication of the dominance there of musical kinds of meaning.

In these great albums, all the strengths we noticed in the Beatles' early work reach fulfillment. George's guitar improvisations move well beyond "riffing": his solo on John's "Good Morning, Good Morning" is the most musically convincing use of distortion ever achieved on the electric guitar, and his conversational "fills" between the phrases of Paul's "She Came in Through the Bathroom Window" contribute wonderfully to that song's oddball comedy. The singing, both solo and background, improves much over that on the early albums, in part because each of the singers develops several distinct vocal styles. These include the *personae* already mentioned, but also softer kinds of singing not possible in concert, for example Paul's folk-like warbling on "Blackbird" or John's mournful chant in "Julia," a song for his dead mother. Rhythmic and harmonic ideas, increasingly sophisticated on the small scale, begin to function on the large scale as well: on side two of *Abbey Road,* the songs actually have a continuous sequence of key relations like a Schubert song cycle; they are also related by repeating chord sequences used motivically and by proportional rhythmic schemes, most obviously in the closely connected sequence from "Mean Mr. Mustard" to "The End." And in ways too subtle and various to list here, all the late albums develop connections between musical and verbal structure.

As any musician knows, the compromising of egos necessary to produce musical ensemble has its costs, and it seems reasonable to infer that when creation, not merely performance, is the goal, the costs are even higher. The talents and egos involved in the Beatles were strong, and sad as it was to witness those final quarrels over the spoils of fame—money, managers, corporations, copyrights—the real wonder is that the inevitable breakup did not occur earlier. Nor was there ever any real hope of a reunion, once the four members had gone their separate and musically disappointing ways. Yet the slightest rumor of some occasion on which they might meet was sufficient for a decade to send a thrill through many of us; the hope that they might somehow regroup, like the hope of the religious for a Second Coming, was a sustaining myth to be cherished in difficult times. As far as popular music is concerned, these are difficult times; in quite different ways, the two dominant styles are both radical rejections of the Beatles' kind of musical communication. Punk, which features crudely revolutionary lyrics, deliberately incompetent playing, and performers selected for their bizarre appearance alone, reduces rock to theater, virtually eliminating music. Disco, which employs monotonously thick chords purged of expressive value, complex total attack rhythms laid on top of a deadly $\frac{4}{4}$ thud, and performers selected for their slick anonymity, reduces rock to Muzak, eliminating any principle of contrast or expression. Faced with that kind of choice, many of us took comfort in the remote hope for a Beatles reunion, and drew sustenance from replaying our Beatle albums. John's death in 1980 deprived us of that unrealistic hope; its anniversary may serve to remind us again of the sustenance.

CREDITS

On the Late Style

Rudolf Arnheim

Our way of looking at the seasons of human life is determined by two conceptions, which I have tried to symbolize in a diagram (fig. 1). One of these conceptions is biological. It describes an arch rising from the weakness of the child to the unfolded powers of the mature person and then descending toward the infirmity of old age. In this view, the late style of life is that of the old man leaning on his cane—the three-legged creature, as the riddle of the sphinx describes him. It is the season of the "winter of pale misfeature," as Keats has it in his sonnet.

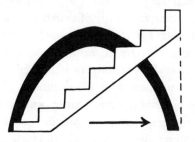

Fig. 1.

The biological view considers not only the decline of physical strength, but also the weakening of what one may call the practical powers of the mind. The acuity of vision and the range of hearing decline, short-term memory begins to fail, reaction time lengthens, and the flexibility of intelligence gives way to a channeled concentration on particular established interests, knowledge, and connections. When these biological aspects determine the view of advanced age, people are afraid of getting old and look upon their capacity for further productive achievement with doubt and irony. *Sins of My Old Age* is the title given by Rossini to a group of late piano pieces; and the unorthodox and uncompromising qualities of late styles in the arts have been attributed often and conveniently to the failing powers of their makers. The Renaissance biographer Vasari observed that Titian, although able to command high prices for his late works, would have done better if in his last years he had painted only as a pastime, in order not to diminish, by weaker works, the reputation of his better years. Most of us nowadays, however, admire Titian's late works as his most original, most beautiful, and most profound. Correspondingly, there is another way of looking at the accomplishments of the aging mind.

This second conception complements the first by finding in the passing of the years an ever-continuing increase in wisdom. In my diagram, the symmetry of the biological arch is overlaid by a flight of steps leading from the limitations of the child to the high worldview of those who have lived long and have seen it all. It is a conception that expresses itself socially and historically in reverence for ancient counselors, prophets and rulers and respect for the older members of the traditonal family. It accounts also for the attention paid to the late works of artists and thinkers. The curiosity of our modern theorists and historians about the particular character of late works is often coupled with the expectation of finding the highest achievements, the purest examples, the deepest insights in the final products of a life of search and labor.

Although reverence for the old probably exists in every mature culture, the theoretical interest in the motives, attitudes, and stylistic characteristics of late styles presumably is limited to periods that have reached a late phase of their own development. This is so not only because history and psychology are favorite occupations of late civilizations, but also because generations discovering in their own conduct the symptoms of a declining age are naturally interested in the great examples of the corresponding stage of individual development. In fact, we may not be able to go very far in a study of late styles without finding parallels to them in certain features of our present aesthetic and intellectual climate and perhaps also in our personal way of life.

Inevitably we begin by looking at works created at the end of long careers. Longevity is one of our indispensable assistants, and only with hesitation do we also consider the late products of short careers. We dwell on the late works of a Michelangelo, Titian, Rembrandt, Cézanne, Goethe, or Beethoven, who all lived long lives; but it takes a special dispensation to include artists like Mozart, Van Gogh, or Kafka, who died young. These short-lived geniuses can concern us only if we assume that death did not strike them blindly in the midst of a career that was structured for a longer duration. Biologists tell us that small, short-lived mammals live at a correspondingly faster pace than large, long-lived ones. I read recently that small creatures breathe faster and have faster-beating hearts, so that all mammals do roughly the same amount of breathing and heartbeating during a normal lifespan. One is tempted to suspect that something similar happens in some of those short but spectacularly rich human careers, in which a maturity of a particular kind distinguishes the last efforts.

Be this as it may, we are not merely concerned with chronological age when we refer to the late works of artists. What we are interested in is a particular style, the expression of an attitude that is found often, but neither necessarily nor exclusively, in the end products of long careers. On the other hand, there are people, and there are artists among them, who live to "a ripe old age" without ever receiving the blessings of maturity.

Much of what is observed about the qualities of the typical aged mind concerns the relation of the person to his or her world. In this respect we may distinguish three phases of human development. An early attitude, found in young children and surviving in certain aspects of cultural and individual behavior, perceives and understands the world only in broad generalities. The various facts of experience are not clearly articulated. In particular, there is little differentiation between the self and the other, the individual and his world. It is a state of mind in which the outer world is not yet segregated from the self, a state that Freud described as the origin of the "oceanic feeling."

This primary lack of differentiation is followed by the second phase, a gradual conquest of reality. The self as an active and observant subject distinguishes itself from the objective world of people and things. This is the most important outcome of an increasing capacity for discrimination. The child learns to distinguish categories of things and to identify individual objects, places, and persons. An adult attitude develops, to which our Western culture offers a historical parallel in a new interest in the facts of outer reality, a curiosity that awoke first in the thirteenth century and created during the Renaissance the age of natural science, scientific exploration, and the cultivation of individual persons, places, and events. It is a state of mind expressed in chronicles, in treatises on geography, botany, astronomy, anatomy, as well as in naturalistic painting and portraiture. This second phase of the human attitude toward reality is distinguished by a hearty worldliness that scrutinizes the environment in order to interact with it.

Perhaps that germinal age of the Renaissance already contained some features of the third phase, in which we recognize the symptoms of aging. But it is in more recent times that the characteristic late attitude has manifested itself clearly. I will mention some of the symptoms.

First, interest in the nature and appearance of the world is no longer motivated primarily by a desire to interact with it. The paintings of the Impressionists, for example, are the products of a detached contemplation. The images depicting the natural and the man-made setting abandon the properties of texture, contour, and local color that report on the material particularity of the objects. The character and practical value of those material characteristics is not considered relevant. A similar attitude can be observed in certain aspects of pure science, especially as it develops in Europe.

Such a detachment of contemplation from practical application is not simply negative. It goes with a worldview that transcends outer appearance to search out the underlying essentials, the basic laws that control the observable manifestations. This tendency is evident in the physical sciences, and it has also expressed itself recently in the exploration of deep-seated structure in anthropology, psychology, and linguistics.

Another symptom of what may be called the late phase of the human attitude is the shift from hierarchy to coordination. Instrumental here is the conviction that similarities are more important than differences, and that organization should derive from consensus among equals rather than from obedience to superordinate principles or powers. Socially, of course, this calls for democracy, the most mature and sophisticated form of human community, which presupposes the greatest wisdom even though in practice, more often than not, it makes do with much less. In the arts it involves, for example, the renunciation of governing compositional schemes, such as the triangular groupings of the Renaissance, in favor of the spread of coordinated units. These units, in turn, forgo the uniqueness that gives each element of a composition an individual character of its own and identifies its equally unique place and function in the composition or plot of the whole. Instead, in works of a late style the viewer or listener meets the same kind of thing or event in every area of the spatial pattern and in every phase of what in earlier styles is narration or development in time. The sense of eventful action gives way in all dimensions to a state or situation of pervasive aliveness. This structural uniformity in the late phase cannot but remind us of the earliest one, in which, as I suggested, discrimination between things as well as between the self and the world is still weak. However, a lifetime of difference separates a state of mind that cannot yet discriminate from one that no longer cares to.

In describing the three phases of the human attitude I have already anticipated much of what can be said about the characteristics of works of art in a late style. Let me dwell for another moment on the tendency to homogenize the structure of a work as a whole. In painting, the various objects and parts of objects lose their distinctive textures, which once defined them as individual characters in the picture story. In earlier portraits, the smoothness of a woman's hair contrasted with the heavy flow of the brocade, and the skin differed from the fabric as in landscapes the foliage of trees differed from granite and marble. In a late work, all these subjects have become creatures of the same kind, characterized by the community of their fate and mission. Similarly, in late musical works, e.g., in Beethoven's last string quartets, timbres of the various instruments blend into the rich sounds of a kind of superorgan, and the antagonism of phrase and counterphrase gives way to an articulate flow.

Such evenness of texture goes with a lack of interest in causal relations. The dynamics of cause and effect presuppose agents and targets distinguished from each other by differences in character and different places in the whole. For example, in classical French tragedy it is the profound difference between, say, Queen Phèdre and Prince Hippolyte and between their positions in the constellation of human relations that generates the propulsive energy of the drama. Compare this, say, with the late mood of the novelist Flaubert, in whose stories characters of ambiguous motivation and muted impulse drift toward, and away from, one another.

The assimilation and fusion of elements, indicating a worldview in which the resemblances outweigh the differences, are accompanied in late works of art by a looseness of the work's fabric, a diffuse-looking kind of order creating an illusion of the various components' floating in a medium of high entropy with interchangeable spatial locations. The second part of Goethe's play *Faust* as well as that of his novel *Wilhelm Meister* gives the impression of loosely strung episodes, united by a common theme. Or compare an early version of Rembrandt's *Return of the Prodigal Son,* in which father and son have rushed toward each other and are hooked together like tongue and groove, with the very late version, in which five human apparitions, each reposing within itself, interact mainly by their common immersion in darkness. Or notice how much coordination rather than hierarchy there is in the late-style compositions of Rodin's *Gates of Hell* and *Burghers of Calais*. There again, causal interaction is replaced by common fate.

This brings to mind a related feature of comparison between styles, which I can best describe by saying that in typical works of what I called the second phase, the phase of biological vigor, the dynamics of the total action originates in separate motivational centers. This is most easily seen in a figural work, where, let us say, the brutal aggression of a Sextus Tarquinius copes with a Lucretia vigorously defending her virtue. The same kind of dynamics activates the components of a musical conception typical of that active outlook on life, for example, in the interplay of the peasants' dance and the thunderstorm in Beethoven's *Pastoral* Symphony. One might say that the artist, from whose initiative all activity in the work ultimately springs, has delegated his energy resources to the agents of his composition. And these agents behave as though they were acting on their own inherent impulses.

In late works, on the contrary, the dynamics moving the various characters are not of their own making. Rather they are subjected to a power that affects them all equally. As always, the artist has delegated his initiative to his creation, but this initiative no longer animates the individual motors of his characters. It is now manifest as the power of a fate pervading the work's entire world. The living and the dead, the corpse of Christ and his mourning mother, they all are now beings in the same state, equally active and inactive, aware and unaware, enduring and resisting.

This changed mechanism for generating and distributing energy in the late works manifests itself in a different handling of the formal means of expression, for example, in the role of light in painting. In an earlier style, light is produced by a well-defined source, which, as a distinctive agent of its own, casts illumination upon the recipients, upon human figures or architecture, and they in turn display their individual reactions to it. But in a late Titian or Rembrandt, the entire scene is aglow. The state of being inflamed is possessed and shared by all. One might describe this phenomenon more generally by saying that the imports from the world of reality, in which discrete forces act upon one another, have been metabolized by the aging mind so fully as to be transformed into characteristics of the presentation as a whole. They have become attributes of what we call style. The late style fuses the contributions of the objectively given in a unitary worldview, the outcome of long and deep contemplation.

A single example from the visual arts may serve to illustrate some of these properties of the late style. Titian's *Christ Crowned with Thorns* (fig. 2), painted six years before his death as the reworking of an earlier composition, all but hides the central figure of the flagellated Christ in a pattern of coordinated figures. They are knit together by a weave of sticks that makes us look in vain for a dominant hierarchy—the kind of structure that would focus on the principal theme in its cause-and-effect relations with the subordinate elements. The torturers and the victim are not clearly distinguished. They are intertwined in a pervasive but not excessive action, an action that fills much of the pictorial space as an overall property of the represented world as a whole. A loose network of connections leaves each figure somewhat detached from the others, and a diffuse glow of golden light seems to emanate from each head and limb rather than strike the scene from some external source.

The differences between late and earlier styles point to a worrisome consequence in teaching for the relation between master and disciple. If the differences in outlook and procedure are so great, how are teaching and learning possible? Pedagogy is at its most powerful when the truly wise serve as teachers to the truly youthful. But how can there be any give and take if there is no common base? Indeed, the conflict between what the master has attained and what the disciple is striving for can be observed in all productive instruction. But this conflict is only one aspect of the relation. The art historian Kurt Badt, whose observations on our subject are reflected in much of what I have said here, has maintained that the late works of artists do not influence the style of their successors. It is rather the works created by the great men in their middle years that act as examples and guiding images to posterity and thereby make history. But "the late works of the great masters, which come about at the same time as the period style of a subsequent generation, tower above the flow of history as solitudes [*Einsamkeiten*] inaccessible to the context of time."[1]

Such an outcome would follow logically from the differences between young and old that we have observed. But what actually happens may be more complex. One can think of examples in which the late works, although indigestible to the immediately following generation, powerfully affect a later one. This is true for the poetry of Hölderlin, the music of Wagner, and the late paintings of Cézanne. In such instances a

Fig. 2. Titian. *Christ Crowned with Thorns,* 1570. (Alte Piakothek, Munich.)

new generation assimilates from a late style those aspects it can accommodate to its own outlook. As a relatively recent example we may recall the influence of the late works of Claude Monet on the American abstract expressionists. In Monet's last landscapes we see the final outcome of a lifelong development, during which the subject matter was gradually absorbed by an ever more conspicuous texture, fully realized in his water lilies, his footbridge paintings, and other late works. Essential to our appreciation of these works, however, is the fact that, despite the radical transformation of the subject matter, all the fullness and wealth of experienced reality remains present. The greatest possible range of artistic content reaches from the concreteness of the individual things of nature to the uniformity of the artist's all-encompassing view. This we might describe as the final achievement of the human mind when it matures at an advanced age. It is only natural that in the case of Monet, the influence he exerted on the painters of a later and younger generation could not reach the depths he had attained himself.

I can think of no better way to conclude these observations than by quoting a statement written by an artist, Hans Richter, in his mid eighties, when he thought back to an exhibition of the late paintings of Lyonel Feininger.[2] Richter was struck by the spiritualization that had occurred in the work of the painter of landscapes, seascapes, and towns:

> Hardly were there any "subjects" left. In the transparency of the picture plane it no longer mattered whether there was a sky, an ocean, a sail, or a human figure. Here spoke the wisdom of an aged artist for whom the world of objects had shed its disguise. Visible beyond that world, inherent in it and above it, was the unity of Nirvana, the creative nowhere to which the artist had entrusted himself. That was what spoke in those images. A ringing voice without sound, on the border between being and not-being, a man capable of giving utterance in this sphere of the almost divine.

NOTES

1. Kurt Badt, *Das Spätwerk Cézannes* (Constance: Universitätsverlag, 1971), 6.

2. Hans Richter, *Begegnungen von Dada bis heute* (Cologne: Dumont, 1973), chap. 8.

Lawrence of Arabia:
The Man, the Myth, the Movie

Michael A. Anderegg

Lawrence of Arabia. The title of David Lean's 1962 film evokes a potent historical/mythic discourse. "Lawrence," T. E. Lawrence, Thomas Edward Lawrence. The name summons up images of Oxford commonrooms, quiet country villages, London libraries, A Boy's Own Paper, other British Lawrences (D. H., Sir Thomas), England, Britain, Britannia. "Arabia." Exoticism, the East, the Orient, the Arabian Nights, the Crusades, the empire. And the preposition "of"—"of Arabia." Not *in* Arabia, not *and* Arabia, but *of* Arabia: derived or coming from; possessing, having; characterized or identified by. Lawrence of Arabia; Gordon of Khartoum; Clive of India. What a world of imperial glory those phrases suggest! The one among the many, a figure in a landscape, the white man's burden, dangerous journeys through "anters vast and deserts idle"; Occidental heroes in an Oriental world.

Lawrence of Arabia. David Lean's film exemplifies, extends, revises, mystifies, distorts, elucidates, revivifies one of the most compelling heroic myths of the twentieth century. From the moment his exploits became known, the character and actions of T. E. Lawrence captured the imagination of professional and non-professional writers alike—poets and journalists, military historians, psychiatrists, playwrights; the exalted and the humble, the general and the private, the Viscount and the no-account—nearly anyone, it sometimes seems, capable of putting pen to paper. Among so many voices, so many interpreters, one in particular stands out: T. E. Lawrence himself, whose monumental, baroque masterpiece *The Seven Pillars of Wisdom* (together with *Revolt in the Desert,* its abbreviated offspring) has given the myth some of its most compelling and ambiguous expressions. The Lawrence legend has not been an exclusively literary creation, however. Indeed, it was not the printed word that first gave form to the portrait of Lawrence that has come down to us. Although many would credit Lowell Thomas's 1926 book *With Lawrence in Arabia* with the primary responsibility for popularizing and glorifying Lawrence's adventures, it was Thomas's earlier (1919–20) film/lecture program "With Allenby in Palestine and Lawrence in Arabia" that once and for all transformed a fairly obscure young Englishman into a full-fledged romantic hero.

Lowell Thomas's media spectacle of the Arabian campaign, perhaps the most successful "show" of its kind in history, was first presented in New York, initially at the large Century Theater and then at the even larger Madison Square Garden. Encouraged by his New York reception, Thomas took the program to London. A triumphant six month engagement followed. Booked into the Covent Garden Opera House (which had never before played host to the movies), Thomas was forced by the ever-increasing demand for tickets to move into the more spacious Royal Albert Hall, eventually transferring to Queen's Hall and then Philharmonic Hall. Later, he went on a tour of much of the rest of the English-speaking world. The London production, quite elaborate by the standards of the time, began with a live prologue evoking a moonlit evening on the Nile, the sets and costumes—from the opera *Joseph*—courtesy of Sir Thomas Beecham. But it was the film shot by Thomas's cameraman Harry Chase that truly capitivated audiences. Speaking more or less *ex tempore* while the film was running, and accompanied by the Royal Welch Guards Band, Thomas wove an Arabian Nights spell. Eric Kennington, who would become the primary illustrator for *The Seven Pillars of Wisdom,* recalled years later that the first time he saw Lawrence was on film at the Albert Hall: "glorious photography, glamour and oratory. I came out drunk." When he met Lawrence in person, he had a difficult time connecting him with Thomas's "screen seraph." "Mr. Lowell Thomas," Lawrence wrote at the time, "made me a kind of matinee idol."

It is precisely as a matinee idol that Lawrence returns to the screen and achieves an apotheosis of sorts in *Lawrence of Arabia.* The bright packaging of the Lawrence legend thus comes full circle. But before the legend, there was a man. Lawrence, after all, is a hero of our own time, not some dimly perceived figure from a lost age. The details of his life may not be as readily available to us as they were to an older generation, but details—places and names and dates—there are in abundance. In themselves, of course, they explain very little. Even so, a brief and, insofar as possible, factual account of Lawrence's career may ease entry into a discussion of the film that career inspired. Actually, a factual account of Lawrence that does not in some way contradict another factual account is not really possible: the best one can do is point to those junctures where fact, fiction and myth hopelessly intertwine.

T. E. Lawrence was born in Tremadoc, North Wales, in 1888. His father, a minor Anglo-Irish baronet named Thomas Chapman, had adopted the surname Lawrence after deserting his wife to live with his former housekeeper. Thomas Edward was the second son of this illicit but in nearly every other way unremarkable, conventionally bourgeois union. Indeed, so unremarkable was his family life that he probably did not discover his illegitimacy until well into his teens. Thomas's boyhood was marked by frequent moves—Scotland, Jersey, France, the New Forest—dictated by the senior Lawrence's restless nature. The family finally settled in Oxford where he attended the local high school and, in due time, the University. From an early age, Thomas exhibited a precociousness and intellectual curiosity that set him off from his peers. He became interested in the Middle Ages and traveled by bicycle and foot over parts of Europe and throughout the Near East, researching what would become his senior thesis, "Crusader Castles." After taking a "first" in the Honours School of History, Lawrence went to the site of the ancient Hittite city of Carchemish, on the banks of the Euphrates, as a member of an archaeological expedition. While there he immersed himself in Middle Eastern culture and learned (well or poorly, depending on your source) Middle Eastern languages. The myth would have it that Lawrence spent more time spying on the Turks and the Germans than he did digging up artifacts. Certain proof for this is lacking, but we needn't doubt that any true-blue Englishman of Lawrence's generation, finding himself in a foreign and potentially hostile part of the world (in this case, the Ottoman empire), would have instinctively kept eyes and ears open.

Soon after the outbreak of World War I, Lawrence, logically enough given his background and studies, was offered a minor position with British Intelligence in Cairo. A fairly nondescript second lieutenant assigned to making maps, he nevertheless had an impact on his superiors (negative as well as positive) disproportionate to his rank and duties. Soon, he found himself involved with a projected revolt of the Arab tribes against their Turkish masters. Here, conflicting testimony becomes particularly dissonant. Lawrence, depending on which account you follow, (*a*) personally chose Prince Feisal as the nominal leader of the Arab revolt, but in fact led the revolt himself; (*b*) was merely an unimportant liaison officer who transported gold from English coffers to Arab pockets; or (c) operated somewhere in between these extremes. Whatever his role, most accounts agree that Lawrence affected Arab dress, mingled freely with Bedouin tribesmen, was involved in the Arab conquest of Akaba, and spent much of the war blowing up Turkish trains. What is certain is that Lawrence eventually came to be seen far and wide as the leader of the Arab revolt, the uncrowned Prince of Mecca, a modern Arabian knight. His exploits, as I've noted, were publicized after the war first by Lowell Thomas and subsequently by others in England and America. Lawrence, in part because he was unsullied by the madness and mud of trench warfare, became one of the few genuine heroes of the First World War.

After the war, Lawrence—disillusioned, it would seem, by the compromises and cynical worldliness of the Peace Conference, perhaps guilty about his ambiguous role in the Arab Revolt, seemingly disgusted by his new-found celebrity status—retreated into obscurity. First as Private Shaw in the Royal Air Force, briefly as Private Ross in the Tank Corps, and then once again in the RAF, Lawrence became the best-known anonymous soldier in the British Armed Forces. While in the ranks, Lawrence/Shaw/Ross wrote his memoirs of the revolt, *The Seven Pillars of Wisdom,* but withheld publication for reasons that remain hard to fathom. In 1926, his abridgement of *Seven Pillars,* entitled *Revolt in the Desert,* was published to great acclaim and Lawrence's fame grew. He nevertheless remained in the ranks until February, 1935. Three months after his discharge, Lawrence was fatally injured when he was thrown from his motorcycle on a quiet country road near Clouds Hill, his modest retirement cottage in Dorset.

This drastically foreshortened outline of Lawrence's life barely hints at the complex myth associated with his name. Virtually from the moment he became a public figure, Lawrence inspired contradictory responses from those who came under his spell. Hostility and mistrust exist side by side with an admiration frequently verging on hero-worship. His stock has risen and fallen at regular intervals. Both as a private individual and as a public figure, Lawrence's reputation suffered a particularly severe blow with the publication, in 1953, of Richard Aldington's *T. E. Lawrence: A Biographical Inquiry.* This curiously shrill exercise in debunking calls into question virtually every claim Lawrence has on our interest and sympathy. But even if we refuse to give credence to Aldington's hatchet job, a dispassionate look at the record reveals a man whose actions and indeed whose very being can only be apprehended through a haze of ambiguity and paradox. Which may explain why, quite apart from our current preoccupation with the notion of imperialism and with the politics of the Middle East, he continues to intrigue and fascinate us.

The paradox, or rather, the cluster of paradoxes inherent in the Lawrence myth undoubtedly was what inspired David Lean and his colleagues to undertake their cinematic project. Three particularly absorbing contradictions find roughly equivalent expression in the film. These might be schematized as follows:

1. *The Weakness/Strength Paradox*. The slight, short, pale, ascetic T. E. Lawrence, an Oxfordian with a schoolgirl giggle, connoisseur of fine printed books, collector of brass rubbings, perhaps homosexual, perhaps asexual, almost certainly masochistic *versus* the courageous, dashing, magnetic Oriental Lawrence, Prince of Mecca, uncrowned King of Arabia, bravely enduring torture, thirst, hunger, and hundreds of other miseries and discomforts in a noble cause. Wrote W. H. Auden (employing categories borrowed from Christopher Isherwood): "To me Lawrence's life is an allegory of the transformation of the Truly Weak Man into the Truly Strong Man."

2. *The Good/Bad Imperialist Paradox*. The Lawrence who wants to lead an oppressed people from bondage to freedom, who loves the East, the desert nights, the strength and courage of his Bedouin comrades, who can love an Arab boy with passion and kindness, who fights for Prince Feisal at Versailles; and the Lawrence who wants to make Arabia the first "brown" dominion, who hides knowledge of the infamous Sykes-Picot agreement from his Arab friends, who sells Feisal out at the Peace Conference, who finds himself personally soiled by contact with the Arabs, who can write that "for an Englishman to put himself at the disposal of a red race is to sell himself to a brute, like Swift's Houhynyms."

3. *The Paradox of Self-Promotion/Self-Abnegation*. On the one hand, the posturing Lawrence, posing for the camera of Lowell Thomas's photographer dressed in flamboyant white robes, collaborating on biographies with Thomas, with Robert Graves, with Basil Lidell-Hart, constructing a massive literary edifice on the foundation of his heroic exploits; on the other hand, the Lawrence who hides out in a London attic, who discourages biographers, who continually delays publication of his memoirs, who enters the RAF and the Tank Corps as a private, constantly changing his name: Ross, Shaw, Chapman, "T. E. Lawrence."

It is on these paradoxes, much more than on any specific account of Lawrence's life, that David Lean and his screenwriter, the playwright Robert Bolt, constructed their version of Lawrence. In doing so, they limited their narrative to selected key events from the Arab campaign. We see nothing of Lawrence before or after the war outside of the opening sequence which dramatizes his death. The remainder of the film—a flashback of sorts—focuses on four events in particular: the conquest of Akaba, Lawrence's capture and torture in Deraa, the massacre at Tafas, and the fall of Damascus. Two military victories—the first relatively minor strategically but almost unambiguously glorious, the second major but fraught with ironies—frame two personal crises central to Lawrence's psychic life. Interspersed throughout are various confrontations, journeys, and military skirmishes, all of which enrich and complicate the meaning of the film's larger structural units.

Lawrence of Arabia does not attempt to present or to explain the "real" T. E. Lawrence (whoever he was); it is, like all films—even those that aspire to documentary truth—a fiction. The person who was T. E. Lawrence does not and could not exist in the film. As soon as he appears on the screen, the Lean/Bolt/Peter O'Toole Lawrence takes on a life independent of historical fact. All the same, the film from time to time draws upon extracinematic Lawrences (Lowell Thomas's Lawrence, Richard Aldington's Lawrence, and, of course, Lawrence's Lawrence). At such moments, we the audience are able to compare other texts to the filmic text, insofar as those texts are available to us. Nevertheless, the film presents its own, self-contained world. *Lawrence of Arabia* is, among other things, an essay on the paradox of heroism, on the inevitable, unfathomable fissures that separate impulse from act, history from myth, the self from the image of the self. Lean and his collaborators make no attempt to resolve the paradoxes I have outlined above; rather, they interknit and transform them in such a way as to enrich, in filmic terms, the texture of the Lawrence myth.

The first paradox—Weak Man/Strong Man—finds expression in *Lawrence of Arabia* primarily in terms of Lawrence's psychosexuality: as is true of the various written accounts of the historical Lawrence, suggestions of homosexuality, masochism, and sadism inform the film's text. Here, ambiguities are especially pronounced: censorship, in 1962, maintained its strong grip on the commercial cinema. Thus, homoeroticism is simultaneously repressed and exhibited by the text. For many viewers, this coyness probably resolves itself into an assertion of Lawrence's homosexuality. Since sexual "deviancy" has nearly always been treated obliquely and ambiguously in the mainstream cinema, obliqueness and ambiguity themselves signify the presence of what is absent. Even a hint of the forbidden equals the forbidden when the forbidden can only be hinted at. The homosexual subtext serves primarily as metaphor, however, and is to some extent displaced by the foregrounding of sado-masochism as a thematic issue. In any case, insofar as Lawrence's psychosexual anxieties might, from a normative point of view, be considered a weakness, it is part of the film's project to transform that weakness into a strength. Lean and Bolt create a Lawrence who achieves heroism, however qualified that heroism might be, precisely because, in Christopher Isherwood's phrase, he "suffered, in his own person, the neurotic ills of an entire generation."

Whether or not we finally see the film's Lawrence as genuinely a homoscxual is thus of secondary importance; of more interest is the film's equation of a conventionally coded set of mannerisms with effeminacy and, hence, weakness. This equation is stated at the outset; indeed, it is built into Peter O'Toole's performance as Lawrence. His manner and bearing, his gestures and body language, while suggesting a combination of diffidence and quirky individuality, also signify a stereotypical "gayness": O'Toole, particularly in the early scenes, projects a—for the lack of a better word—"fey" image, looking uncomfortably rumpled and decidedly unsoldierly in uniform. None of this is lost on General Murray (Donald Wolfit), the commanding officer whose contempt for Lawrence ("you're the kind of creature I can't stand") seems in excess of any motivation explicitly provided by the discourse. After agreeing to let Lawrence set off on an arduous and dangerous journey to find Prince Feisal, Murray remarks "who knows—might even make a man of him." The comment, in retrospect, is deeply ironic. On the one hand, becoming a "man," in the sense of passing from boyhood to manhood, is precisely what stirring adventure stories like *Lawrence of Arabia* are supposed to be about. Specifically, the film shows how an epicene young Englishman proves himself as courageous, resourceful, and strong as any hardened Arab chieftain. At the same time, Donald Wolfit's pointing of the phrase "might even make a man of him" suggests something else: the distaste of the man of action, sexually self-confident, unthinkingly heterosexual, for the (seemingly) sexually neuter, perhaps homosexual, aesthete. Do Lawrence's subsequent experiences make a man of him? In Murray's terms, they do. Lawrence becomes a great military hero. But he becomes a "man" in another sense Murray could not have intended, for what Lawrence discovers at the end of his Arab adventures is his own humanity, his "manhood" as a member of the human race. Along the way, he is tempted by "godhood," a temptation that transcends "manhood" entirely and ends by making a mockery of Murray's straightforward wish.

The temptation of godhood as a theme in *Lawrence of Arabia* hardly needs elucidating, so self-consciously have Lean and Bolt woven it into their text. This theme manifests itself in Lawrence's increasing isolation, in his donning of spotless white robes which give him visual predominance over the particolored Arabs, in the worshipful attitudes of his followers, and, most notably, in his abrogating to himself the right to execute a man ostensibly because, as an Englishman, he stands above petty tribal rivalries and age-old blood feuds. By presenting Lawrence as a kind of god to the Arabs, the film seems to reenact one of the hoariest clichés found in Hollywood films set in "primitive" cultures and among "savage" tribes: the white westerner who is mistaken for a deity by the dark, superstitious natives. Normally, however, this scenario involves a woman, the "White Jungle Queen" of Edward Field's poem. Which suggests an intriguing speculation. In a film where women are conspicuous by their absence, Lawrence—pale, effeminate, a blond and blue-eyed seraph—becomes a surrogate woman, figurative white goddess. An ambiguous exchange of dialogue points nicely in this direction. Immediately after the fall of Akaba, Sherif Ali (played by the darkly handsome and self-consciously masculine Omar Sharif) brings Lawrence flowers, tossing them on the water at his feet. "Garlands for the conqueror, tributes for the prince, flowers for the man," Ali says. "I'm none of these things, Ali," Lawrence responds. If Lawrence is not conqueror, prince, or man, we might reasonably ask, what is he? Without pushing an admittedly shaky speculation any further, we can note that Lawrence constantly seduces the various Arabs to his view of things, making them love him as well as follow him. "You trouble me like women," Auda says to Lawrence and Ali in the course of one of the most important of these "seductions." However we read the line, Lawrence's manipulative tactics with the Arabs are here clearly exposed as "feminine" wiles. A supposed weakness—Lawrence's effeminacy—is thus transformed into a strength.

Textually allied to Lawrence's effeminacy is his masochism. Moments after the film introduces us to the young Lawrence, an army lieutenant stationed in Cairo, we see him demonstrating his physical self-control by slowly snuffing out a burning match with his fingers. Right off, Lawrence's status as "hero" is complicated and qualified. It is notable that Lawrence performs this trick in front of puzzled but admiring "other rankers"; already, he is an exhibitionist, albeit on a small scale. When one of the soldiers tries to repeat Lawrence's performance, he quickly pulls his hand away from the match, complaining that "it hurts." "Of course it hurts," Lawrence replies. "What's the trick, then?" the soldier asks. "The trick," Lawrence responds, "is in not minding that it hurts." Soon afterwards, having received permission to go into Arabia, Lawrence lights another match, but this time he blows it out in the normal way. By cutting from an enormous close-up of the match to a shot of the burning desert, Lean implies that Lawrence's penetration of Arabia, whatever else may motivate him, functions as a displacement of his masochism, a painful/pleasurable testing of the self. By stages, both the pain and the pleasure increase to an extent Lawrence could not have foreseen. When pain and pleasure, even at their most intense, can no longer be distinguished from each other, Lawrence has reached the breaking point: beyond it lies madness.

The breaking point comes at Deraa, but even before Deraa, his experiences force Lawrence to question his own actions and motives. He knows that war is progressively corrupting him, that he has failed to gauge how much his own dreams and plans involve bloodshed. Most frightening of all, as he confesses to General Allenby (Jack Hawkins), he has come to enjoy the bloodshed. Faced with such self-knowledge, he can only ask Allenby to relieve him from further duty with the Arabs. But Allenby can't let him go, for Lawrence has become a hero, and his heroism is too useful a weapon to cast aside. At this point, there is a break in the filmic text, a break of such magnitude that it must be covered by an intermission. The intense young hero of the film's first half turns into the cynical and vainglorious poseur of the second half while the audience buys popcorn in the lobby. With a boldness remarkable in the commercial cinema, Lean simply omits what would appear to be a crucial transition and thus leaves the audience to its own devices.

When, after the intermission, the film resumes, the first figure we see is Bentley (Arthur Kennedy), the cynical newspaperman very loosely modeled on Lowell Thomas (who was never cynical, at least in public, about Lawrence). Bentley's appearance underlines the shift in focus between the film's two major parts. Lawrence is by now a public figure, a "hero" created by Bentley; ironically, his fame seems to have diminished his responsibilities. Now more of a sideshow than anything else, he and his guerrilla bands derail and loot Turkish trains. A hero in the eyes of the Arabs, he appears vain and childish in ours. The film, at this point, credits Lawrence's debunkers. When Lawrence says of the Turks, "they can only kill me with a golden bullet," his words seem not nearly as ironic as he would like them to be. Soon afterwards, in his "mercy killing" of an adoring Arab servant, Lawrence finds himself once again responsible for the death of someone close to him (he earlier executed Gassim, the man he brought out of the Nefud desert, and he lost his other servant boy, Daoud, in quicksand). Being a god means sacrificing merely human bonds. Shortly after this, through his experience in Deraa, Lawrence finally comes face to face with his simple mortality, his need for a "ration of common humanity."

The film's presentation of the Deraa episode may fairly be criticized as irritatingly oblique. Lawrence, disguised as a poor Arab, enters the Turkish stronghold at Deraa on a reconnaissance mission. Picked up by Turkish soldiers (after making himself quite conspicuous), he is brought before the local Bey (José Ferrer), who appears to be more than professionally interested in discovering an Arab with fair skin and blue eyes. In resisting the Bey's clearly sexual advances, Lawrence knees him sharply in the groin. The Bey's guards, degenerate-looking specimens who take obvious sadistic pleasure in their task, flog Lawrence mercilessly and then throw him out into the night. Lawrence, in *The Seven Pillars of Wisdom,* describes his experience with some hesitation and circumlocution, but nevertheless with an overall frankness that caused him considerable retrospective pain. As he vividly tells it, the guards not only beat him but also played "unspeakably" with him; when the beating was nearly over, Lawrence felt "a delicious warmth, probably sexual," swelling through him. After one final slash of the whip into his groin, he tells us, "my eyes went black: while within me the core of life seemed to heave slowly up through the rending nerves, expelled from its body by this last indescribable pang." Nothing in his account, however, altogether explains his summary judgment of his experience: "in Deraa that night," he writes, "the citadel of my integrity had been irrevocably lost."

I cite Lawrence's account—the only one we have of the Deraa experience—not so much to counteract as to rationalize the film's obliqueness. Censorship aside, both Lawrence's own mysteriousness and the film's constant refusal to explain away complex experiences justify an indirect approach. Whatever else Deraa may mean, it signifies that moment when Lawrence recognizes the fundamental frailty of his flesh as well as his frightening ability to transcend that frailty. The Truly Weak Man and the Truly Strong Man come acutely together for a moment, and the Lawrence who emerges from the experience is a different Lawrence from the one who walked boldly into Deraa. That the Truly Strong Man turns briefly to sadism can then be seen as a necessary prelude to self-awareness, to a final revulsion from and abdication of his godlike heroism: having entered into the heart of darkness, Lawrence discovers a horrible image of himself.

The Conradian allusion may aptly preface a look at Lawrence's relationship with the Arabs, or what I have termed the Paradox of the Good/Bad Imperialist. We need to read this aspect of the film with particular care, since Lean and Bolt are not always as conscious of the paradox as we might like. The truly "bad" imperialists are certainly easy enough to identify. The suave, cynical Dryden (Claude Rains) and the seemingly apolitical Allenby ("I'm just a soldier, thank God") epitomize the political/military complex we know as imperialism. Lawrence, as we would expect, is relatively enlightened. When he invades the Officer's Club in Cairo—clearly a hotbed of racism—dressed as an Arab and accompanied by his Arab servant, we are made to feel, along with Lawrence, superior to the obvious imperialists. Actually, Lawrence merely asserts his ego in this scene; politics has been subsumed by private virtues, and private virtues, as we all know, all too often become public vices. Here and elsewhere, the film suppresses the central issue of imperialism: that it is the "good" imperialists, idealists like Lawrence, who prepare the way for the bad ones. "The English," Prince Feisal tells Lawrence, "have a great hunger for desolate places." Lawrence clearly shares that hunger, and though his appetite may be personal rather than national, born of admiration rather than ambition, it is equal to the hunger of a Dryden or an Allenby.

Idealist or no, Lawrence, like all imperialists, wishes to dominate, to impose *his* will, *his* vision, *his* understanding of what is good for *them* on the Arabs whose life he shares and whose aspirations he claims to value. The film in fact presents the Arab world with some ambivalence, as the casting strategies alone might lead one to expect. Some of the actors (notably the Egyptian Omar Sharif) are Orientals; Feisal, however, is portrayed by Alec Guinness, very much an Englishman, and Auda Abu Tayi by the Mexican actor Anthony Quinn. These three characters embody the range of stereotypes one may hold of Arabs. Feisal is sage, calm, softspoken, prophetlike; Auda is childish, excitable, vain, avaricious—all emotionalism and sensuality; Ali incorporates elements of both, while additionally contributing attractive exoticism and "Oriental" glamor. Insofar as *Lawrence of Arabia* presents the Arabs as greedy, irascible, quarrelsome, "simple," earthy, and so forth, it fails to escape the preconceptions of much of its audience; instead, it enters into the dilemma of its protagonist. Lawrence attempts to identify with the Arabs by becoming one. Having no identity of his own (he is, as he explains to Ali, a bastard), he is willingly adopted—literally—by his Arab friends. But identities cannot be acquired so easily; he is not, after all, an Arab, and the more he tries to be one, the more emphatic his alienation becomes. We see this immediately after the fall of Akaba when, alone, Lawrence rides his camel by the seashore, cut off from human contact, incapable of relishing a victory that isn't really his. But taking on an Arab identity does help Lawrence further the imperial project. He wins the Arabs over primarily by demonstrating that he is as good as they are; he is then perceived—in the film, at least—as better. For Lawrence seemingly conquers fate; for him, "nothing is written." He thus combines the virtues and strengths of the Arabs with a freedom from their strict ethical and social codes. His power, which gives him the upper hand, grows from these attributes.

In stages, as I've already noted, Lawrence becomes like a god, neither English nor Arab, deciding who shall live and who shall die, executing justice free of emotional involvement, responsible to no one but himself. So, in order to prevent his followers from disintegrating on the eve of the battle for Akaba, he cold-bloodedly executes a man he had earlier rescued from certain death. The ambiguities of his role are perfectly symbolized by this act: seemingly dealing even-handed justice, he actually serves the imperial will. In the end, the idea that nothing is written, that man makes his own fate, becomes Lawrence's greatest delusion, for he forgets, as we are seldom allowed to, the nature of the powers that circumscribe his actions. Thus self-deceived, Lawrence becomes himself a victim of imperialism, an ideology that frequently prefers to give the illusion of independence while keeping a tight hold on the reins of power.

Simultaneously an imperialist and the victim of imperialism, Lawrence must fail equally in his attempt to transcend political realities and personal limitations. The ambiguities in Lawrence's character, his inability to come to terms with his own actions, his progressive alienation from everything around him, signify an overwhelming guilt that can be read as the projection of the collective disease we call imperialism. Lawrence, like Robert Bolt's Sir Thomas More in *A Man for All Seasons,* finds himself caught between the demands of the world and the promptings of his conscience; unlike More, however, Lawrence cannot bring the conflict into absolute clarity. And so, also unlike More, he cannot see his way out of the dilemma. A hero who has outlived the age of heroes, Lawrence finds no decisive victory at the end of his quest. The capture of Damascus is a bitter anti-climax, the Arabs remain as divided as ever, British masters are substituted for Turkish ones, and even Prince Feisal turns to cynicism. "Colonel Lawrence," he tells Allenby, "is a sword with two edges: we are equally glad to be rid of him, are we not?"

But if Lawrence is quintessentially modern in his heroism, it is not because he fails in his quest—other heroes have failed before him—but because of the intensely self-conscious way he acts out his heroic role. Lawrence simultaneously performs as a hero and watches himself performing. And we, of course, watch him performing as well. The Paradox of Self-Promotion/Self-Abnegation is transformed into the tension between role and identity. It is here that David Lean most brilliantly employs film in such a way that its formal properties reflect the thematics of the fable. A theatrical medium, film perfectly captures the undeniably exhibitionist constituents of Lawrence's personality. Lean and Bolt eagerly borrow upon and expand details of fact and myth that stress Lawrence's self-consciousness, his bent for playacting, his awareness of the value of gesture and pose. (In *Seven Pillars,* Lawrence writes of his "detached self always eyeing the performance from the wings in criticism.") Peter O'Toole calls attention throughout to Lawrence as performer, which inevitably makes us aware of his own "performance" as Lawrence. Indeed, one of the film's special pleasures lies in the playfulness O'Toole brings to his characterization, a playfulness that suggests his own enjoyment at playacting on such a grand scale—and in his first film at that! Performance thus becomes an issue outside of as well as within the diegesis. By casting the virtually unknown O'Toole as Lawrence, Lean complicates the categories of actor, role, and identity. Since, in the cinema, character and actor cannot easily be distinguished, O'Toole—with no "star" persona to interfere—at once embodies and individualizes Lawrence. And O'Toole is supported by well-known stars whose very presence insures immediate identification: Jack Hawkins, lending his solid, gruff Britishness to General Allenby; Alec Guinness, providing Feisal with dry wit and gentle intelligence; Anthony Quinn doing his turn as aging macho ethnic. Because these actors are not fundamentally mysterious, their characters are not mysterious. They thus serve to emphasize by contrast O'Toole's unknownness, an unknownness which then encompasses Lawrence himself. These casting strategies also contribute meaning to a subsidiary but related theme: Lawrence, the young upstart lieutenant, takes over the Arab revolt supported by the older and more experienced Allenby, Feisal, and Auda, just as O'Toole, the young upstart actor, takes over the film supported by seasoned actors like Hawkins, Guinness, and Quinn.

Self-dramatization, in one form or another, nearly always colors Lawrence's behavior. Even his most heroic moments are qualified by self-conscious gesture. The climactic event in the film's first movement—up to the fall of Akaba—shows us Lawrence courageously and with single-minded determination retracing his steps through the murderous Nefud desert to rescue a lost Arab comrade. Lean uses all of the tools at his disposal, including photography, composition, editing, and music, to construct one of the film's best-remembered sequences. In a rhythmic series of alternating shots we see the Arab, Gassim, wandering aimlessly under an ever-intensifying sun, Lawrence determinedly riding toward him, the servant-boy anxiously waiting at the desert's edge, and finally a culminating image of Lawrence, baked and parched, his face seemingly sandblasted to a gray mask, galloping out of the desert on his camel, the half-dead Gassim holding on to him quite literally for dear life. Interestingly, Lawrence's account of this episode in *Seven Pillars of Wisdom* is, as is usual with him, self-deprecatingly unheroic; in the film, his doubts, qualifications, and hesitations are suppressed. Nevertheless, the whole sequence is so formal in its structure, so manipulative and yet meticulous in its construction, as to simultaneously draw us in and keep us at a distance. We are made uncomfortably aware that Lawrence acts as much to demonstrate his courage and heroic temper—to the Arabs and to himself—as he does to save the life of a fellow human being.

Very soon after this exploit, Lawrence, at the instigation of Ali, assumes Arab dress, a costume—in every sense of the word—of spotless white. Emblematically, at least, Lawrence is now an Arab. At the same time, he looks like no other Arab in the film; rather than taking on the identity of his comrades, he assumes a visually unique role. Lean stresses the theatrical nature of the transformation by having Lawrence ride off by himself as soon as he has put on his new costume. Finding an isolated spot, Lawrence dismounts and begins to prance and posture to his own shadow, allowing the flowing robes to balloon behind him in the breeze. He is a little boy dressing up, acting out Arabian Nights heroics. Here, in particular, we sense the actor behind the role. Lawrence and O'Toole seem to be both revelling in and in awe of the part they are playing, uncertain of what to do next but at the same time aware that from now on there is no turning back: destiny calls. The moment is privileged; Lawrence will never again seem at once so winning and so vulnerable.

If Lawrence is an actor, Arabia is his stage. The metaphor, as Edward Said more than once suggests in *Orientalism,* implicitly informs much of the Western literature that concerns itself with Arabia. "The Orient is the stage on which the whole East is confined . . . ," Said writes, "a theatrical stage whose audience, manager, and actors are *for* Europe, and only for Europe." Lean fills *Lawrence of Arabia* with flamboyantly theatrical shots of Near Eastern topography, but those critics who fault the director for indulging in breathtaking vistas for their own sake miss the point entirely. Just as, in earlier films, he painstakingly used plaster and lath as a method of recreating a subjective reality (Dickens's London in *Oliver Twist,* for example) so here he takes great pains to formalize the real world until it begins to resemble an impossibly elaborate studio set. Lean's remarkable pans and tracks of the desert sands, his complicated zooms, his compositions revealing the mysterious mirages of the desert, his dramatic visual surprises—as when a ship looms over the edge of a sand dune—are all directed toward establishing Arabia Deserta as a series of fabulous backdrops for Lawrence's exploits.

But the more Lawrence penetrates the landscape, the more he seems to absorb it into himself: Arabia is a theater in Lawrence's mind. "The passage of the mythological hero," Joseph Campbell reminds us, "may be overground, incidentally; fundamentally it is inward—into depths where obscure resistances are overcome, and long lost, forgotten powers are revivified." Lean's epic style depicts Arabia as both a magnificent stage set and a metaphysical landscape, his elegantly tracking camera capturing the grandeur and barrenness of the desert, his slow dissolves and subliminal editing suggesting the illogical continuity and dreamlike texture of the forbidding terrain. Initially dwarfed by the desert's vastness and buffeted by its inexorable brutality, Lawrence learns to come to terms with it, to become at once part of it and apart from it. He inhabits this world, as he does everything, self-consciously: grandiloquent of gesture, ostentatious, vainglorious, he plays his part as well as he can for a man who does not know what his part really is.

Such role-playing inevitably leads to the borders of schizophrenia. Twice in the film, Lawrence looks at his own reflection in the blade of his knife. In the first instance, he is still relatively innocent. He has just put on his white robes for the first time, and he studies the image reflected back to him in puzzled admiration, not quite believing that he has been able so thoroughly and drastically to change his identity. The second time, much later in the film, the context is very different. Lawrence, after giving the order to take no prisoners, participates in the massacre at Tafas. The white robes are now soiled with blood, and the face Lawrence submits to reflective scrutiny seems to be that of a madman. Neither man nor role are recognizably what they were before, and Lawrence can now only retreat from heroism, put aside his Arab dress, and return to England and the absurd, perhaps not entirely accidental death with which the film began.

The paradoxes I have been discussing do not, in David Lean's film, resolve themselves into a solution to the enigma of Lawrence's character. *Lawrence of Arabia* ends, as it began, a deeply ambiguous film; indeed, it ends and begins simultaneously. Lawrence enters the film in order to die. As his motorcycle speeds along a country road, his intense face is illuminated by areas of light and shadow in alternation, an effect that becomes more and more bizarre as his velocity increases. Swerving to avoid hitting someone on the road, he loses control of his machine and, thrown offscreen, quite literally disappears. Here, in the first moments of the film, we have the essential Lawrence: brave but foolhardy; a thrillseeker who seems to invite disaster; manic intensity; a self-sacrificial bravado; a fatal gesture; the superhuman will in conflict with human possibilities; the hero as scapegoat.

Such a beginning to what most viewers would rightly consider a rousing adventure story should warn us to expect a film that constantly questions itself, not only in terms of plot, character, and theme, but also as a particular kind of discourse, as a method of presentation. Lowell Thomas's film created a hero; Lean's film, at least in part, is about the power of the cinema to create a hero. Though Lawrence's motives may be beyond recovery, his image speaks eloquently to our hopes and needs. Time and again, Lean's camera closes in on Lawrence's face as if to penetrate its mystery, and each close-up leaves us with a deeper enigma than before. The image cannot be questioned; it is inviolate. But if he refuses to solve the puzzle of Lawrence's character, Lean brilliantly depicts Lawrence's world. He thus transcends and at the same time pays homage to film as spectacle. Allusive, open, self-conscious, mystifying, unfinished, complex, *Lawrence of Arabia* remains one of the richest and most satisfying of modern epics.

Three: The Personal Voice

Bankrobbers and Bodysnatchers

William Holtz

On the night of September 7, 1876, two University of Michigan medical students were engaged in a curious task incidental to their education. The place was a cemetery near a small town in Minnesota; their tools were pick and shovel and dark-lantern; and their object was grave-robbing. As they worked, sweating and heaving between the mounds of earth, they peered nervously into the surrounding darkness, uneasy not because they feared mere apprehension, but because they feared having to face at any moment the wrath of Frank and Jesse James.

It is a strange story, this—a minor thread in the web of history, and just odd enough to seem improbable, yet possessed of the compelling probability of fiction. As history, we can place it in a context of similar narratives of the "resurrectionists" who supplied human bodies for dissection. But even within this context, the apparently simple sequence of events is vibrant with implication that teases the mind to supply what history omits. The result is an odd conception neither history nor fiction, but compounded of the truth of both.[1]

Probably never have thought and feeling been so sundered as by the dilemma which sent these young men—and many before them—prowling graveyards by night. For there is grim irony in the fact that the high aims of medical science require its students to probe the secrets of life in ways that fill the mind with instinctive dread. Except for such pockets of enlightenment as Paris and Bologna, where great medical schools flourished, the study of human anatomy labored under severe difficulties, both social and legal—in England until the mid-nineteenth century, and almost until the twentieth in the United States. For as medicine grew more sophisticated, and as the number of students increased, the need for cadavers rose, and the meager sources of supply officially sanctioned had to be supplemented in other ways, which were frequently ingenious, occasionally scandalous, and generally illegal.

The situation at the University of Michigan's medical school, and to varying degrees throughout the other states, had its roots in an extremely complex situation in England. Public opinion simply would not tolerate dissection of respectable people: yet surgeons commanded high fees, teachers of surgery could grow wealthy from their students, and the system needed bodies. The earliest English law allotted to the College of Barbers and Surgeons four bodies of executed criminals yearly for dissection; and by the mid-eighteenth century, grave-robbing was a recognized means of increasing the supply. No less a body than that of the Reverend Laurence Sterne, the preacher-turned-novelist, is supposed to have come by this route to the dissecting table at Cambridge, where he had matriculated years before, and where a student recognized with a start the well-known features of the humorist who passed in London society by the name of Yorick: if the story is true, his skull is yet among those in the Cambridge collection, though no one knows which is his. Generally, however, the victims were the poor, who could afford neither deep graves nor honest guards, nor the vaults and patent coffins that some resorted to. But money worked both ways, and one famous surgeon, Astley Cooper, would offer high prices for the remains of particularly interesting cases: he testified that "there is no person, let his situation in life be what it may, whom, if I were disposed to dissect, I could not obtain." An earlier anatomist, John Hunter, in 1783 paid over £500 to get the body of the seven-and-a-half foot "Irish Giant," Charles Byrne.

An ordinary body, however, would fetch from £8 to £10 on the London market in the early nineteenth century. Most surgeons and students had neither the unique knowledge nor daring required to obtain "subjects," and only rarely did they steal bodies themselves. Rather, they bought them, in a fiercely competitive market, from a corps of professional "resurrectionists" (also known as "sack-em-up men," or "grabs"). These men, recruited from the dregs of society, had to be able to break gates, climb walls, dig furiously yet quietly, bribe sextons, battle watchmen, and haggle with the surgeons at the end of their night's labors: they were a special breed who could earn more in one night of grave-robbing than in a month of honest work, and they strove against rival gangs, and against their employers, with the zeal of trade-unionists. As with any tradesmen, they soon developed a distinctive vocabulary, special tools and techniques, and an awareness of relevant laws. The body itself was a "thing"; wooden shovels were used for silence and a special pry-bar to force coffin-lids once the head of the box was exposed—for it was not necessary to excavate the entire grave to get a set of ropes on the "thing's" shoulders and snake it to the surface. The professionals were careful to leave the shroud behind, for British law recognized no property right in a human body—it *belonged* to no one—and although the resurrectionists, if caught, might be jailed on a number of minor charges, they could not be convicted of stealing if they took only the body itself. Their employers paid their fines, and used influence to protect them; but all things considered, they probably earned their money. Some grew wealthy; most drank their lives away; and a few ended on the dissecting table themselves.

Thus was medical and anatomical science dependent for its day-to-day existence on the efforts of the most depraved elements of society. Some surgeons dealt directly with the resurrectionists, but others delegated this to subordinates, and thus widened the gulf between their own commendable work and the system that supported it. The more successful the surgeons, the more students they drew; the more "things" required, the more vicious became the resurrectionists and the more outraged the general citizenry. Despite the social and educational distance between them, the surgeons and the resurrectionists were joined in a conspiracy against the common citizen, who could not achieve the necessary scientific detachment, but persisted in regarding the "things" as persons who deserved respect and protection, and whose burial rites reflected a fundamental sense of life's continuity. Groups of volunteers patrolled the cemeteries, where they dealt severely with anyone they apprehended; and more than one surgeon's home was attacked by angry mobs.

Inevitably, some suppliers decided that there were easier ways of procuring bodies than by digging them up. Some tried to intercept them before burial, as did a man named Wight, who generously helped a friend's widow lay out her husband's body in his coffin—then stole back by night to transfer the body to another box, leaving a weighted coffin for the widow. He was caught, but his defense was ingenious: the woman was so poor, he said, that he hoped to get enough money for the body of her husband that she could give him a proper funeral. Less altruistic, and more efficient, were a pair named William Hare and William Burke, who together in a year murdered sixteen Edinburgh slum-dwellers and delivered them to a local surgeon, who was remarkably incurious as to their manner of death. Burke, especially, fired the public imagination, perhaps because of his cool complaint after his trial that the surgeon still owed him £5 for his last delivery—a sum that he would like for a new waistcoat for his execution. His public hanging was marked with a deep roar of execration, and his name entered the language as a term for the kind of murder he practiced: "to kill secretly by suffocation or strangulation, or in order to sell the victim's body for dissection, as Burke did" (*OED*). Somewhat more refined was the technique of two London suppliers, who were apprehended after only two murders: these burkers drugged their victims with a mixture of rum and laudanum, then hung them head-down in a well. It seems clear that for some, at least, murder appeared less risky than grave-robbing, and obviously it was easier.

It took outrages such as these, and an enlightened inquiry by Lord Warburton, to move Parliament to act. A bill passed in 1832 did much to alleviate matters; essentially, it provided that unclaimed bodies in hospitals and workhouses might be sold for dissection, and it made grave-robbing or moving a dead body a crime. Such a law could not reconcile the populace to the need for legitimate anatomical studies, but it released the surgeons from their dependence on the resurrectionists, and it closed the legal loopholes the sack-em-up artists had enjoyed for years.

In 1832 the University of Michigan was still a set of unrealized plans evolved from the Catholepistemiad of Michigania, instituted but unrealized in Detroit in 1817. Classes would not be opened until 1841, in Ann Arbor. There would be no actual medical courses until 1850. The first dissection, however, took place as early as 1846, when Dr. Moses Gunn, then a private physician but later Professor of Anatomy, arrived in Ann Arbor just fifteen days after his graduation from Geneva Medical College in New York. Among his baggage was "a box of suspicious shape and size and unmarked content." It contained a body that Gunn had appropriated from the Geneva school on his departure and that he used for his first lectures on anatomy in Ann Arbor. Twenty years after, when he left Michigan for Rush Medical College in Chicago, he apparently repeated his coup, for he was alleged to have absconded with the entire Michigan supply—about forty bodies—after having bound and gagged the janitor of the Medical Building. The Regents were assembled in emergency session, but took no action, doubtless as a result of Gunn's threat to expose how the University had obtained the bodies in the first place.

Gunn's story might well have been a lurid one, if we can judge by the few remaining records. Michigan was now facing England's problems of a generation earlier. Whereas in the first years of medical instruction fifteen or twenty cadavers annually had met all needs, the much larger classes after the Civil War required at least 125 to 140 bodies a year. They were not to be found easily, for the old dilemma appeared, now codified into law: practical anatomy was required by statute in medical instruction, but exhuming bodies—the only way to get them—was a penal offense. Needless to say, the Demonstrator in Anatomy had to be a resourceful man, and he generally spent more time in procuring than in demonstrating. An early appointee recorded that he had to "get up" thirteen cadavers with his own hands his first winter. "I was chased sometimes by constables," he remarked, "but never caught, and I supplied the University." This same man had agents as far afield as Buffalo and Chicago, and as near as Wayne. Transportation was sometimes furnished by teams hired from the sheriff of Washtenaw County, who kept a livery stable.

The mark of the professional resurrectionist soon appeared, as evidenced by an account of a broken coffin, an abandoned shroud, and a half-filled grave in a nearby cemetery. The Medical College was suspected, and a mob was prevented from burning the building only by the intervention of a hundred armed medical students. Generally, however, Ann Arbor citizens were not much disturbed, for the Demonstrators in Anatomy were usually careful not to allow local exhumation. They were busy afield, though; one traveled 1,500 miles in less than four months, negotiating for cadavers with his twenty or thirty agents, with whom he also kept up a lively correspondence. His superior described his work in a secret letter to one of the Regents:

> He cannot go into the field in strange places. He must find men willing to undertake such illegal and dangerous work. They have to be bribed and they are not reliable. Money must be spent. Arrangements to escape detection must be made. After a body is received, it must be boxed, carted, and transported. All by unreliable persons who must be bribed!

These unreliable persons were remarkably diligent at times, however. In 1878, three such agents were captured in Toledo, and confessed to a contract for seventy bodies for Ann Arbor. Sixty had already been shipped. At about the same time, another Ohio crew, also with an Ann Arbor contract, was discovered to have stolen and sold to the Medical College of Ohio the body of John Scott Harrison. Only chance, it seems, prevented this son of William Henry Harrison and uncle of Benjamin Harrison from gracing a dissecting table at the University of Michigan.

This was the situation in the 1870s, when Ann Arbor was a country town but a growing center for the study of medicine. The campus was surrounded by a fence, with stiles at convenient places, and at the northwest corner (State and North University) one might enter by a main gate, across which was a line of low posts "with room enough between for one man at a time, but not for a cow." From this point a plank walk stretched along a path still marked by the two parallel rows of trees just north of the present diagonal; it led to what was then the Chemistry Building and thence east to the original Medical Building. Here it was that the dissecting took place. Bodies, supplied by a network of agents, arrived frequently in barrels marked "Pickles"; and although the regard for public relations kept Ann Arbor cemeteries fairly safe and local people rather unconcerned, there were well-founded suspicions about the Department of Anatomy. One Demonstrator, asked where the school got its subjects, replied candidly, "We *raise* 'em"; and there was a campus joke to the effect that "a medic is never happier than when he finds a fellow man in a pickle." For these fellow men, the medic paid fees of from twenty to forty dollars, a fact that the University accounts acknowledged in carefully imprecise language. We can only guess how many secrets died in 1900 with the passing of "Doc" Nagele, the German-immigrant janitor of the Medical Building, who in more than a generation of watching dissections became so proficient in anatomy that he frequently helped students with their work. Part of his job was to hide the bodies that came in, and he was apparently the custodian with whom Dr. Moses Gunn contended when he looted the University of its forty corpses. Nagele was on occasion called upon to testify in cases of grave-robbing, but at such times he conveniently lost all command of English, and no one could be found to master his particular German dialect.

In September of 1876, two barrels arrived at the Medical Building marked "Fresh Paint" rather than the usual "Pickles." These were unique in other ways, too, for they were a link in one of the most bizarre of resurrectionist episodes. This was the work of an amateur, a medical student who, in an amazing reduction of the whole problem, shot down his dissecting material in the middle of a main thoroughfare. The story was to end a half-century later, when a skeleton—the last bony remnant of an obscure sidekick of Jesse James—was destroyed by fire in a small town in North Dakota.

Young Henry Mason Wheeler, a medical student at the University of Michigan (Med. class, 1877; M.D. Columbia, 1880) was nearing the end of his summer vacation as he sat in front of his father's drugstore in Northfield, Minnesota, on September 7, 1876. Strangers are seldom unnoticed in a small town, and Wheeler was probably aware of a number of unfamiliar persons on the street. There were in fact eight, members of the James-Younger gang: the notorious Frank and Jesse James, Cole Younger and his brothers Jim and Bob, and three lesser figures whose names were Miller, Stiles, and Pitts. Frank and Jesse, accompanied by Cole Younger, sauntered into the Northfield Bank, across the street from where Wheeler sat, while the rest of the gang took up positions outside. The first sign of trouble appeared when a merchant attempted to enter the bank: one of the outlaws seized him and warned him back. He read the situation in a glance and fled down the street, giving the alarm. Two of the bandits then mounted their horses and rode up and down the street, ordering the citizens to disperse. There was a shot within the bank, then another in the street, as a Swedish immigrant who knew no English was gunned down for not taking to his heels. There was another shot as the bank door opened and the rest of the outlaws emerged. In the bank was a dead cashier who had refused to open the vault.

Wheeler and a hardware merchant named Manning offered the only active resistance. Manning seized a rifle from his store and began firing from the end of the street as the gang mounted up, while Wheeler ducked into the Dampier Hotel, grabbed an old Army carbine, and climbed to a second-floor window. Manning's first shot felled Bob Younger's horse; his next killed Stiles, passing directly through his heart. Meanwhile, Wheeler had fired upon Cole Younger, but had missed; his next shot killed Miller, who fell at the opposite end of the street from Stiles. Manning then wounded Cole Younger in the arm, and as he reloaded, the horseless Bob Younger stalked him along the sidewalk with a drawn revolver. From the hotel window Wheeler fired again, wounding Bob Younger before he could fire on Manning. Bob Younger then mounted behind one of his brothers and the gang fled, carrying two wounded and leaving behind two dead and an unopened bank vault. The street filled with people. A posse was hastily formed.

One of the first on the scene was Clarence Edward Persons, a friend of Wheeler's and a classmate at Michigan (Med. '77), who arrived so soon that he was able to retrieve one of the black felt hats the bandits had dropped in their retreat. His account, preserved by his son, further reveals Wheeler's presence of mind. As he saddled up to join the posse, Wheeler called Persons aside—and we must read his words against the background of a wild scene preserved for us by years of Western movies: "Clarence, you had better see if you can get the bodies of the two fellows who have been shot, and perhaps we can land them in Ann Arbor for dissecting material. You see what you can do while I am gone."

Or so the record reads, the voice coming down to us through two generations of reminiscence. That night, as Wheeler pursued the fugitives, Persons and Charles Edward Dampier, son of the owner of the Dampier Hotel and also a Michigan medical student (Med. '78), resurrected the freshly buried bodies, fearing each moment, Dampier recalled, the return of the outlaws who had terrorized the town. They put each body into a keg labeled "Fresh Paint" and marked the kegs for shipment to Ann Arbor.

Jesse and Frank James both escaped; the rest of the gang was captured two weeks later; and the kegs were transported to Ann Arbor, where they arrived in time for the fall semester. Wheeler and Persons were no doubt the best-equipped medical students on the campus, until friends of Stiles claimed his body for re-burial. Under the law, he had to be yielded up, and the students were left with one corpse between them. No one appeared for Miller, the victim of Wheeler's skill: he, apparently, belonged to no one. Weeks passed, and little by little the probing knives of the students separated nerve from sinew and tendon from flesh. Occasionally the blades would click upon bone.

It is here that the mind begins to stir uneasily at what the records omit, at the gap in history that invites conjecture. For there is something profoundly disquieting in Wheeler's long intimacy with his victim—searching day in, day out, among the lax fibers and empty veins of one whose thread of days he had himself snapped short in a single hot and lusty moment. What occupied Wheeler's mind during these weeks of dissection? What did he talk of to Persons as they worked? There is more to ponder here than the fact that Miller died of a severed subclavicular artery: there is a ferment of guilt and bravado and self-justification that has left no mark on the pages of history. Or almost none. We have only the laconic notes of Person's son, recalling a fragment of conversation worn smooth with many tellings. For after the two students had scraped the bones clean, Wheeler asked: "What shall we do with the skeleton?" In Person's reply we can hear something very like the fall of tumblers in a lock, as a special responsibility was confirmed. "He's yours," Persons said. "You shot him."

Am I my brother's keeper? The question echoes here, although it probably was never spoken. Wheeler seems to have accepted Person's judgment, but whether he received the relic as an honorable trophy or as a monstrous, rattling albatross, bound to him in dark kinship, we cannot tell. He took it with him, somehow (by what conveyance now, we wonder: how does one pack a skeleton?), to his practice in Grand Forks, North Dakota. He installed it in his office, where it remained his companion for almost fifty years.

A curious companionship it must have been—and, perhaps, an uneasy one. We can be almost certain of the banal jokes with his patients; but we can also sense a deeper, unvoiced dialogue with the quiet watcher in the corner. What accusation is there, and what reply, as Wheeler, his ear tuned to the rhythmic surge within a living chest, suddenly glances across the room to where the sunlight slants idly through a cage of barren ribs? Other questions murmur here than those answered by poultices and morphia powders. Whether Wheeler heard them, whether he ever articulated the thoughts that writhe beneath the bare recital of these events, we can never know. We can merely note how history rounds off this tale. Late in Wheeler's life—he must have been in his seventies—his office was destroyed by fire, and with it, in a belated cremation, the remains of Miller the outlaw. The story, finally, was over.

And so, despite the grim logic that drives through this episode, a whorl of ambiguity lies at its heart. Murder and mutilation, but both properly sanctioned: again we find outselves grappling with the essential split between thought and feeling that has plagued studies of the human body from the beginning. The objectivity of the scientist is powerful against those obstacles to knowledge raised by human feeling, but as a consistent posture it is inhuman; and although reason and justice seem to be on

Wheeler's side, there is a horror that will not be exorcised. Only a little imagination is needed to see the mark of Cain upon Wheeler's brow, and a curse like the Mariner's upon the rest of his days.

Since Wheeler's time, laws have regularized the supply of anatomical specimens, but they are still generally those who, through improvidence or bad luck, have ended their lives unable to provide for their own burial, and with no one to provide for them—paupers and criminals, the misfits of our society. It is interesting to speculate on the fate of anatomical study if our affluence should ever eradicate poverty, for few people come to the dissecting table who can pay to go elsewhere. The split continues, or even widens, for one of the marks of our affluence is the decadence of our burial rites, which have too often become a sentimental evasion of reality, an elaborate pretext of corporeal permanence, rather than a ritual affirmation of human endurance in the face of change. This debasement is abetted by the assiduous funeral director, who studies "grief psychology" and cosmetology as well as embalming, and who has a commercial interest in absurd laws that make an intelligent and properly serious handling of death difficult if not impossible. As Jessica Mitford and others have made us aware, it is more complicated to get our bodies out of this world than into it.

On one side of the gulf, then, is Everyman, his face averted from death. On the other is the man of medical science, whose mask of objectivity perhaps hides a certain fear as well—for according to recent accounts, the budding doctor is typically more aware of death, and more uneasy, than those about him, who are his future patients. Thus his course of study becomes an early grappling with an adversary he devotes his life to forestalling, and his objectivity serves as armor. Can these poles ever be reconciled? There are hopeful signs, as witness the occasional tough-minded citizen who subordinates his love of his own flesh to his reverence for the flame of life that flickers upon it, and leaves his body to science, that others might live better, and longer. Is it too much to expect that the anatomist and his students might attain to an equally worthy vision, in which detachment is tempered and humanized by an imaginative apprehension of the "subject," however abject his fate, as a fellow man, victim of the common foe? In such a joining of passion and detachment we might find the conflict basic to this whole subject resolved in a humanly significant gesture, realistically cognizant of painful facts yet suffused with a sense of identity and continuity with the community of man.

Thus if Wheeler strikes us at first as something monstrous, a version of the mad scientist of modern folklore, we yet can find the possibility of redemption in his half-century of companionship with the bones of the man he slew. For the objectivity of the scientist is a mask, and it cannot be worn always: certainly during those years, as his heartbeats ticked away the measure of his own mortality, there were times when he came to know the silent sharer of his room as something other than the durable part of a man named Miller. Perhaps even in those first weeks of work in Ann Arbor he began to discover the figure beneath the sheet as his other self, as Everyman, as Brother Death.

NOTE

1. I am indebted to Professor Donald F. Huelke of the Department of Anatomy, University of Michigan Medical Center, for his history of the Department of Anatomy (*University of Michigan Medical Bulletin* 27:1–27, 28:127–49, 29:133–44), and to Professor F. Clever Bald, former director of the Michigan Historical Collections, who first drew my attention to the Northfield Bank raid and who made materials from the collections available to me. The best account of the English resurrectionists is by Hubert Cole, *Things for the Surgeon* (London, 1964).

Looking for Mr. Ames

Nancy Willard

I was a sophomore at the University of Michigan when I took my first class from Professor Ames. He taught a course called "The Art of Writing." The catalog said "By Special Permission," but I knew of no one who was turned away for lack of skill. Each semester a new crop of stories would attach itself to the lore already surrounding this man.

Fact: He was of slight build yet surprisingly strong; he had twice broken one of the thermal panes in Haven Hall simply by the act of closing the window. At the age of forty he had married one of his students, Madeline Shaw. On their wedding night, which they spent in his tiny bachelor apartment, the new bride thought she had never slept in so uncomfortable a bed in her life. A camel could not have been lumpier. The next morning she lifted up the mattress and discovered the springs were crammed with all the books her new husband had started to read but never gotten around to finishing.

Fact: He loved toys. Russian nesting dolls, treetop angels, Matchbox cars. A young woman in Mr. Ames's Modern Novel class said his office made her feel she was in the waiting room of her orthodontist, who had a shelf filled with amusements for his young patients. The top shelf of Mr. Ames's bookcase held half a dozen Quaker Oats boxes. When you had a conference with Mr. Ames, those good-natured witnesses beamed down at you.

Over this chaos presided a small silver Byzantine madonna. She hung from a shoelace on the wall behind his desk, and she looked as if she had her blessed hands full. Mr. Ames was not Greek Orthodox, though he sometimes went to Christmas and Easter services at St. Nicholas and left before the sermon.

Fact: While leading a discussion of a particularly mediocre story, Mr. Ames gave a brilliant extemporaneous lecture on voice in fiction, during which every student understood, in a deep intuitive way, that the universe is holy, and that every part is connected to every other part. If a butterfly entered this classroom and hurt itself, said Mr. Ames, that hurt would be felt in the farthest galaxy. Before you pick a rose, you must first ask permission of the stars. His performance quite eclipsed the mediocre story; nobody present at the discussion can recall so much as a single detail.

Rumor: Mr. Ames was supposed to be working on a book about writing and teaching.

Fact: Not a student took his class without wondering if he or she was mentioned in it.

In those days I thought all professors of literature, when left to their own devices, dreamed in metaphor and spoke in epigrams. Tweed jackets with leather patches on the elbows were in fashion, and the air of genteel poverty worn by even the lowliest instructors made a great impression on me. I loved their desks bustling with papers and all the paraphernalia of their profession, bluebooks and class registers, pipes at rest on giant glass ashtrays and notes slipped under the door or taped to the frosted glass: *Dear Mr. Ames. I had this great idea for a story but when I wrote it, it wasn't so great. Can I come see you?*

I think it was partly for these things I became a teacher myself. But my office at Vassar is so small I must step aside to let students get to the chair. I have no pipe (I don't smoke) and no space for my books; those that fill the shelves belong to the two previous occupants, now on leave. The boxes of books lined up on the floor once belonged to Elizabeth Bishop; my office mate is doing extensive research on her work. Gladly do we share our space with her wise spirit.

Clutching the poem I hoped would get me into Mr. Ames's class, I sat on the floor outside his office; the English Department had forsworn the luxury of chairs. Part of my mind listened to the buzz of voices behind closed office doors. The other part reviewed Book 7 of *The Republic* for an exam in my Great Books class. *Wherefore each of you, when his time comes, must go down to the general underground abode, and get in the habit of seeing in the dark. When you have acquired this habit, you will see ten thousand times better than the inhabitants of the cave . . . because you have seen the beautiful and just and good in their truth.*

Suddenly a door at the end of the corridor opened and a deep voice floated out.

"Listen, I'm telling you the truth. The linoleum at Sears is actually fifty cents cheaper."

There is a theory of knowledge which says that we are led to the truth by a series of disillusionments. In my universe, such truth isn't worth knowing. What kept my illusions alive at that moment was Mr. Ames, who opened his door and called me into his office. He wore a white shirt and a tie on which he had spilled—good grief, was it egg? The desk was a glorious confusion of books and papers and empty wrappers of Dutch Girl Instant Hot Chocolate. On the wall behind him hung a plaque which read:

> *Fisherman's Code*
> Early to bed
> Early to rise
> Fish all day
> And make up lies.

I read it and glanced back at him.

"That's what writers do," he said.

Speechless, I handed him my poem, written in ultra-free verse. It was called "The Gardener's Song" and today I don't remember a single line. He read it over. He did not say it was wonderful. He said, "I know a poet *you'd* like, Miss Willard. Charlotte Mew."

I wrote down the name: Charlotte Mew. I had never heard of Charlotte Mew. Mr. Ames leaned back in his swivel chair, and I realized how short he was. His feet did not even touch the floor.

"Welcome to 'The Art of Writing'," he said. And he handed me back my poem.

The Class

Mr. Ames's class unfolded in a series of cold grey afternoons, the perpetual November of a Michigan winter. I can still see us, fifteen students shuffling into the classroom in parkas and clumpy boots, waiting for Mr. Ames to arrive, swathed in the old trenchcoat he wore winter and spring. Tuesday and Thursday, Tuesday and Thursday, Tuesday and Thursday—very soon we took him for granted, the way we take air and water for granted till the time arrives when we don't have them.

What did I learn from this man? I seem to remember no single insight of any great importance. Yet I know that for all of us there were days when nothing mattered more than what Mr. Ames thought of your newest story, your nearly finished poem. I remember his office but not what we said to each other in that remarkable place. And I remember his voice, as he read to us Theodore Roethke's lovely villanelle, "The Waking."

> I wake to sleep, and take my waking slow.
> I feel my fate in what I cannot fear.
> I learn by going where I have to go.
>
> We think by feeling. What is there to know?
> I hear my being dance from ear to ear.
> I wake to sleep, and take my waking slow.
>
> Of those so close beside me, which are you?
> God bless the Ground! I shall walk softly there.
> And learn by going where I have to go.
>
> Light takes the Tree; but who can tell us how?
> The lowly worm climbs up a winding stair;
> I wake to sleep, and take my waking slow.
>
> Great Nature has another thing to do
> To you and me; so take the lively air,
> And, lovely, learn by going where to go.
>
> This shaking keeps me steady. I should know.
> What falls away is always. And is near.
> I wake to sleep, and take my waking slow.
> I learn by going where I have to go.

Rumor: Mr. Ames was a student of Roethke's at Michigan State in a class which has passed from history into legend. The building in which the class met had windows on three sides. One fateful day Roethke told his students he wanted them to describe a physical action. "Now you watch what I do for the next five minutes and describe it," he said, whereupon he opened a window, climbed out on the narrow ledge of the building, and inched around the three sides, all the while making faces at the students through the glass. The girl who told me Mr. Ames's office reminded her of her orthodontist's waiting room also told me this, so perhaps she was not a reliable source.

And I remember some of the poems Mr. Ames asked us to memorize. We had to learn a new one every other week. You could choose your own, and you could recite it or write it out in class, but you had to know it. This was a task after my own heart, for who knew when I might find myself in a place without books? I loved to dwell in the cool high rooms of the public library on Washington Street, the dark crowded rooms of the secondhand bookshops along State and Liberty. I could not imagine life without books. The summer I turned sixteen my family moved from Ann Arbor, Michigan, to Los Alamos, New Mexico, and I felt as if we were moving from the civilized world to the moon. "The desert is beautiful," my father told me. What was the desert to me? I wanted to hear him say, "The public library is even better than the one in Ann Arbor."

I packed my Emily Dickinson and my Blake, my *Songs and Sonnets of Shakespeare,* and a book with the rather presumptuous title, *One Hundred Great Modern Peoms.* I was sixteen and I wanted to get poetry into my head, so that even in the desert I could say to myself, "My mind to me a kingdom is." And in the middle of the atomic city, while horned toads basked on our patio, I carried out my task of memorizing a new poem a week.

Now years later, I find that though I have forgotten many of the words to the poems, I have not forgotten their music, or what Frost calls the sound of sense. And I have come to believe that one of the most valuable things a writer can do is to memorize poems and passages that he wishes he'd written himself.

Of my "Blake to Keats" class with Mr. Ames, I remember a few of the poems I learned by heart, fewer insights and no dates. But I have not forgotten his voice as he read aloud to us. It rises up clearly behind the familiar words. Will my voice carry that far? I read poems aloud to my students and urge them to read their own work to each other. Nothing so quickly reveals the ill-turned phrase or the sentence staggering under the weight of too many adjectives as reading your own work out loud.

Not long after graduation, I dreamed I had stumbled into a secondhand shop presided over by an angel. The angel led me down aisles crammed with pedestals, wings, dolls, hairnets, chairs, garbage cans, flowerpots, feathers, gloves.

"Nothing is for sale," the angel explained. "It all belongs together. Listen, can you hear it?"

I listened.

"I hear a heartbeat," I said.

The angel smiled.

"That's the poetry of things. Isn't it wonderful? The universe scans."

After I left Ann Arbor, I lost touch with Mr. Ames, except for the cards I addressed at Christmas to him and to his wife, and the cards they sent me in return. The note at the bottom was always in Madeline's handwriting and said how pleased her husband was to see my poems beginning to appear in the quarterlies. I was surprised and comforted to know that Mr. Ames was still aware of me: two stars, one large, one small, both dancing in the same galaxy.

It is odd how news of great events so often arrives in a whisper. Browsing in a Barnes & Noble on Fifth Avenue, I ran into a boy who'd sat two rows behind me in Mr. Ames's writing class. He looked as if he were made up to play the part of a successful middle-aged broker. I don't know what he thought of me; time had written new parts for us both.

"I wonder if Mr. Ames still has those oatmeal boxes in his office," I said.

"You haven't heard? He had an operation to remove a tumor in his stomach. I heard it was cancer. I hope they got all of it."

Several months later I was in Ann Arbor for a Fourth of July family reunion. I called Mr. Ames at home and reached Madeline. The last time I'd spoken with her, years before, I had stopped by the house to deliver a late paper. Now in my mind's eye I saw her clearly, a slender woman with blond braids coiled at the nape of her neck. Her husband was still teaching, she said, though he'd taught the last five classes of the semester from a hospital bed.

"I'm sure he'd be glad to see you. He's in Room 30. I'll be going back to the hospital right after lunch, if you'd like a ride."

I thanked her and said that I couldn't get away till late afternoon. On a summer's day, the one-mile walk from my mother's house to the hospital seems to take no more than a few minutes. Dylan Thomas once said he liked to think of poetry as statements made on the way to the grave. It seemed appropriate that the walk to the hospital took me past Forest Hills Cemetery. The wrought iron gate always stands open. From the street you can see, just beyond the rise in the gravel path, a magnificent stone angel, bigger than life, though I suppose even when they are not magnificent, angels are always bigger than life.

When I arrived at the hospital, I had completely forgotten the number of Mr. Ames's room. The receptionist scanned a computer screen and said,

"He's been moved to intensive care. Are you family?"

"No, but his wife is expecting me."

"You'll need a pass," said the receptionist and handed me a well-worn strip of cardboard, numbered 2.

Fact: The door to Intensive Care is marked Authorized Personnel Only, and the whole wing is as cool and still as the opening of a rose. I peeked into the first room beyond that door. The man in the bed, connected by tubes to a monitor and an IV bag was certainly Mr. Ames, though in an edited, sallower version, as if an evil spell had diminished him. His wife sat on the edge of his bed. They were laughing together; she was waving her hands, telling him a story.

I knocked and they both looked up.

"Good morning," I said and remembered it was the middle of the afternoon.

Mr. Ames's face broke into a smile. He was still Mr. Ames, but he was dying. Madeline stood up and said she was going to sneak off for a cup of coffee. She had not left his bedside all morning.

I felt as tongue-tied as on that distant day I'd stopped by his office and handed him the poem that would be my passport into his course.

"How are you?" I asked lamely.

"Since you're here, I'm almost well, at least for the tme being."

Seeing that I could hardly utter a word, he began to talk about his students. This one had just published a poem in the *Virginia Quarterly*—did I remember her? She sat in the back row of our class. That one had given up writing and entered Yale Divinity School. Mr. Ames knew all of us by name. He knew what we had done with our lives, and he knew what our lives had done with us.

"How do you remember us all?" I asked.

He chuckled.

"It's easier to remember you all than to forget you. My great aunt taught fourth grade for forty years. The last five years of her life she had Alzheimer's. She stayed in her room at the nursing home and spent her days scolding forty years of students, invisible, rows and rows. Wasn't that strange? She no longer remembered their names, only their faults. Tell me, how do you like teaching at Vassar?"

"I love it. And I don't believe I've ever worked harder in my life."

"And isn't it wonderful work? A teacher affects eternity; you can never tell where your influence will stop."

"Oh, I wish I could sound wise in class, the way you do."

Mr. Ames chuckled.

"There's a large element of luck in teaching," he said. "So often those words of wisdom are not what you meant to say at all, and you can't even imagine why you said them. I hear you have a book of poems coming out soon."

"Not till next fall. I'll send you a copy."

Another silence. Mr. Ames broke it.

"I regret that I shall not live long enough to finish all the books I want to read. Perhaps there will be a library in heaven where I can catch up. A room with a window seat and cushions and hot chocolate. Blake says dying is like walking from one room into another. I want to go on learning. I hope there are good teachers in heaven."

A month later he was dead. My mother sent me the obituary. There was no memorial service and no good cause to which I could send the money I would have spent on flowers.

We are led out of Plato's cave through a series of disillusionments. The strong light of reason puts even our own shadows to flight. But at night, when our lives return to us in dreams, who gives a hang about reason? Suddenly, night after night, I was a student again. In my dream, I couldn't finish my Blake paper on time, and I was trying to telephone Mr. Ames at his office. The phone rang and rang and rang, till at last I heard a click and Mr. Ames's voice saying to no one in particular, *I cannot come to the phone now. Please leave a message. Do not start your message till you hear the tone.*

The tone never came.

The English Department has installed this devilish device, I thought. In the empty silence that followed, I left a message for him to call. Every night I wondered why he didn't return my call, and every morning I woke up knowing.

A year after his death I received a letter from Madeline, asking if I would help her put together a book on her husband's teaching. She'd written to dozens of his former students, asking them what they remembered most about his class.

From a letter written by Rachel Beth Ryan.

What has stayed with me is not what Dr. Ames taught me about success but what he taught me about failure. I still have the comment he wrote on one of my worst stories:

"This isn't your best work. But don't worry. Sometimes you have to write the piece wrong before you can get it right. You're clearing space, making room for it, just as you would for a long-awaited guest."

My biggest problem was structuring my stories. I'd see the scenes in my head but halfway into the writing I'd lose the sense of how everything fit together. I tried making outlines, but the stories only got duller and duller. Dr. Ames urged me to write the scenes I wanted to write, regardless of their order in the narrative. When he found out I was addicted to playing bridge he said, "The next time a scene occurs to you, write out a brief summary on a 3 × 5 card. When you've got—shall we say, a full deck?—sit down and arrange them. If you're lucky, the story will find you, and it may be a far better story than the one you set out to write. Don't use an outline. Wait for the story to show you where it wants to go. Remember, the story is the master, the writer is the servant."

Dr. Ames had great faith in the healing power of literature. The right author taken at the right time, he felt, could set a bewildered writer back on course. Sometimes I almost felt he was giving me a prescription. "Your metaphors are tired. Two ounces of Neruda and one of Emily Dickinson, to be taken at bedtime. Any book you love can be your teacher," he said, "if you read it as a writer. Study it paragraph by paragraph, sentence by sentence, word by word."

From a letter by Jay Cohen.

It shames me to remember my class with Ames. He must have found me insufferable. I was a sophomore, and I had this big crush on Alexander Pope. I wanted to be T. S. Eliot and spoke with what I hoped was an English accent. I even bought a Parker 51, though I lose pens at the rate of one a week. Unfortunately I loved all the trappings of being a writer and none of the work. Ames kept a box in his office that held fifteen slots, and above them he had written the names of his writing students. Every Friday he expected us to leave our papers in the designated slot. One day I left a note saying my poem was in progress. To my surprise, he called me in and said, "If something is in progress, you can mark it *don't read,* but you must hand it in."

I was dumbfounded.

"What's the point of handing it in, if you're not going to read it?"

"The point is, you will let go of it. And then the teacher in yourself can speak."

He used to say, "I'm trying to make myself obsolete." Months passed before I could acknowledge that letting go is not giving up but a way of getting distance on the poem or story, of seeing how to work on it.

Something else he taught me: there are two kinds of beginnings in fiction, the sentence that gets you started and the true opening sentence, which may not find you till you are well into the work. Ames loathed outlines. Especially in poetry, he believed logic was a terrible impediment to good writing, and he worked hard to make me forget what I'd been taught in freshman English: topic sentence, examples, conclusion. He'd cut up my poems in class and rearrange the stanzas, sometimes even the lines. Then we'd discuss other possible arrangements, and I'd leave class with all these tiny slips of paper crushed into my back pocket, looking as if I'd just run amok over a box of fortune cookies.

From a letter by William Klonsky.

Nothing that Ames told me when I was in his class helped me as much as a letter he wrote me three years ago. I was writing my third unpublished novel. And one day I took a look at the hundred or so pages I'd been grinding out for the last five months, and I realized they were no good. It wasn't just a question of revision. The whole thing was wrong: story, characters, everything. Why had it taken me so long to realize this?

At that point I decided to give up writing. And I wrote a long letter to Ames explaining why, because I felt he was the one person besides myself who would care.

Within the week he answered my letter.

Dear Bill,

You have mistaken the failure of one writing project for the total failure of yourself as a writer. Try to separate them. Put the novel aside and write something completely different. Nonfiction, perhaps. If you still feel blocked, write me a letter describing a story you'd like to write. Make it a very detailed letter. Trust me. Somewhere along the way, the letter will turn into the story itself.

From a letter by John Petty.

When I signed up for "The Art of Writing," I thought I was joining a workshop. We'd read each other's work in class and discuss it. That's the kind of writing class I'd taken before. I'd have time to write, and I'd write what I pleased. It was a great shock to discover that Ames gave assignments.

"The point of assignments," he said, "is to take your imagination to a new place. Some of you may find yourselves going back to these exercises long after you've left this class."

He liked the word exercises, because it reminded him of the study of music. I had no trouble with the fiction assignments, but the poetry assignments were maddening. Write a poem without adjectives. Write a poem developed from a first line. Write a poem of which the first and third stanzas are provided. Write a dialogue in verse. Write a revision of somebody else's bad poem. There were other assignments, but I've forgotten them. Later I found Ames had borrowed them from Roethke's essay, "The Teaching Poet."

Of all his assignments, the one I liked best was what he called writing in the instructional mode. He told us that his passion for odd instructions began when he was traveling to the Canary Islands on a Spanish ship and found the following notice posted over a life jacket on his cabin door:

> *Helpsavering aparata*
> *In emergings behold many whistles! Associate the stringing apparata about the bosoms and meet behind. Flee then to the indifferent lifesavering-shippen obediencing the instructs of the vessel!*

Ames was charmed. He saw great possiblities for poetry. He asked everyone in the class to write a poem in which we instructed somebody to do something. To help us get started, he brought to class a small handmill, the kind used for grinding coffee.

"This mill has a venerable history," he said. "It is first cousin to the mill in the fairy tale that ground an avalanche of porridge because its owner couldn't remember the words to make it stop. And it is second cousin to the mill that sits at the bottom of the sea, grinding salt till the last Judgment. Now, write me the instructions for using this mill."

There was nothing obviously magical about Ames's coffee mill. But aren't all objects magical if you consider them in the right light? Spinning wheels, brooms, rings; in fairy tales they show us their dark side.

Whatever I wrote has gone into the great Waste Basket in the sky. But I do remember what one student wrote, because it was mimeographed for class, and I liked it well enough to save it. Unfortunately I didn't save his name.

This mill is good for just about everything except there are a few things you must take note of.

1) Always turn the crank counter-clockwise, for it produces always against the motion of the earth and time—the product is a result of friction against time.

2) Never turn it clockwise—for to do so is to compete with the stars, the moon, the sun, the earth, and all of their generative forces. They will become jealous and you will disappear, never to have been born.

3) Because of the above, never let anyone else use it, touch, see it, or even know of its existence for this could prove fatal. This is not like those natural treasures which lack all traces of human horror.

[Note: the piece was written by Will Ostrow.]

The advantage of an instructional poem is its focus. You have your subject and you have your audience. Stephen Sondheim, whose songs I love, put it this way: "If you told me to write a love song tonight I'd have a lot of trouble. But if you tell me to write a love song about a girl with a red dress who goes into a bar and is on her fifth martini and is falling off her chair, that's a lot easier, and it makes me free to say anything I want."

From a letter by Jane Stewart Briggs.

In Dr. Ames's class I was writing fiction. I loved revising and reworking my stories. But I hated to end them, and one day in class I asked, "How do you know when a story is finished?" I shall never forget his answer. "There's this difference between the great artist and the Sunday painter: the great artist knows when to stop. It's almost like baking bread; you can smell when it's done, the work itself tells you."

Endings, endings. Stephen Vincent Benét wrote, "When I was in school, I knew poetry was not a dead thing. I knew it was always written by the living, even though the dateline said the man was dead."

You there, Mr. Ames, six feet under a stone in Forest Hills and sleeping in the back row, far from the gaze of the angel who presides over the graves like a teacher—and what a quiet class!—you there, she's calling on you to recite, to tell the truth. Mr. Ames, what have you to say for yourself?

We think by feeling. what is there to know?
I hear my being dance from ear to ear.
I wake to sleep, and take my waking slow.

Of those so close beside me, which are you?
God bless the ground! I have walked softly there.
And learn by going where I have to go.

The "Passing" of Elsie Roxborough

Kathleen A. Hauke

Driving her fashionable Ford roadster from Detroit to Ann Arbor, Elsie Roxborough arrived at the University of Michigan as a freshman in the fall of 1933. She was the first Negro student to live in a University dormitory. Her classmate Arthur Miller, an aspiring playwright and fellow reporter on the campus newspaper, called her "a beauty, the most striking girl in Ann Arbor. She was light-skinned and very classy. To a kid like me, she seemed svelte, knowing, witty, sexy."[1] With her own group in Detroit, the Roxane Players, she produced Langston Hughes's play *Drums of Haiti,* and charmed Hughes as she had charmed boxer Joe Louis some years earlier. Elsie Roxborough was "the girl I was in love with" in 1937, Hughes wrote in his autobiography.[2] Upon graduation, Roxborough "passed" into the white world. The next time most of her friends heard of her was in 1949 when an eight-column headline in the black newspaper *Michigan Chronicle* announced her death from an overdose of sleeping pills. Hughes kept her photograph over his writing table for the rest of his life.

Who was Elsie Roxborough? What became of her, and what did she represent? A piecing together of her life suggests that her fate was to dramatize the truth of Hughes's poem "House in the World":

> I'm looking for a house
> In the world
> Where the white shadows
> Will not fall.
>
> There is no house,
> Dark brother,
> No such house
> At all.

Elsie Roxborough started out to shake the stigma of color; when that proved impossible, she joined step with the oppressor. Her life as a disguised alien in the middle reaches of the white social register did not satisfy here ambition or her pride. Perhaps no happy ending awaited her. The welcome thawings of racial prejudice after the war, and the first signs of a civil rights movement, would only have mocked and embittered her in the years of her deception. A happy child become desperate, she is a case study of the "dark sister" excluded by the American Dream.

Elsie Roxborough came from an elite Michigan family. In 1930 her father, attorney Charles Anthony Roxborough, a Republican, was elected from Detroit's Third District as the state's first black state senator. He attempted to implement the Civil Rights Bill of 1885 by his own Resolution #11 which called upon the state "to investigate the discrimination at the University of Michigan."[3] Colored coeds had been denied space in the University residence halls by the Housing Director, the Dean of Women, and President Alexander Ruthven, who told the press he would allow the Union Trust of Detroit—since the funds for the women's dormitory, Mosher-Jordan, came from that source—to select who could live on campus.[4] Roxborough's uncle, John Roxborough, who started "policy" or "the numbers" (gambling) in Detroit, was one of the wealthiest men in town during the Depression. She became close to Uncle John during her high school and college years because he financed her, her sister Virginia, and their brother John at the University, just as he had helped to support young men with althetic potential who came to his attention.

In 1932, after graduating from Northern High School, Elsie Roxborough stayed in Detroit for a year reporting on cultural events and writing gossip for the weekly newspaper her father owned, the *Detroit Guardian*. During that year, her life became intertwined with Joe Louis's. Uncle John had discovered Louis at the Brewster Athletic Club in 1930, and groomed him, as he would Elsie, to prove the splendor of blackness—its strength, beauty, artistry, and character. Louis, who wrote "I always followed other people," followed his promoter with blind faith, for John Roxborough was a gentleman who wore tailor-made suits and held power in the black community. Louis later recalled in his autobiography:

> He told me to drop by his real estate office . . . . The office was just a front. . . . In those days it was hard living. . . . If you were smart enough to have your own numbers operation and you were kind and giving in the black neighborhoods, you got as much respect as

Elsie Roxborough

a doctor or lawyer. . . . I'll never forget the day Mr. Roxborough took me over to Long's Drugstore and told the owner to give me anything I wanted and charge it to him. First time I ever had so many clean bandages, rubbing alcohol and such. . . . Sometimes he'd invite me to his house for dinner. It was a beautiful house, and he had a good-looking and gracious wife. I loved it. I never saw black people living this way, and I was envious and watched everything he did.[5]

Many of their peers remember a romance between Elsie Roxborough and Joe Louis. Sometimes Louis accompanied the Roxboroughs to Idlewild, the American black society resort community near Manistee in northern Michigan. Elsie had spent all the summers of her childhood there, playing softball, riding horseback, "posing" on the beach—she did not swim—and dancing in the clubhouse each evening to the jukebox. Neighbors at Idlewild included author Charles W. Chesnutt, and physicians Daniel Hale Williams, who first performed open-heart surgery, and Charles Drew, who discovered blood plasma. Nella Larsen referred in her novel *Passing* (1929) to Idlewild as "quite the thing" for blacks who had "arrived."[6]

"Every girl wants love," Elsie Roxborough's friend Julia Duncan says. "Joe Louis had money, and for Elsie it was a fantasy dating him. She said she would marry him, but I never paid any attention. She was seventeen years old!"[7] When Louis's eyes wandered, Elsie broke the windows of his new Packard. Ulysses W. Boykin, who wrote a column "With the Younger Set" for the *Detroit Tribune* in the 1930s, and served as vice president of WGPR Radio and TV 62, the first black-owned station in the United States, recalls that "Elsie was in love with Joe Louis; it wasn't just rumor, yet it wasn't a hot love affair. People here felt the romance would blossom into something, but Joe was not cultured."[8] A member of the Roxane Players, Nimrod Carney, conjectures, "There was a class thing among blacks. Uncle John would have tried to break it up because John Roxborough was a very proud man. The cultural differences would be too great."[9]

In June, 1935, Joe Louis was big news in the black press and beginning to be noticed in the white. The *Chicago Defender* got wind of an impending engagement and asked both parties if it were true. On 13 July 1935 its front-page banner read, "'NOT ENGAGED,' SAY JOE LOUIS AND GIRL FRIEND: Co-Ed Denies Rumor That She Will Wed." It quoted Elsie

Roxborough's wire to the *Defender:* "Joe and I are merely friends and my career as a writer is much more important to me than the thought of marriage." Joe Louis answered, "I think Elsie is a fine girl, but . . . she has her books to think about." The Roxborough-Louis romance ended suddenly when Louis became engaged to Marva Trotter, the secretary to his other manager, Julian Black, in Chicago.

The Roxborough her friends describe was too spunky and inner-directed for the placid, outer-directed Louis. Her brother-in-law, Ben Brownley, remembers that "Elsie had the most exciting life of any black girl of her time." And Peter W. Cassey, Jr., who retired as acting direc-tor of the Bureau of Taxation for Wayne County, says:

> As a young kid, I was fascinated by her. Elsie seemed to have everything she wanted—her own car. We lived on the same street, Chandler. I can still hear my mother say, "There goes *EL*sie!" Peo-ple envied her. She always created a stir. Today they would call her flaky, but she was far from flaky. She was an extremist; she thought she was Hollywood.[10]

Class pride was essential to Elsie Roxborough's self-definition. Her fore-bears had gained wealth and position through education and native intel-ligence, and she was not going to forfeit that by stepping into the unrefined class Joe Louis represented. And perhaps a feminist yearning to achieve success by her own talents, not just as the lovely consort of a celebrity, kept her from taking Louis seriously.

Even with Louis out of her personal picture, life for Elsie Roxbor-ough looked bright. The University of Michigan was a white person's milieu for which she felt an affinity due to her social status and fair color. She had prevailed upon her sister to come to Ann Arbor, in January of 1935, and they were roommates in the beautiful new Mosher-Jordan dormitory on the hill. Until Senator Roxborough had persuaded the state legislature that there was discrimination in housing at the Univer-sity, by unwritten code black students had lived in private Negro homes or in a Negroes-only league house on East Ann Street. Mary Taliaferro, wife of Senator Roxborough's law partner, recalls:

> Her father opened the doors to her; he made a legal issue of it. It had to be unpleasant for her. Others didn't want to room with her and yet she was probably superior to most of them. [In Detroit] she

lived in a nice home, with good maids, good equipment, the best
of whatever was to be had at the time. It must have been hard on
her that people wouldn't want to room with her at the University.[11]

The Roxborough family had protected their young from the damage
prejudice inflicts, but when their accomplished, hard-driving daughter
entered the mainstream of American life in Ann Arbor, she didn't have
the usual emotional defenses and thus was more vulnerable, more easily
scarred.

Jean Blackwell Hutson, a peer of Roxborough's at the University,
who later became Chief of the Schomburg Center for Research in Black
Culture, part of the New York Public Library system in Harlem, described the psychological atmosphere of which white students were unaware: "I remember the bigotry of Dean Alice Lloyd. She pretended to
be concerned about Negro students and wrote kind letters to parents,
but she stood firm in holding the line [against integration of the dorms]."
Hutson admits that Roxborough seemed like a snob to her then: "Elsie
had been reared like a princess and was accustomed to having her own
way."[12] Her snobbery produced a tension between Roxborough and
other blacks on campus who had not enjoyed her privileges. To white
students she was an exotic, not like other Negroes yet not like themselves either. A hothouse flower, she was rudely awakened when she
went on academic probation her first semester. She flunked a science and
a history course. But by her junior year she had adapted to the rigors of
the University, raised her grades, and plotted her future.

In the fall of 1935 the Theatre Guild of Detroit produced her play
Wanting at the Frogs Club at Beaubien and Madison. Her sister helped
out by acting in it as an artist, Dodsie, best friend of the heroine. In
February 1936, *The Crisis* had a two-column photo of Roxborough,
captioned "Young Playwright," to publicize *Wanting*. On 20 March 1936
the play was presented in Chicago but received a poor review in the
Chicago Defender from Enoc P. Waters, Jr., who wrote:

> That the play was a disappointment to a majority of the audience
> was indicated by the unfavorable comments of many as they left the
> building. Beginning 50 minutes behind schedule, the long, loosely-
> woven play . . . told the story of Russell Terrill, a young socialite
> who, tiring of [her] vivacious artists' group . . . seeks . . . experi-

mental social service work. Here she contacts Sandy, a habitual drunken widower with a daughter and some . . . communistic notions. There follows a period of sordid infatuation during which she takes up residence in Sandy's quarters. The spell is broken when Sandy becomes abusive and deserts her. . . . The play was not of the type in which a Race [Negro] cast could be at its best. Plans to go cycling in Italy, the idea of one owning a stable of ponies, or of one making another a present of a yacht becomes ridiculous in the mouths of Race actors and actresses because these situations are so far from reality.

Roxborough submitted substantially the same play to the Hopwood Minor Drama contest in April 1936, but with a new title, *A World of Difference*. It placed third of those entered. Arthur Miller won first prize. One judge called her play "artificial." He was "bored by it." Another considered "all contestants . . . not up to last year's entries," and the third commented, "No plays revealed any indications of talent."[13]

Perhaps Roxborough was trying to say something in her play that neither her black audience in Chicago nor the white Hopwood critics realized. She was showing a slice of life as she knew it. The play was rooted in a familiar, elite group of black people who had the same money, advantages, interests, vices, and ambitions as white civilization that already knows luxury does not bring happiness. The world-weary lead with the androgynous name, Russell Terrill, "dressed in long, white satin" though she is also described as "tomboyish in appearance," is a mocking and ambivalent self-portrait that foreshadows Roxborough's own rejection of the caste comforts she had enjoyed as a child.[14]

On 24 April 1936 Roxborough's play *Flight* was produced in Detroit. Her pretty friend Ruth Webb played a white woman who persuades a golden-haired Creole, Mimi Daquin, disillusioned with her own people, to flee from them and find lasting happiness with others. It may be prophetic that both plays, *Flight* and *Wanting/A World of Difference,* feature heroines who leave the group they are born into for a radically different one. Roxborough, a romantic, believed in the pursuit of happiness, but hers, she felt, would lie among whites. There would always be a low ceiling above her if she tried to rise in the black world— as the writers of the Harlem Renaissance had discovered when white critics patronized and ghettoized even their finest work. Nor could she think of marriage and children, for children might turn out colored, and impede her progress in the dream world her talent seemed to make accessible.

In the same season Roxborough crafted her first play, fall of 1935, Langston Hughes's play *Mulatto* opened at the Vanderbilt Theatre on Broadway. It dramatized the agony of a loyal son when he sees all the privileges of American citizenship open to one parent and denied to the other. *Mulatto* did not provide a solution to the racial dilemma. It claimed that blacks try to give love and tenderness to whites, who receive such affection covertly but deny it overtly. Unlike Roxborough's plays it offered blacks no hope for social mobility across the color line.

On 7 November 1936 Roxborough's play *Father Knows Best* was presented by the Roxane Players in the little theater of the Detroit Institute of Arts. (Because no scripts are extant and it was not reviewed in surviving papers, its content is unknown.) She ran the Roxane Players, wrote for the campus newspaper, and kept her studies up. She got her dramatic group off the ground, according to Nimrod Carney, because "she was Elsie Roxborough!"

> There were half a dozen black groups in Detroit then. For example, [poet] Robert Hayden worked backstage with the Roxane Players and in time started his own group, The Paul Robeson Players. Other groups had more direction than Elsie's. Hers operated on the force of her personality and went out of existence until she came back to town. She had soirees upstairs at the Frogs Club, and she used that as a rehearsal place.
>
> She was a little older than I. I hadn't anything and was unsophisticated. I was abusing myself in those plays: it was an inside group and I was not on the inside. But I didn't mind because those plays showed me the way to the trough and I was happy to reach the trough.
>
> Elsie was a charming . . . young lady who had a talent. It was unusual for anybody to get such a group together, but it was extraordinary that people would follow the lead of a black female in the thirties. It was much harder for the female then than now to reach out and grab a piece of the world that she wanted.

Following her theatrical debacle in Chicago, on New Year's Day, 1937, the *Defender* printed a new, two-column photo of Roxborough on its society pages. The caption said she was spending the holiday in Cleveland visiting Evelyn Jackson. Langston Hughes was also in Cleveland then, visiting his mother. The two playwrights probably discussed their work, for in March 1937 Hughes was in Detroit viewing rehearsals of his *Drums of Haiti* that the Roxane Players were preparing for presentation on 15, 16, and 17 April. It was a historical play about Jean-Jacques Dessalines, a rebellious slave who freed his people to become black emperor of Haiti.

Roxborough had heard about Langston Hughes ever since she was a child. She was six when Hughes, at eighteen, published his first poem in *The Brownie Book,* the NAACP magazine for children; seven when his famous "The Negro Speaks of Rivers" came out in the June 1921 issue of *The Crisis*. He was a leading figure in the Harlem Renaissance and a member of the radical group of Negro "actors" invited to the Soviet Union in 1932 to make a movie about racism in America. Roxborough must have assumed that the black flowering of the twenties that Hughes helped create had broken the way for other writers and that she, too, would find a niche thanks to her theatrical activities.

On the personal level, rumors abounded. Len Reed, in the *Pittsburgh Courier,* said, "Elsie Roxborough is doing it again. This time the play is by Langston Hughes. He's the fellow who wrote the book for *Mulatto.* With so much in common between the two, the play should be a success." William Smallwood, in his *Afro-American* column, "Social Skits," wrote:

> Last weekend, éclat Detroit probably packed into their Lucy Thurman YWCA to witness Langston Hughes's *Troubled Island,* the title of which dashing Mr. Hughes allowed equally dashing Elsa Roxboro [*sic*] to change to *Drums of Haiti.*
>
> The quidnuncs would have you swoon in your best Melanie fashion over the Hughes-Roxboro duo because . . . these two are supposedly in the throes of love. . . . [Elsie] has what the girls call "flash."[15]

When Hughes was questioned by the *Afro-American* about impending marriage, he replied, "I'm afraid that my marital intentions have been greatly exaggerated. . . . I am a professional poet and while poetry is so frequently associated with romance, there seems to be little compatibility between poetry and marriage, especially where one must depend upon it to support a wife."[16] Elsie Roxborough and Langston Hughes were alike in being educated and dreamers, and involved in the theater. But she had always lived among the upper-crust; Hughes identified with the street black. She was tall—5'7"—and he was short—5'5"—and twelve years older. She lived in style; he shared his mother's basement flat where his stepfather was building custodian. Although Hughes seemed close to Roxborough as an artist, he was still, like Joe Louis, a lower-class figure.

In 1937 Joe Louis became heavyweight boxing champion, and black America exploded in jubilation. The eyes of the Roxborough family were on Uncle John's protégé to whom experiences would come that had never before been known by an American Negro. Was this triumph connected to Elsie Roxborough's decision the same year to leave her race? Her rationale was the lack of opportunities in the theater, a problem she had discussed with Langston Hughes:

> I agreed . . . that it was difficult for any colored person to gain entrance to the American entertainment field except as a performer—as a director or technician almost impossible—and for a colored woman I would think it harder even than for a man. Elsie was often mistaken for white in public places so it would be no trouble at all for her to pass as white.[17]

Hughes disapproved of "passing" on principle; his works on the subject emphasize the emotional cost.[18] But Roxborough had already discovered the emotional cost of failure as a playwright. The rejection of her plays by critics and judges contrasted with the nearly incredible success of Uncle John's golden boy. If making it as a black in America demanded masculine brute strength, she would flee to the genteel white world in which a woman's arts would be appreciated.

Roxborough changed her hair color from raven black to auburn, eliciting a pun from columnist Boykin, "She's just dye-ing to get away."[19] In her roadster she headed to Pasadena, looping through Mexico to test her high school and college Spanish and make herself sufficiently familiar with Hispanic culture that she could feign foreign origins if her racial background were questioned.

Roxborough illustrated what you could do if you were light-skinned and had enough money. From the autumn of 1937 on, most black reporters were never sure whether she was in Hollywood or New

York, and her family wasn't saying. On Christmas Day, 1937, William Smallwood headlined his *Afro-American* column, "Elsie Roxborough Reported Living Incognito in Gotham":

> Though none of the metropolitan lads who pound typewriters for a living know it, Elsie Roxborough whom Detroit affectionately dubbed the colored Connie Bennett, has been living in Gotham for the past few months as Nordic—much to her family's undisguised disgust. You can imagine poor La Roxborough shuddering each time she slips into an uptown subway train.[20]

Roxborough was so determined to succeed that she put blinders on and forged ahead despite the consequences. Others couldn't "pass" but she could, and if passing was her only option, she would take it. Furthermore, passing was an adventure. It was exciting to play out the historic black American folk trick of "fooling ole massa"—to slip through to the white world and witness that no one could tell the difference. In her case the trick worked extra well: she rose to a position where she represented the epitome of Aryan beauty. She took the name Pat Rico, and for a while flourished as a model and owner of a modeling studio.

After less than a year in California, she moved to New York and lived "downtown," but she did not abandon black life completely. She would go up to Harlem and be photographed in Bill "Bojangles" Robinson's beautifully-appointed cocktail and supper club, the Mimo Club, on Seventh Avenue just below 132nd Street, when Uncle John and Joe Louis came to town. On 13 July 1938, when Langston Hughes sailed for Europe to attend a peace congress sponsored by the International Association of Writers for the Defense of Culture, his friends recognized the woman who reached the dock too late to say goodbye as the person in the picture in Hughes's Harlem apartment.[21]

By the summer of 1939, Roxborough—as "Pat Rico"—had a telephone number in New York and lived at 77 Washington Place in Greenwich Village. Under this name she published a story, "Charming Escort," in the September 1939 Street and Smith's *Love Story* magazine. In that story the heroine is a model torn between her attraction to a sensuous top-fashion photographer who uses her, and a more homespun photographer who helps her get established with good pictures of herself and introductions at the right studios. The theme of this wish-fulfillment fantasy is that the too-successful man does not understand the feelings of the woman whose emotions he exploits. A racial analogy would be that the white American does not understand the feelings of the mulatto who lives beside him.

By the time World War II started, Roxborough had assumed a third new name, "Mona Manet," and moved to a final residence, across the street from the future site of the United Nations buildings. The 21 October 1943 issue of the *New York Times* says that Mona Manet was in charge of makeup and coiffures for the *Times's* "Fashions of the Times" style show. And she had opened her modeling salon, Mona Manet, Inc., at 48 East 52nd Street, by 1944.

In February of 1946 a new, internationally flavored magazine, *Fascination,* was launched in New York by Hungarian emigré Geza Herczeg, who had won an Oscar in 1938 for writing *The Life of Emile Zola* for the screen. Elsie Roxborough/Mona Manet joined the staff, and wrote a column on new cosmetics in hyperbolic, artificial language. The high point of her ethnic deception is her description of a reception in Atlanta:

> Your beauty editor had the thrill of her lifetime when she was commissioned as Beauty Stylist to do the make-up and hair-styling for Atlanta's overwhelming "Fashionata of 1946." . . . With us on the trip to Atlanta were 12 of New York's most versatile models, selected because they had grace and acting ability as well as beauty. . . .
>
> Antoine's Salon at Rich's did the hairdos for me and kept the girls groomed for their many changes at each performance.
>
> We enjoyed plenty of good old Southern hospitality in that magnificent town of fabulous homes and exquisite gardens and clothes. Governor and Mrs. Arnall turned out for the very elegant opening night. . . . They say no one has been received as royally as our company since Clark Gable was down there for the *Gone With the Wind* premiere.[22]

As trickster, Roxborough succeeded in fooling white Atlanta, where blacks and whites still did not mix socially. With whom could she laugh about her supreme ruse, however?

While Roxborough/Manet lived and worked in midtown Manhattan among white professionals, in little ways the slow but continuous emergence of black consciousness and black pride went on without her. Concealing her identity, living with a white roommate, she could not

rationalize bringing *Ebony* magazine into her apartment when it unosten-
tatiously appeared in November 1945. She could not invite her Uncle
John or her friends Joe Louis, or Langston Hughes, or even Arthur
Miller—who had known her only as Negro—to her apartment, or even
mention to anyone that she knew them. She would feel uncomfortable
discussing the headlines about President Truman's attempts to establish
a Fair Employment Practices Commission—the precursor of Equal Opportunity and Affirmative Action. Trying to act like a real Caucasian,
Roxborough/Manet became a caricature, a poor imitation of mainstream
society and its values.

Novelist and screenwriter Ernest Lehman—the script for *North by
Northwest* is one of his credits—was a fellow writer for *Fascination*. He
used to gossip with editor Herczeg about the mysterious Mona who
year-round was wrapped in mink, as if the ultimate in furs provided
protection against the psychological chill. From Lehman's account it is
obvious that she went through a metamorphosis of personality in making
her race change. No longer was she aggressive, dynamic, "wild." As
white, Roxborough/Manet became passive, defenseless. Lehman writes:

> I had no idea that Mona was "passing." She was vulnerable and
> appealing and glamorous without being threatening to anyone. . . . I
> had the impression that Geza was doing whatever he could to help
> her survive. He definitely gave her her job with the magazine. He
> was certainly her protector, perhaps a father-confessor.
>
> Mona was unattached. There were no men in her life that year
> [1946]. She never seemed to come on to men in a noticeably sexy
> way, even though she was young and attractive and a kind of
> woman about town.
>
> We were always happy to see each other when our paths crossed.
> She told me one reason she liked me: I reminded her of Arthur
> Miller, the playwright. . . .
>
> Mona moved in the magazine world, the world of fashion, res-
> taurants, and nightclubs. She enhanced any gathering she was in.
> She was sweet, self-effacing, low in self-esteem, tinged with sad-
> ness. I doubt whether there was anyone who didn't like her. As far
> as I know, she never connected in New York with any truly impor-
> tant magazine. *Fascination* was not first-rate, and soon folded.
>
> If in "passing" she seemed to have lost some of her drive and
> intelligence, it probably was due to the pernicious effects of the

thousand ploys one would have to indulge in. . . . In those times, it was a hopeless adventure leading nowhere.

I think she remained in my memory . . . because of the dramatic quality of her story, once it was revealed, and the suddenness of her untimely end. To me she was like a character out of a novel or a play, such as Edna Ferber's "Julie" in *Showboat*.[23]

When her roommate returned to New York one Sunday night after a weekend in Connecticut, she found Mona dead in bed. She called Mona's sister in Detroit, who went with Uncle John's wife "Cutie"— they both looked white—to claim the body and bring it back to Detroit for burial. They told Mona's New York friends that the funeral would be private, trying to conceal her racial identity even in death. There was no obituary in the New York papers under her name or either of her pseudonyms. The death certificate lists "Mona Manet, writer, white, 865 First Avenue, Manhattan, age 35," as having died of "congestion of the viscera."

America was in the throes of a steel strike that weekend with 500,000 workers idle, 12,000 in Detroit. Louella Parsons was extolling the movie *Pinky* for "attacking a daring subject in a daring way. Jeanne Crain is superb as a Negro girl who realizes the folly of trying to pass as white." In the movie *Lost Boundaries* Mel Ferrer was starring in the true story of a Negro doctor and his family who did "pass" in New Hampshire. Roxborough's former rival for the Hopwood drama prize, Arthur Miller, had a box office and critical success with *Death of a Salesman*. The drama section of the *New York Times*, which she may have read on her last morning, featured University of Michigan professor Valentine Windt for directing a Shakespeare festival in New York. Windt had been Roxborough's teacher in Ann Arbor and she had interviewed him for the *Michigan Daily*—but she would not have dared to approach him as "Mona Manet." In Detroit, the *American Weekly* supplement to the *Times* contained an article on the numbers racket, noting that John Roxborough had served two years in the Jackson Federal Penitentiary (1944–46) for payoffs to police and city officials who had "protected" his business.

Elsie Roxborough's final passing hit the front pages in Detroit's black press. The weekly *Michigan Chronicle* spread a banner headline, "ELSIE ROXBOROUGH DIES," and attributed the cause to nerves rather than suicide because she had left no note. Whether she actually committed suicide will never be known. Her stockings were soaking in the wash bowl, a sign of her probable intention to go out the next day. She had telephoned family the previous week for money. Nevertheless, she may have desired to end her existence for a long time, like the unsuccessful writer-heroine Russell Terrill in her Hopwood entry, *A World of Difference*. Terrill has a speech on her wish for death:

> When I go to bed at night, I don't care whether I live until morning or not—most times I fall asleep praying for death. I feel all lost in a great vastness, and beaten. . . . I go through the usual automatic rituals, eating tasteless food, talking meaningless talk, laughing soulless laughter. I'm too much of a coward to really die—I've only prayed to sneak out in my sleep. . . . If I were only of some use to the world![24]

Elsie Roxborough knew that black Detroit expected much of her. The expectations she had for herself may have been even greater. Detroit had told her: you are the best; you have had every chance; here you are powerless; go elsewhere and shine brighter than the whites. So Roxborough maneuvered and schemed, wriggling through all the possibilities she could devise. Ambivalent about how to express herself racially, she may have wanted to communicate a message to both her white and black peers: "Be careful of appearances. People of *both* colors are talented and beautiful. We have hidden riches." However, when she passed to a professionally acceptable identity, her writing as a "mixed" sensibility became garish, as in *Fascination,* or maudlin, as in "Charming Escort" for *Love Story*.

Elsie Roxborough had felt unique when she set off for Ann Arbor in 1933, as if all she had to do was play her cards right and the game was hers. But being Negro, she was programmed for failure. Barbara Christian has said of Jean Toomer, a light-skinned Negro fiction writer, that "as a result of the touching of two cultures [his] women's lives are painfully truncated, their spirits abused and repressed."[25] Alice Walker has noted that Toomer's intellectually repressed black women "stare out at the world wildly, like lunatics, or quietly, like suicides."[26] Like one of Toomer's desperate women, Elsie Roxborough vigorously sought a way out, and then lost the gaiety and energy of her youthful ambition. It is ironic that both her suitors, Joe Louis and Langston Hughes, "made it" in the white world by pursuing their talents as Negroes, whereas

Roxborough, aping whites, did not. Having lost the finest elements of her personality by choosing to pass, she could find no place out from under the long white shadow; there was "no such house at all."

NOTES

In addition to others mentioned in the notes, I wish to acknowledge the help of the following people for information, interpretation, and support: Kermit Bailer, George H. Bass, Pat Booker, Gwendolyn Brooks, Ben M. Brownley, Nellie Ann Bush, Geneva Cassey, Edward Caulkins, Arthur T. Crump, Helen Pease Devlin, Vickie Burnett and Roberta Doran, Stepin Fetchit, Fred Guinyard, Hamilton (Ontario) Public Library, Nellie M. Hauke, Nathan I. Huggins, Rowena Jelliffe, Robert J. Kearns, S. J., Blyss B. Lewis, Richard B. Lyons, Pat Rollins McPherson, Michigan State Library Services, Blanche, America and Lorenzo Nelson, Edith Richardson Phelps, Mary Jo Pugh and the Bentley Historical Collection of the University of Michigan, Arnold Rampersad, Charles A. Roxborough, II, Carol Roxborough, Marshall Shulman, Leona Simmons, Harry Solomon, Indu Suryanaryan, Tallulah Taliaferro, Tuure Tenander, Helen Thomas, Bessie Ware, Vilma Zuliani, and especially Richard L. Hauke, and the Katy Hauke Research Fund.

For discussion of the issues raised in this article, I am indebted to John C. Dancy, *Sand Against the Wind* (Detroit: Wayne State University Press, 1966); William H. Grier, M.D., and Price M. Cobbs, M.D., *Black Rage* (New York: Bantam Books, 1969); Gerri Major, with Doris E. Saunders, *Black Society* (Chicago: Johnson Publishing Co., 1976); Howard H. Peckham, *The Making of the University of Michigan, 1817–1967* (Ann Arbor: University of Michigan Press, 1967).

1. Arthur Miller, personal letter, 11 December 1982.

2. Langston Hughes, *I Wonder As I Wander* (New York: Hill and Wang, 1964; rpt. 1956), 328.

3. *Journal of the Senate of the State of Michigan,* 1931 Regular Session, Vol. I (Lansing: Franklin DeKleine Co., 1931), 108, 115. See also "Discrimination at University Hinted," *State Journal* (Lansing, Mich.), 12 February 1931, 1, col. 8; "Probe Student Segregation, Mich. Legislature Asked to Investigate," *Chicago Defender,* 21 February 1931, 3; "Klan Plans to Block Segregation Probe," *Chicago Defender,* 28 February 1931, 3; "Maj. Gen. Carr Has New Fields to Conquer," *Mich. State Digest,* 19 February 1931, 10; and "The Hand of Klan in Case Against Mich. Senator," *Chicago Defender,* 14 March 1931, 6.

4. *Chicago Defender,* 21 February 1931, 3.

5. Joe Louis, with Edna and Art Rust, *Joe Louis: My Story* (New York: Berkley Books, 1981), 26–27.

6. Nella Larsen, *Passing* (1929; rpt. New York: Collier Books, 1971), 52.

7. Julia Hunton Bradby Duncan, telephone interview, Detroit, Mich., 9 October 1982.

8. Ulysses W. Boykin, telephone interview, Detroit, Mich., 7 May 1983.

9. Nimrod Carney, telephone interview, Detroit, Mich., 8 May 1983.

10. Peter W. Cassey, Jr., telephone interview, Detroit, Mich., 5 April 1983.

11. Mary Taliaferro, telephone interview, Detroit, Mich., 27 August 1982.

12. Jean Blackwell Hutson, personal letter, New York City, 25 April 1983.

13. Judges for 1936 were Alfred Kreymborg, Edith J. R. Isaacs, and Alexander Dean. Their comments are preserved in the Department of Rare Books and Special Collections, University of Michigan.

14. "A World of Difference," Department of Rare Books and Special Collections, University of Michigan Library.

15. William Smallwood, *Baltimore Afro-American*, 24 April 1937, 22.

16. Langston Hughes, "Poet Denies That He Will Wed," *Baltimore Afro-American*, 27 March 1937, 2.

17. Hughes, *I Wonder As I Wander*, 328–29.

18. See "Passing" in *The Ways of White Folks* (1933; rpt. New York: Vintage Books, 1971), 49–53, particularly. In it a "passing" son passes his dark-skinned mother on the street and doesn't greet her, then writes her a note of apology; praises her for not giving a sign she even knew him, then, "I will take a box at the Post Office for your mail. I'm glad there's nothing to stop letters from crossing the color-line," he says; also, "Who Passing for Who?" in *Something in Common and Other Stories* (New York: Hill and Wang, 1963), 40–44; and the poem "Passing," in *Selected Poems*, 257–58.

19. Ulysses W. Boykin, *Detroit Tribune*, 10 July 1937, 7.

20. William Smallwood, *Baltimore Afro-American*, 25 December 1937, 9.

21. Faith Berry, *Langston Hughes: Before and Beyond Harlem* (Westport, Conn.: Lawrence Hill and Co., 1983), 248–49, 253–54, 277–79.

22. Mona Manet, "New and Fascinating," *Fascination*, May 1946, 10, 12.

23. Ernest Lehman, personal letters, Los Angeles, Calif., 21 December 1982 and 28 March 1983.

24. "A World of Difference," 13.

25. Barbara Christian, *Black Women Novelists: The Development of a Tradition, 1892–1976* (Westport, Conn.: Greenwood Press, 1980), 55.

26. Quoted in Christian, 181.

Bel Air: The Automobile As Art Object

Daniel L. Guillory

On one of those high, dry October days when the sunlight spills warmly into your field of vision and the icy tang of winter clings to the edge of consciousness, I found myself driving over the bad farm roads of east central Illinois. The countryside was geometrically neat and planar: corn and bean fields fell in regular intervals like squares on graph paper or the blue lines of a surveyor's notebook. I was heading toward the Indiana line, and even now the land was no longer as flat as a table top but began to undulate and dip into ravines, hills, and little sandstone cliffs. The roads turned serpentine and narrow, enclosing an apple orchard here or a herd of fat Holstein there. Everywhere the sunlight was falling in big, manageable chunks, illuminating the farmhouses as formal as postage stamps and the sharp-edged red barns that must have been cut out with scissors and pasted to the horizon.

Everyone feels rich at harvest time, and perhaps that is why these farm folk who raise the corn and apples delighted in horse-trading, auctioneering, flea markets, barn sales, and open-air swap sessions. I had already passed two auctions in progress, and I would have passed up the next one except for an especially severe glint, a blister of light that emanated from the heavily chromed snout of a 1936 Packard. I half expected FDR to be sitting on the back seat. This sedan stood tall and stately, and the farmers approached it with a certain air of hesitation and respect. A 1929 Model A seemed more democratic and inviting, even though it did have traces of rust on the rear fenders. But the showpiece was a 1950 powder-blue Ford Tudor, "slick as a bar of soap and smooth as a sewing machine," according to the old farmer who owned it. Clearly, this was no ordinary flea market; serious collectors were sprinkled among the farmers in overalls, plaid shirts, and John Deere caps. Although the sermons were better, the prices were too steep for my professorial salary. "Tell you what I'm gonna do," said the owner of the blue Ford. "Feller up the road, friend o'mine, has a Chivvy fer sale," he explained, as he pointed toward a hill some two or three miles distant. "You jog left at the crossroad and follow the hard road up the hill. You can't miss it."

The crudely lettered sign *Car For Sale* was planted in the front yard of a white frame house that might have served as an archetype of the region. No one seemed to be around, so I ambled into the inviting red barn, with its rich texture of smells: timothy, alfalfa, manure, and mud. The cracks between the old barn boards were thinner than knife blades, allowing the cool October light to squeeze through like thin sheets of glass. Dust motes hovered everywhere. There was just enough light to discern the strawcovered outlines of an automobile resting in the corner like some found object. Here was no Victrola or tacky butter churn; here was a piece of pure Americana, a 1958 Chevrolet Bel Air sitting glumly on tires that were squashed flat and useless. A bale of hay had fallen on the roof. A rusty-colored chicken sat pensively on the back seat. Yet the sheet metal, lacquered in alternating bands of metallic blue and creamy white, still glowed impressively. This old sedan arched its metallic eyebrows over the four intact headlamps, and the front bumpers were puckered open and spread wide like a shark's jaw filled with numberless teeth. I was drawn especially to the turquoise blue interior, the dashboard and instrument panel composed in sweeping parabolic curves punctuated by conical knobs and switches in a style that was pure Buck Rogers. A shape reminiscent of the fabled V-2 rocket had provided a decorative motif that was repeated on the upholstery of the doors and seats.

This Bel Air was Everyman's Space Ship for 1958, an artifact from a happier and dreamier time when space ships and their telltale fins had charmed the national imagination. In the year before this Bel Air left the assembly line in Detroit, Sputnik was launched. Eisenhower was ensconced safely in the White House, Elvis was king, and the Cold War was turning icy-hot, as suggested by the Civil Defense "Conelrad" logo on the radio dial. Somehow this car had cheated the inexorable march of time, like the strange, captured moments of a prized photograph. But unlike the photograph, the Bel Air was not a ghostly image but a three-dimensional presence, enticing and seductive in its pure physicality. I dimly understood that by possessing this car I was retrieving part of my past and—through a kind of Proustian logic—expanding my present. The good hard money of the 1950s could still be spent; the music persisted, not merely the music of lovers' lanes and hamburger heavens but the deeper strains of a past recaptured. Rock and roll pounded in my temples; the hiked-up bass lines of electric guitars ricocheted in the close, cabin-like interior of the old Chevy. Some dark-haired singer in a gold lamé suit intoned pleadingly into a microphone; the rhythms grew stronger and stronger, overwhelming in their intensity. Like so many before me, I found my virtue and good sense powerless before this onslaught. And I bought that car.

Some days later a tow truck deposited the Bel Air in the driveway of my house on Faculty Row, adjoining the grounds of the starchy liberal arts college where I taught literature and writing. Something was dreadfully out of place. The car was older than most of the students. Surely the Prof was off his rocker for buying such an old junker! A neighbor and colleague, indignant and peeved, demanded that I remove that "relic" from the driveway. Property values were going to suffer, he insisted. As if to exacerbate my feelings of guilt and squeamishness, the local Chevrolet dealer refused to touch the car. The service manager, in fact, broke into peals of laughter when I timidly admitted that the car was a '58. Apparently, Mr. Goodwrench was as phony as any other character on television. No independent garage wanted the work, either. Even a so-called custom shop saw no profit in the undertaking. I now owned a piece of collectible kitsch, something to frame and elevate as an art object in the manner of Joseph Cornell, the artist who spent a lifetime making glass-framed boxes which he filled with various *objets*.

But if the automotive establishment wasn't interested in a disabled 1958 sedan, many other people obviously were. The doorbell began to ring daily, and inevitably a stranger appeared, asking about The Car. Was it for sale? How had I found one in such excellent condition? Was it a straight six or a small-block eight? Did I plan to exhibit? The most interesting visitors were those who, like the rural antique dealers, wanted to swap stories. One fellow recounted in vivid detail a trip that he and his family had taken to the Yukon in a 1958 Bel Air. Others rehearsed first dates, proms, traffic tickets, and other small moments of family and personal history. Although the stories, for the most part, amounted to trivial and corny tales, the act of nostalgic recollection and the process of retelling were genuinely impressive. An American paradox was parked in the driveway, an assemblage of insensate rubber, steel, and glass parts that somehow triggered poignant human feelings. A college dean, who usually spoke in terms of "cost benefit analysis" and "management by objective," arrived one morning, asking to inspect the ancient oil-bath air filter. He then gave me an impromptu sermon on the virtues of this 250-cubic-inch straight six engine, closing with the colloquial observation that "these here motors will run forever. You could hit 'em broadside with a bazooka, and they'd still keep running." I had never heard those tones in the official memoranda he sent through campus mail. By this time, I suspected that I had fulfilled every anthropologist's secret dream: the discovery of an authentic tribal totem. When these visitors spoke of the Bel Air, their tones shifted, and their voices fairly rose in song. One man produced a billfold in which, next to snapshots of his wife and kids, were pictures of the three '58 Chevies he had owned, including an Impala convertible, black and shiny as a hearse. The Bel Air had provided an entrée for each of my visitors, and something indisputably human in their own past had suddenly become larger and more accessible. Like the car itself, memories were being towed out of some red barn and made ready for restoration.

Buck and Larry appeared on the doorstep like all the other strangers who had come to see The Car, but from the very first moment I sensed that our association would be different. For one thing, in dress and manner they resembled dropouts from some Tantric California commune of the late 1960s. Larry was a vegetarian who sported a red beard down to his chest, and he generally spoke about the beauty of "natural and organic" ways—when he spoke at all. Buck was a dark and loquacious fellow with old-fashioned wire-rim glasses that bobbed up and down on his nose as he laughed nervously and launched into frequent jokes or sarcastic anecdotes. Although they tried to pass themselves off as young innocents, I later learned that Buck had a degree in anthropology and that Larry had completed everything but the dissertation for a Ph.D. in biology. During the time I knew them, they asked me more pertinent questions about philosophy, literature, and world affairs than did most of my students—or even my colleagues, for that matter. They read voraciously, and they fixed old cars. Lesson number one: a book is a tool.

They sized up the car with a cool, professional savvy, checking tie-rods, A-frames, wheel bearings, gear lube, and throttle linkage while petting the metallic flanks of the old Bel Air as if it were a pony about to receive its first saddle. At first I thought these automotive guardian angels fit into some convenient sociological niche, like "hippie hot-rodder" or "blue-collar car buff" or "nostalgic collector." Actually, they belonged to a more original category that I dubbed *homo mobilis,* self-reliant, Emersonian types who believed that "less was more" and that maintenance was a way of life. Keep it running, keep it running, and above all, do it yourself. Since the age of twelve or thirteen, Buck and Larry had torn down and reassembled every kind of engine they could get their hands on: motorcycles, lawn mowers, outboard motors, even garden tillers. They had learned to trust the palpable reality of the well-tuned motor as much as they learned to distrust and despise automotive dealerships with their sinister wiles and shoddy business practices. Well, I had started off in the right direction, they assured me, by buying the car from another individual (never from a dealer, new or used) and by buying a used vehicle that was *potentially* road-worthy. At this point, I had my doubts. The thing hadn't run in years. Belts were loose, gaskets were brittle, valves and rocker arms were painfully out of adjustment. The carburetor sprayed gasoline in fan-shaped spumes over the entire engine compartment. Could this lethal, incendiary weapon be transformed into a civilized sedan, after all? As if to answer my question, Larry shuffled over to his pickup and returned with a tube of industrial-grade sealant and a small crescent wrench. After a few minutes of tinkering and a boost from the truck's oversized battery, the old Chevy fired up, coughed throatily, and began to turn over in a rough but regular rhythm. "Needs work," observed Larry.

That laconic utterance translated into six weeks of intense physical *and* intellectual exertion of a kind and combination I had never experienced before. We all had jobs, but every afternoon, Larry and Buck appeared faithfully with whatever tools, jacks, torches, lights, and meters were dictated by the task at hand. In the end, we stripped the car down to its bare bones, piece by piece, even the maddening watch-like interiors of the carburetor, speedometer, and clock. When we finished, some six weeks later, at a time when the first snow was beginning to dust the ground, the car was mechanically perfect and aesthetically pleasing, with one small exception. The electric clock proved intransigent to the very end; Buck concluded that it would always gain five minutes per week, that it was probably a design defect. I never learned if that was a face-saving rationalization on his part, but it was the only time Buck or Larry ever offered an excuse. In their view, everything on a car behaved according to immutable principles of logic and right reason. If anything malfunctioned on the car, there was always an exact and assignable cause for the problem. Unlike the world of men and ideas, where reality was surrounded by a nimbus of confusion and doubt, the systems of the automobile obeyed laws of a Platonic and Newtonian kind.

I began to appreciate the subtle meshing of one part with another and the larger coherence of whole *systems* of parts (engine, drive train, brakes). Precise articulation was the goal here as in the teaching of rhetoric. If the front wheels were out of alignment, then the tires would wear unevenly and commence to wobbling at high speeds. This vibration, in turn, would weaken the tie rods, and eventually grind down the rubber bushings until the car would be next to impossible to steer. On the other hand, if one had the precise point of alignment for every system, the whole car began to behave with a beauty that was proved in flawless acceleration, cornering, and braking—and in the knowledge that these small parts of the universe hummed perfectly. Hence, the ignition points must be separated by a gap of exactly thirty-five thousandths of an inch for reasons of engineering as well as aesthetics. So too, the timing was adjusted exactly five degrees from "top dead center." I never heard Buck rhapsodize about the special beauty of the automobile, but one splendid afternoon when the western sky was flaring and we had finally returned the last pieces of chrome trimming to their proper places, Buck caught me staring at the finished product. For once, he was speechless. His face crumpled into something like a smirk or a wink before he loaded the last of his tools on the bed of the truck. He and Larry drove away, looking for all the world like the Robin Hoods of the automotive kingdom.

Although Larry and Buck might have earned hundreds of dollars apiece for the work they performed, I knew better than to offer them money—despite the fact that the Bel Air had quadrupled in market value. Our exchange had been more educational than mercantile. Buck and Larry would have never used the word, but they surely taught me that an automobile, first, in its operating parts and, second, in its repair and maintenance, amounts to a kind of *logos,* a self-contained system of causes and effects, a wholeness of truth and reason. Automobiles, which had heretofore baffled me with their perverse and irrational breakdowns, now seemed tractable and sane. Furthermore, working on an automobile provided one with a sense of control that carried into every department of human life. No one would want to be guided by the strictures of *Chilton's Repair Manual,* but how refreshing it would be if our scholarly and political discourse approached the clarity of the manual. Words like *knurled, tapered,* and *pitted* were semantically pure in a way that terms such as *liberal, symbolic,* and *axiomatic* rarely were. One night after reading chapters on gears and ratios in *Chilton,* I picked up a recent issue of the *Publications of the Modern Language Association* and found myself translating the critical jargon into something like plain English. Other tilts occurred, also. Even though I punished my hands and arms with special soaps and brushes, ultimately I could not conceal my secret life as a devotee of oil and pistons. Immovable sludge from the heart of the old engine lodged permanently under my fingernails and cuticles. Ground-in blackness darkened the whorls of my fingerprints and the tiny crosshatchings of my knuckles. Was it sacrilege to teach Shakespeare and Keats with hands in such a state? Perhaps. But in ways that daily surprised me, I was becoming more and more sensitive to the struts and supporting members of literary creations. Any poem is infinitely more complex than any engine, but going from one to another in the intimate way I was doing proved instructive and enlightening. One did not need to lapse into the breezy generalizations of Robert Pirsig in *Zen and the Art of Motorcycle Maintenance.* Whether one called it zen, logos, or *ratio,* the inherent discipline of repair work sharpened the hands, the eyes, and the mind, leaving one with a self-sustaining sense of liberation. Once I grasped that fact, my apprenticeship was over, the *rite de passage* was accomplished, and Larry and Buck disappeared forever, leaving me with a car that stayed out of doors during the worst winter in one hundred years. It never failed to start on the first turn of the key.

The experience with Larry and Buck released a whole complex of memories which I had conveniently tucked away or repressed once I entered the rarefied atmosphere of academe. In those sacred precincts, automobiles were not a proper subject of discourse, except perhaps as counters in a game of fiscal or economic analysis. And one learned quickly to drive the right kind of automobile, namely, a foreign one. Preferences varied from one ivory tower to another, but certain makes were always in favor. For the economy-minded, a used Hillman Minx or Morris Minor might be ideal. An MG, old or new, was always popular, as was the Mercedes, particularly the diesel-powered models. But the ultimate in academic chic was the Volvo, sold in advertisements as the thinking man's car. And I believed that I shared vicariously in that cool Swedish rationality as long as I owned my Volvo 145 station wagon, despite the fact that the SU carburetors were untunable, that the points wore out every 2,000 miles, or that the camshaft collapsed after 50,000 miles (for which the factory did partially reimburse me). I needn't cite the thrown piston rod from my new Mercedes or the VW Square Back that greeted the front passenger with a cascading waterfall (via the glove compartment) every time it rained. And while my two MG's were delightful to drive, both leaked notoriously, and the electric systems were abysmally inefficient. And I did drive three hundred miles (in a borrowed Plymouth) to buy a fuel pump for the last MG. I had been duped with advertising techniques long since documented by Vance Packard in *The Hidden Persuaders*. When the Volvo left me on a snow-packed road in the middle of January, I vowed to find an American car that most resembled the one I had almost forgotten: my father's pride, a 1950 Chevrolet De Luxe.

That Chevy had been my father's first new car, and I knew it as our family car, as well as the car on which I learned to drive. My first lesson on the correct operation of clutch and brake pedals ended with the destruction of our wooden garage doors and a few flecks of white paint permanently embedded in the front bumper of the Chevy. The car cost $1,800 new in 1950, and except for tires, batteries, brake linings, belts, and hoses never cost another penny. We performed all the work on it right in the driveway, with a few simple tools and the jack as provided by the factory. The car came with a service manual, no radio, and a "lap robe" for chilly evenings. I don't recall ever thinking of it as anything but transportation or work since I held the wrenches, pumped the pedals, or cleaned up the mess while my father did the interesting jobs. Once a month we checked every fluid, bulb, and belt, changed the oil and greased everything. No one ever touched the car except me or my father. When I inherited it, that old Chevy had 99,000 miles on the odometer. When I sold it five years later, the total was up to 133,000— and I sold it to a service station owner who used it to haul wrecks and boost batteries on cold winter mornings. The luminous days with Larry and Buck may have allowed me to relive these days from the past, and perhaps the restoration of the '58 Bel Air was a strange way of reclaiming the lost '50 De Luxe. Sometimes I would be driving late at night across the prairie during the dead of winter. The world had turned glacial; time and distance melted into one another. The radio cracked and fizzed as station signals faded in and out from all over the country: WABC (New York) . . . WSM (Nashville) . . . WLS (Chicago) . . . WWL (New Orleans). The wheel vibrated ever so slightly through my thick gloves, and for an instant this car was every car I had ever owned. I thought of grandfather's Model A, bought new in 1929 and kept running for twenty-five years. The thing rocked and pitched like a buckboard through the cotton fields. The roof was kept tight with yearly applications of tar. It came to be a part of him, like a horse or mule. I half expect to find it one of these days, waiting at the edge of a green pasture, where he left it over twenty-five years ago.

All this telescoping of time and distance seems especially ironic since the American automobile is the supreme example of planned obsolescence in the world's largest consumer economy. What had been designed as a piece of ephemera, something to be forgotten as soon as the annual models appeared, became instead a preserver of the past and the trigger mechanism for a whole cluster of nostalgic feelings and associations. Automobile travel became a species of time travel; we found ourselves going backward in time while moving forward in space. Aristotle was deprived of the opportunity to define the exact nature of the automobile, but I suspect that with his keen concern for causation and movement generally, he might look at the automobile as the art of movement in the machine age. In *The Poetics* Aristotle described the plot or mainspring of action in a play with the Greek word *dunamos* (English "dynamic"). Perhaps we have thought of automotive dynamics in rather narrow and unimaginative ways. The term "dynamics" is a staple in the critical vocabulary of disciplines as diverse as engineering, psychology, and aesthetics. In ways not yet fully understood, the automobile belongs in all three areas of inquiry. As such, it represents a nexus of many human skills and undertakings.

Precisely because the automobile can be viewed from so many different perspectives, it possesses an unusually high visibility within American culture. Automobiles are probably the most recognizable and identifiable artifacts shared by most Americans. Literary critics might call this charismatic power "resonance," while an anthropologist might see the auto as our source of *mana*. But the copywriters seized upon and enhanced this mythic potency almost from the outset. Here is a representative sample from a 1951 Ford advertisement:

Today the American Road has no end: The road that went nowhere now goes everywhere.... The wheels move endlessly, always moving, always forward—and always lengthening the American Road. On that road the nation is steadily traveling beyond the troubles of this century, constantly heading toward finer tomorrows. The American Road is paved with hope.

It isn't the Ford as such that is being sold here but a sort of Whitmanesque dream of the future. In an analogous way, the central importance of the automobile today is suggested by a recent Chevrolet Chevelle spread in which a gallery of American types (hardhats, housewives, and professionals) are grouped around the car which is parked conveniently in front of the neighborhood Roxy. The marquee proudly announces "A Fresh New Slice of Apple Pie." Even though the photograph is clearly staged, the overall advertisement is clever and convincing because we all recognize ourselves in it. The movie is over; the car is parked at the curb, waiting for its driver. Any member of the crowd might hop in and drive away. That intoxicating promise of power, that irreducible pleasure in moving from here to there is what the automobile finally means.

There isn't a Roxy in my town, but there is an architectural clone called The Cinema, and nearby lives an old gentleman who owns two 1965 Chevrolet Corvairs. One is "Sea Green," the other "Fathom Blue." If the old fellow has heard of Ralph Nader's *Unsafe at Any Speed,* he won't admit it—at least not to me. I've been eyeing the blue one, always discreetly and with no apparent haste. In matters like these timing counts for everything, so I'm waiting for another one of those high-domed October days. When the conversation hits a lull and the light softens on the contours of the old Corvair, I'll incline my head gently toward the car and make him an offer he can't refuse.

The Female Body

Margaret Atwood

". . . entirely devoted to the subject of 'The Female Body.' Knowing how well you have written on this topic . . . this capacious topic . . . "
—letter from *Michigan Quarterly Review*

1.

I agree, it's a hot topic. But only one? Look around, there's a wide range. Take my own, for instance.

I get up in the morning. My topic feels like hell. I sprinkle it with water, brush parts, rub it with towels, powder it, add lubricant. I dump in the fuel and away goes my topic, my topical topic, my controversial topic, my capacious topic, my limping topic, my near-sighted topic, my topic with back problems, my badly-behaved topic, my vulgar topic, my outrageous topic, my aging topic, my topic that is out of the question and anyway still can't spell, in its oversized coat and worn winter boots, scuttling along the sidewalk as if it were flesh and blood, hunting for what's out there, an avocado, an alderman, an adjective, hungry as ever.

2.

The basic Female Body comes with the following accessories: garter belt, panti-girdle, crinoline, camisole, bustle, brassiere, stomacher, chemise, virgin zone, spike heels, nose ring, veil, kid gloves, fish-net stockings, fichu, bandeau, Merry Widow, weepers, chokers, barrettes, bangles, beads, lorgnette, feather boa, basic black, compact, Lycra stretch one-piece with modesty panel, designer pegnoir, flannel nightie, lace teddy, bed, head.

3.

The Female Body is made of transparent plastic and lights up when you plug it in. You press a button to illuminate the different systems. The

Circulatory System is red, for the heart and arteries, purple for the veins; the Respiratory System is blue; the Lymphatic System is yellow; the Digestive System is green, with liver and kidneys in aqua. The nerves are done in orange and the brain is pink. The skeleton, as you might expect, is white.

The Reproductive System is optional, and can be removed. It comes with or without a miniature embryo. Parental judgment can thereby be exercised. We do not wish to frighten or offend.

4.

He said, I won't have one of those things in the house. It gives a young girl a false notion of beauty, not to mention anatomy. If a real woman was built like that she'd fall on her face.

She said, If we don't let her have one like all the other girls she'll feel singled out. It'll become an issue. She'll long for one and she'll long to turn into one. Repression breeds sublimation. You know that.

He said, It's not just the pointy plastic tits, it's the wardrobes. The wardrobes and that stupid male doll, what's his name, the one with the underwear glued on.

She said, Better to get it over with when she's young. He said, All right but don't let me see it.

She came whizzing down the stairs, thrown like a dart. She was stark naked. Her hair had been chopped off, her head was turned back to front, she was missing some toes and she'd been tattooed all over her body with purple ink, in a scrollwork design. She hit the potted azalea, trembled there for a moment like a botched angel, and fell.

He said, I guess we're safe.

5.

The Female Body has many uses. It's been used as a door-knocker, a bottle-opener, as a clock with a ticking belly, as something to hold up lampshades, as a nutcracker, just squeeze the brass legs together and out comes your nut. It bears torches, lifts victorious wreaths, grows copper wings and raises aloft a ring of neon stars; whole buildings rest on its marble heads.

It sells cars, beer, shaving lotion, cigarettes, hard liquor; it sells diet plans and diamonds, and desire in tiny crystal bottles. Is this the face that launched a thousand products? You bet it is, but don't get any funny big ideas, honey, that smile is a dime a dozen.

It does not merely sell, it is sold. Money flows into this country or that country, flies in, practically crawls in, suitful after suitful, lured by all those hairless preteen legs. Listen, you want to reduce the national debt, don't you? Aren't you patriotic? That's the spirit. That's my girl.

She's a natural resource, a renewable one luckily, because those things wear out so quickly. They don't make 'em like they used to. Shoddy goods.

6.

One and one equals another one. Pleasure in the female is not a requirement. Pair-bonding is stronger in geese. We're not talking about love, we're talking about biology. That's how we all got here, daughter.

Snails do it differently. They're hermaphrodites, and work in threes.

7.

Each female body contains a female brain. Handy. Makes things work. Stick pins in it and you get amazing results. Old popular songs. Short circuits. Bad dreams.

Anyway: each of these brains has two halves. They're joined together by a thick cord; neural pathways flow from one to the other, sparkles of electric information washing to and fro. Like light on waves. Like a conversation. How does a woman know? She listens. She listens in.

The male brain, now, that's a different matter. Only a thin connection. Space over here, time over there, music and arithmetic in their own sealed compartments. The right brain doesn't know what the left brain is doing. Good for aiming though, for hitting the target when you pull the trigger. What's the target? Who's the target? Who cares? What matters is hitting it. That's the male brain for you. Objective.

This is why men are so sad, why they feel so cut off, why they think of themselves as orphans cast adrift, footloose and stringless in the deep void. What void? she asks. What are you talking about? The void of the Universe, he says, and she says Oh and looks out the window and tries to get a handle on it, but it's no use, there's too much going on, too many rustlings in the leaves, too many voices, so she says, Would you like a cheese sandwich, a piece of cake, a cup of tea? And he grinds his teeth because she doesn't understand, and wanders off, not just alone but Alone, lost in the dark, lost in the skull, searching for the other half, the twin who could complete him.

Then it comes to him: he's lost the Female Body! Look, it shines in the gloom, far ahead, a vision of wholeness, ripeness, like a giant melon, like an apple, like a metaphor for *breast* in a bad sex novel; it shines like a balloon, like a foggy noon, a watery moon, shimmering in its egg of light.

Catch it. Put it in a pumpkin, in a high tower, in a compound, in a chamber, in a house, in a room. Quick, stick a leash on it, a lock, a chain, some pain, settle it down, so it can never get away from you again.

Venus and Others

John Updike

"Thy navel is like a round goblet, which wanteth not liquor," says the male voice in *The Song of Solomon,* "thy belly is like a heap of wheat set about with lilies. Thy two breasts are like two young roes that are twins." Robert Graves quotes a popular version of these verses which goes, as I roughly recall, "Thy belly's like a heap of wheat, /Thy breasts like two young roes, / So come to bed with me, my sweet, / And take off all your clothes." A naked woman is, for most men, the most beautiful thing they will ever see; on this planet, the female body is the prime aesthetic object, recreated not only in statuary and painting but (as Ms. Atwood points out) in the form of doorknockers, nutcrackers, lampstands, and caryatids. For the Victorians, it was everywhere, naked in brass, while their real women were swaddled and padded and reinforced like furniture; in this century, the female body haunts merchandising from top to bottom, from the silky epidermal feel of a soft cigarette pack to the rumpy curves of a Porsche 911. The female body is a masterpiece of market design, persuading the race to procreate generation after generation, extracting semen from mesmerized men with the ease of a pickpocket at a girlie show.

This captivating mechanism pays a price for its own complexity: cancer attacks breasts and ovaries, menstrual cramps and hysteria impair performance. Its season of bloom, of potential fertility, is shorter than that of the male body, though more piquant and powerful. Kafka, in a male-bonding letter to Max Brod, unchivalrously remarked of women, "Not until summer does one really see their curious kind of flesh in quantities. It is soft flesh, retentive of a great deal of water, slightly puffy, and keeps its freshness only a few days." He goes on, with his scrupulous fairness: "Actually, of course, it stands up pretty well, but that is only proof of the brevity of human life." Just so, the actuarial longer-lastingness of the female body demonstrates the relative biological disposability of the male, hormonally inclined toward reckless exertion and indulgence, and the salubrious effects of lifelong exercise in the form of housework.

If the main social fact about the female body is its attractiveness, the main political fact is its weakness compared with the male body. There may be some feminists ardent enough to dispute this, but the truth is elemental. As Elizabeth Hardwick, reviewing Simone de Beauvoir's *The Second Sex*, put it with admirable firmness, "Women are certainly physically inferior to men and if this were not the case the whole history of the world would be different. . . . Any woman who ever had her wrist twisted by a man recognizes a fact of nature as humbling as a cyclone to a frail tree branch." This fact lies behind many facts of feminine circumstance, such as the use of women as domestic drudges and beasts of burden in the world's fundamental economy, or the superior attentiveness and subtlety of women in the private maneuvers of advanced societies. Watching a movie, women as well as men, scientific research has disclosed, will watch the face of the woman on the screen. In a female face, the things that can open, the eyes and the mouth, open wider. Women talk, women see. "The fastidiousness of women," Stendhal wrote in *On Love*, "is the result of that perilous situation in which they find themselves placed so early, and of the necessity they are under of spending their lives among cruel and charming enemies."

This physical weakness and the cruelties that result are the truth but not all the truth, and from the standpoint of the species not even the main truth. An interesting thought-experiment, for an adult male, is to try to look at a prepubescent girl, one of ten or eleven, say, with the eyes again of a boy the same age. The relative weakness, the arresting curves, the female fastidiousness are not yet in place, but the magic is. The siren song, the strange simultaneous call to be kind and to conquer, the swooning wish to place one's life beside this other. To be sure, cultural inducements to heterosexuality bombard us from infancy; but they fall, generally, upon terrifically receptive ground.

The female body is, in its ability to conceive and carry a fetus and to nurse an infant, our life's vehicle—it is the engine and the tracks. Male sexuality, then, returning to this primal source, drinks at the spring of being and enters the murky region, where up is down and death is life, of mythology. The paradoxical contradictoriness of male attitudes toward the female and her body—the impulses to exalt and debase, to serve and enslave, to injure and comfort, to reverence and mock—goes back to some point of origin where emotions are not yet differentiated and energy has no distinct direction. The sex act itself, from the male point of view, is a paradox, a transformation of his thrusts into pleasure, a poke in the gut that is gratefully received. Sadism and masochism naturally flirt on the edges of our, as Katherine Mansfield said, "terrible need to make contact."

And naturally modern women feel a natural impatience with being mythologized—being envisioned (talk about hysteria!) as madonnas and whores, earth-mothers and vampires, helpless little girls and implacable dominatrices—and with male inability to see sex simply for what it is. What is it? A biological function and procedure, presumably, on a plane with eating and defecation, just as women are, properly regarded, equally entitled human beings and political entities with minds of their own. Well, men have been known, inadvertently, in lapses of distraction or satiety, to see the female body as just a body, very like their own, built for locomotion as well as procreation, an upright watery stalk temporarily withstanding, with its miraculous molecular chain reactions, the forces of gravity and entropy. It is a lucid but dispirited moment, seeing a nude woman as a kind of man, only smaller, lighter-framed, without a beard, but matching us tuft for tuft otherwise, and with bumps, soft swellings, unmale emphases stiffened with fat, swayed by gravity . . . a heap of wheat set about with lilies . . . those catenary curves, that curious considerate absence . . . the moment of clear vision passes.

We can only appeal, in asking forgiveness of women for our mythologizing of their bodies, for being *unreal* about them, to their own sexuality, which is different but not radically different, perhaps, from our own. For women too there seems to be that tangle of supplication and possessiveness, that descent toward infantile undifferentiation, that omnipotent helplessness, that merger with the cosmic mother-warmth, that flushed pulse-quickened leap into overestimation, projection, general mix-up. *The Song of Solomon* has two voices; there is a female extoller as well, who claims, "My beloved is white and ruddy, the chiefest among ten thousand. His head is as the most fine gold; his locks are bushy, and black as a raven . . . his belly is as bright ivory overlaid with sapphires," etc. The male body, can it be?—its defenseless boneless belly above the one-eyed priapic oddity—may also loom as a glorious message from the deep, with an Apollonian (to be exact, a Martial) beauty beyond the bodily. In Ms. Atwood's last novel, *Cat's Eye,* the heroine, in one of the many remarkable passages about growing up female and human, reflects upon the teenaged boys she talks to on the telephone: "The serious part is their bodies. I sit in the hall with the cradled telephone, and what I hear is their bodies. I don't listen much to the words but to the silences, and in the silences these bodies re-create themselves, are created by me, take form." Some of this is sexual, she reflects, and some is not. Some is purely visual: "The faces of the boys change so much, they soften, open up, they ache. The body is pure energy, solidified light." For male and female alike, the bodies of others are messages indicating what we must do—they are the glowing signifiers of our own existence.

Four: The Artist's Perspective

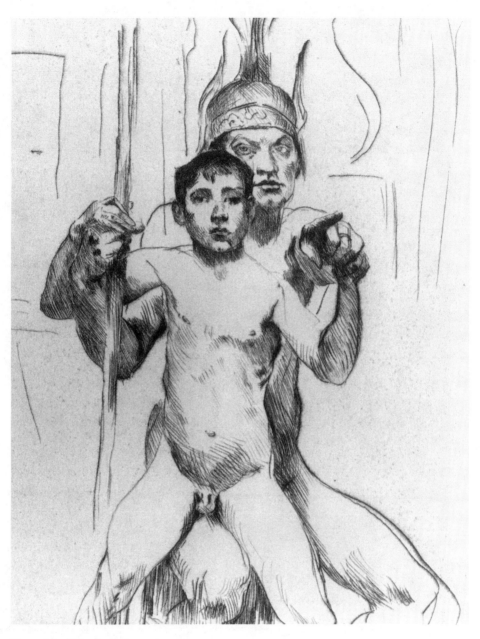

Kriegerlehre (Warrior's Lesson), 1914.
By Lovis Corinth (German, 1858–1925).
Drypoint etching.

Moses Descending Mount Sinai, 1982.
By Karen Rasco (American, born 1956).
Photo collage.

Thom Gunn, 1968.
By Don Bachardy (American, born 1934).
Pen and ink drawing.

History of Art, 1989.
By Virginia Maksymowicz (American, born 1952).
Cast paper and acrylic.

Blossom, 1988.
By Charles Dickson (American, born 1947).
Mixed media.

Man with Meissen Figurine, 1982.
By Viola Frey (American, born 1933).
Oil on 1100 lb. arches.

Journey into Dark, 1984.
By Misha Gordin (Born in USSR, 1946).
Photograph.

Besy (Devils), 1989.
By Lius'en Dul'fan (Russian, born 1954).
Oil.

Five: Six Short Stories

The Woman in the Reeds

John Fowles

The wind was quite strong.

It blew the lazy arms of the willows sideways, and roughened the water of the long reach. Over the flat lush fields and the wooded hills to the west, ragged shadows chased sunshine, and far above the gray and white puffs of summer cloud a high fan of delicately fingered cirrus reached southwards. Gong back toward Oxford, two punts and a skiff ran quickly with the wind and current. One solitary punt, with a young man and a girl, struggled upstream. The boy was wearing jeans and a scarlet T-shirt that contrasted unpleasantly with his freckled skin and his crewcut ginger hair. His neck and wrists were disagreeably red; and his biceps were weaker than even his rather short, skinny figure warranted.

Lying back on the faded khaki plush cushions in the bow, the girl watched him thrust the pole down, then the wood slide through his wet fingers till the soundless dunk on the river-bottom, when he heaved down, then stood up, wobbling a little, and inexpertly controlled the drive forward. In the short time before the wind halted the forward impetus, he would glance at her; but their eyes rarely met, because she took good care to watch him only when he was thrusting and recovering. What he saw was a small sideways-looking girl of nineteen or so, with smudged eyebrows in a plain white face, her not very long dark brown hair done back in an alice band; small and neat-looking, but quite without any special attraction, any sexiness; on the contrary, rather peaked, private, inward, always with a small snubbing air of deserving to be somewhere better than where she actually was. She worked as a typist-assistant in a coal-merchant's down by the station. He was an undergraduate, reading chemistry.

He drove the punt inshore, squatted, and caught the projecting branch of a fallen willow; then held the boat moored by the pressure of the pole against its side. She sat forward, her hands on the tangerine knees of her slacks.

"You're doing ever so well."

"Was before the bloody wind blew up. If you want to do a bit of punting be sure the bloody wind'll start up." He lengthened into an *oo* the short *u* in words like "punting," "bloody" and "up." "Should've brought some beer with us. It's going to be too far to the pub with this lot."

"I don't mind. Reelly." She looked diffidently round. "Anywhere'll do."

Another punt with two couples in it slipped past them going downstream. In the forward seat a dark young man wearing a white shirt and a college square sat with his arm round a girl. She was very pretty, with a loose skein of blonde hair. Her head rested on his shoulder, against his cheek, and the hair flowed over his encircling arm. They stared at the couple in the stationary punt, cool, appraising, dismissing. The young man punting, also in white shirt and square, glanced at them. And the voice of the fourth member of the punt, another girl, sitting by herself while her partner poled, came to them momentarily over the ruffled water—the high-drawling and affected voice of a girl from the upper middle classes. They passed very swiftly, yet the two in the punt by the willow felt themselves obscurely slighted, outclassed, and avoided each other's eyes.

"We'll just go on up past the bend. There's a cut up there. Eh?" He had an ugly Northcountry way of saying "Eh?" after a decision, as if by so doing he made it mutual. He jerked the pole out of the mud.

But she pointed; almost desperately. "Oo! Aren't those flowers pretty!" About fifty yards away a cloud of brilliant yellow shivered in a sudden rush of sunlight—a clump of ragwort.

"Want to pick some?"

"Oo yes."

He poled the punt on a little, wedged it against the low bank, and tied the painter to a willow-root. She waited till he was on the bank before standing up, steadying herself shakily, and making an unnecessarily nervous stride onto land. They walked through the long grass toward the ragwort. They were both short, but he walked loose-shouldered, simply, while she moved with a slightly mincing step, which her tight trousers accentuated. She was not natural in trousers, but self-consciously petite; a girl friend had once told her that she looked like Princess Margaret.

She knelt and pulled at the stems. They broke roughly, with back-curling shavings of fiber that she tore off, in a pernickety little way, before pulling at the next stem. The flowers were very vivid. He stood over her, watching her pick them. When she had a small yellow cloud in her left hand, some ten stems, she looked up at him. It was the first time that day they had really looked at each other.

"Sit down," she said.

He sat beside her. She fluffed out the umbels of flowers and spoke without looking at him.

"I've thought about . . . you know."

He felt his heart constrict. "Yes."

"I was . . . ," she glanced quickly at his averted face and plunged on. "I wasn't going to say anything."

He pulled silently at a head of grass. "Go on then."

"Well . . . "

The great weight that had been crushing his mind for the past forty-eight hours suddenly slipped away. "The answer's no?"

She nodded, fingering the flowers. She wished now that she hadn't picked them. They had rather a coarse look, and many of the petals were eaten by some insect.

"I see then." He tried to sound and look downcast.

"I have thought. Reelly. Very carefully. I do like you, Peter. When you first came, I didn't. Like I told you, didn't I? But I do now." She consciously lowered her voice. "I wouldn't say it if I didn't mean it."

"I was a mug to ask."

"I don't think I'm good enough for you, anyhow. You're so clever and look at me—I'm only a typist, reelly." She waited in vain for him to contradict this. "I'd like us still to be friends," she added. "And of course I won't tell a soul. I didn't even tell mother."

"I shouldn't ever've asked." He was staring at the grass. "I knew it was daft. Soon as you said you'd have to think, I knew it was daft. You say yes at once, or else it's no bloody good." He managed to put a little despair into his flat voice.

"I didn't know. Reelly I didn't." She spoke at her flowers with a self-absorbed air of tender sincerity he could see she was enjoying. He was glad the business had been got over quickly, that he hadn't got to argue her out of his daft proposal; and yet he was, after all, hurt.

They fell into an embarrassed silence. She fidgeted with the ragwort, and he picked at the heads of bennet, so that specks of yellow pollen fell among the freckles on the back of his hands. She looked surreptitiously at him, at his rather sullen face. The only nice things about it were the blond, thick eyelashes. A shadow came; then sunlight burst back over them.

"Peter?"

"Well?"

"You do understand."

"It's all right, Doreen." He stood up.

"Let's go then. Eh?" He held out a hand to pull her up, but she looked up at him reproachfully.

"You *are* offended."

"No I'm not."

"I know you are."

He said nothing, but his mouth widened in an expression of stubborn contradiction and self-dissatisfaction. He stared down at her. He thought of a word he had heard someone use the day before: "bedworthy." She wasn't that. She looked up and misunderstood his expression.

"You've been ever so sweet."

She had heard the other two undergraduates who had come to lodge at her mother's house at the beginning of the university year calling him the Yorkshire Pudding. It was not fair. He was ungracious, sometimes uncouth, but he was not a pudding. He had a certain shyness; and it had taken him two terms to pluck up courage to ask her to go out with him. After that they went out once a week to the cinema, and occasionally at weekends. In the cinema they held hands; and she let him kiss her goodnight, the conventional reward, before they went into the house; one night he had tried for more but she hadn't liked it, and made it clear that she hadn't; there was a for-lack-of-a-better-ness in their relationship that they both sensed. Then had come his blurting-out of the astonishing question, two evenings before. Yet even that was sweet, when she thought about it in the wind and sunlight, teasing out flowers—sweet because it was absurd, like a baby trying to lift something impossibly heavy. Of course it had been no; but it had been nice to be given an opportunity to say it.

"I've been a damn fool." He lay back, staring up at the sky. "A bloody fool." He wanted to get a blow in at her.

"I never reelized you were so serious."

"I wasn't. That's what's so daft."

She looked at him, hurt, and in the end her silence made him go on.

"I meant it when I said it. Only I knew, you see. What you'd say."

She picked at the grub-eaten petals, thinking of the man she would like to marry. He would see her hidden loveliness, the delicate loveliness that until now had never been recognized by anyone but herself. She repeated to herself, not in words, but in emotion, her favorite phrase, once read in a magazine: "She seemed to be made of an exquisite, fragile porcelain." She was not totally unaware that it was a silly sentence, but, ever since reading it, she had always tried to emphasize her fragility—if she moved where she might fall, if ever coarseness or roughness threatened. It was less the touch of Peter's hand in the darkness of a cinema that pleased her than the difference in size that was established; her smallness, her daintiness, her girlishness.

"I know exactly who I want to marry," she said. "It's silly. I don't expect I'll ever meet anyone like him."

"Bet you won't."

"But I want to be sure first."

"I know just who I'd like to marry," he said. He was lying on his back, his eyes shut. She was surprised, and defensive again, but she felt curious.

"Go on then. Tell me."

"I don't care much what she looks like. Long as she's not fat." He opened his eyes, searching the sky for words. "I don't care if she's North or South. But no class, no accent. She won't mind me and my accent, but she won't have any. She won't have any truck with all the bloody class distinction business and all that." He sat up, avoiding her eyes. "No blooming wanting to be what she isn't. Just a nice girl who knows what's what. Who I am and what she is. And likes a bit of fun."

"Have I got an accent?" She hastily conceded a fault. "I know I say words wrong. I say 'reelly' wrong. They laugh at me in the office. Really. Really." She savored the word. "I don't know why I say 'reelly.'"

"You're all right. It's when you start putting it on."

"Oh I don't!"

"You go all middle class and all that. Ever so genteel." He slipped a look at her and saw she was wounded. "I don't mind. It's normal down here. Have to start pretending you're better than you are the moment you're born. Down here." He heeled at a tuft of grass.

"Why did you ask me if you don't like the way I speak?"

"'Cause I think accents are bloody daft."

"I'm not at all like what you said, am I?"

He looked at her and grinned. One of his side-teeth was broken, and it gave him a battered air that his rather bony face accentuated. "Beggars can't allus choose, lass," he said, broadening his accent, trying to pass it off as a joke.

She gave him a veiled look from under her eyebrows, picking mechanically at the flowers. He recognized that she was about to topple into resentment; beneath the daintiness, the studied weakness, there was a small dark will, that lurked in her eyes and sometimes refused to back down.

He reached forward and rather timidly touched one of the white tassels that fringed the bottom of her trousers. "I like you very much, Doreen. But you have just turned me down."

"You're glad I did."

"I still asked. I've never done that to anyone before."

"Shouldn't think you've had much opportunity." Her voice was sharp.

"I haven't."

"You're just getting your own back now."

He pushed at her knee. "Come on. We can still be friends."

"You started it."

He held out his hand and after a moment's hesitation she gave a small, still hurt, smile and shook the ends of his fingers. But then she selected a ragwort stem and passed it to him.

"I'll wear it next to me heart for ever and ever." His miming was clumsy, and she looked away; she searched for something that would sound kind and yet put him in his place.

"I feel you're like a brother, reelly." She was an only child. Her father, a college butler, had died six years before. "When I'm with you I feel... protected." She looked at him to see how he would react to these little tendrils of indebtedness.

Something in his science-orientated mind jibbed at this glossing-over of reality. Rolling on his back again, he spoke quickly, rather indistinctly. "Every night at No. 29 I look down and I see your bedroom light below and then it goes out." He stopped and folded his white arms over his face, stretching, trying to be casual. "What I think about you then isn't anything a brother ought to think."

After a pause she spoke with a put-on reflectiveness. "That's the trouble."

"What?"

"That sort of thing. It's why liking's not enough."

"I know. You needn't tell me." He sounded curt.

"I'm sorry."

He stood up. "No crime, no punishment." She saw that he wanted to break the mood. The sun had gone in for a long spell, and her arms were goosy. With a dour smile, he pulled her to her feet. "Come on. You've sent the bloody sun in." He put his hand on her shoulder for a moment as they walked back to the punt. To both of them, it was a relief, the end of the saying of what had to be said; and to feel that there had been nothing really ugly in it all; and they had both scored.

In the punt she put on a cardigan. "I hope it won't rain."

"Want to go back then?"

"D'you?"

"We got our lunch."

"I'd like to go on," she said, in her bright-little-woman voice. "If you would. It's nice. Even with the wind."

"Don't mind me if you'd rather go back."

"No reelly." She gave him a shy straight look from under the smudged eyebrows. "I'd like us still to be friends."

"I'm your man then. Come on."

He kept the punt in the lee of the bank. Long waving banners of willow-leaves brushed the girl's head. She snatched off one of the leaves as they slid past. It had a dazzling rose-red gall on it. Her mother called them willow-fairies. "Do you know what this is?" She held it up; he was meant to say no.

"Insect. Changes the bio-chemical set-up of the leaf. Like a cancer."

Cancer frightened her, and she flicked the leaf idly back into the water, to show him his science had made it boring. "*Reel* cancer isn't caused by an insect, is it?"

He grinned and shook his head. She was like his mum—could never understand, was determined never to understand.

He had to leave the bank and began to pole energetically up the center of the reach. He thought of his parents. They had visited him last term. After going round the colleges, he had taken them punting. Though they had professed to like it, he knew that in some obscure way, it had shocked them. It was too leisurely, too "southern." And he had shocked them, too, trying to explain what Oxford meant to him. They were very superior working-class, but their world was limited by

Wakefield, by the shop. Peter had tried to explain what he was going to be: a good chemist earning a good salary—not a wage—and not necessarily in the North, indeed probably not in the North. Home was the North, but life was the South.

He brought the punt round the sweep at the end of the reach, shaving the right-hand bank, to save distance. Then the going was easier. The wind pushed the snout of the punt toward the bank, but it ran forward more smoothly. After a hundred yards they came to the cut. It was a dyke that had been made many years before, at right angles to the main river, between two long meadows of unmown grass. The footpath was on the other side of the river, and by the cut there was an old peeling notice that said: "Private. Landing forbidden. By order."

Another punt lay moored there. Three young men were sitting in it, reading, an open bottle of beer between them; the black caps and unbroken labels of two more quart bottles poked up behind the stern seat. As Peter poled and glided past, the three looked up briefly, eyed the girl without interest, and went on reading.

Peter pushed slowly up the cut. In one place it was choked with the rubbery stems and leaves of water-lilies, though there were no flowers. Then the punt brushed through white-starred platforms of dropwort and encroaching spear-jungles of reeds.

"Won't this do?"

"Bit further. Eh?"

The reeds and bulrushes grew so thickly from either bank that ahead they formed a thin curtain across. But there was another little stretch of water just visible through the curtain and Peter decided to make that their goal. Doreen turned to see where they were going, and her pink cardigan had fallen open. He could see the sharp small forms of her too perfect breasts. He wanted to be in a secluded place with her; to get, perhaps, some sort of money's worth, not that the prospect was very bright. He steadied himself and thrust down hard to give the punt enough momentum to plunge through the curtain.

About halfway through the bow of the punt struck some soft obstruction, tilted a little and stopped. He was thrown off balance, but recovered in time to see Doreen craning forward, parting the reeds with her hand.

She flung back, twisting around, and buried her face in her hands.

"What's wrong?"

"Go back!" Her voice sounded stifled.

"But what is it?"

She had her face buried in her knees, and all she would do was rock her head from side to side. He put one foot over the back seat of the punt. The reeds covered whatever it was that she had seen.

"What's wrong, Doreen? What've you seen?" His voice sounded faintly exasperated.

"Go back." Something in her tone, and in the force of the look she at last gave him, sent him back. He picked up the pole and thrust it forwards, and then levered the punt slowly backwards. It seemed to be held for a moment in the reeds, and then it slid smoothly back into the more open water.

"Now for Christ's sake, lass, what is it?"

Her eyes fixed his, rather like a child's, as if asking him to tell her she was wrong. "It was a leg." She hissed the word.

"A leg!"

"A woman."

He stared at the green curtain of reeds. Nothing was visible. "You're joking." His eyes went from her to the inscrutable reeds again.

"She's face down. It's horrible. It's horrible." Her face was drawn with the shock.

"I'm going to take a look." He glanced back to the other punt, some eighty yards away. They were still reading quietly. He pushed into the side. "You stay here."

He walked along the bank, trailing the pole through the long sweet-smelling grass. There were clumps of purple hyssop and pink willow-herb. The reeds grew higher and thicker where the curtain was, and he could see nothing. He looked back and saw Doreen was on the bank, coming toward him with a frightened expression.

"Just there," she called.

"All right. You stay back." For a moment she seemed ready to disobey him; but she stopped some ten yards away.

He poked the long punt-pole through the reeds, pressing a long swath sideways. He could see nothing but green stems and water. A shimmering blue demoiselle dragonfly fluttered toward him. A warbler reeled off an irritated song from further down the cut. He moved a pace or two on and tried again.

At the end of the green clearing his pole made, something gleamed. He pushed the pole deeper and pressed sideways. A white body lay on its face, its head toward him, in a little cell where the reeds had been

pressed sideways. Horrified, he glimpsed a length of dark hair and a
curve above the buttocks that could belong only to a woman. The bank
had long ago collapsed out into the center of the cut, and she was only
half-submerged; perhaps the water-level had gone down. One arm lay
under the body and the other was flung out through the reeds. She was
quite naked, with a terrible greyish whiteness in the skin.

He sharply withdrew the pole, and the reeds waved stiffly back
across their secret. He turned toward Doreen. "It's a girl," he said across
the space between them.

"I've never seen a dead body before." She had a feeling that she
ought to faint. Her legs felt weak. But nothing was spinning; things
even had an added clarity.

He took her arm. "Lie down if you feel funny."

"I'm all right."

"I'll go and tell those chaps." He began to run down the bank to
where the cut entered the main river. He heard her running behind him.

"Hey!"

They looked up, surprised, vaguely offended. One of them had a
glass of beer in his hand.

"There's a dead body in the reeds up there!" He pointed, and the
three looked swiftly together, as if the corpse might be rising like a teal.
"She's lying half in the water. Got no clothes on." They looked at him
disbelievingly. "We think she's been done in."

The young man in shorts who had been holding the glass of beer,
the oldest of the three, with a Jewish face and a prematurely balding
head, said "I'm a medical student." He climbed out on the bank. "You're
sure it wasn't a dead dog or something?"

"Ask my girlfriend. She saw it first."

"It's reelly horrible. I think she's been dead a long time. She's all
white. You know?" Doreen's voice took on its most genteel tones.

The Jewish-looking student set off down the bank.

"There. In there!" Peter, behind, pointed to the place. The medical
student looked round the grass, then felt his way cautiously down into
the reeds. He stopped a moment and threw his sandals back on the bank.
Then his head disappeared as he bent down. Peter caught a glimpse of
his blue shirt as he shifted position. He seemed to be there a long time.
Then the reeds moved as he came back to the bank.

"You're right. She's dead. Some time. Been strangled."

His face looked grim. They walked back to the others. Doreen was talking animatedly to the two students on the bank.

"It's a stiff all right," said the Jewish-looking student as they came up. "Nothing like a quiet day's revision on the banks of a gentle stream."

"What had we better do, Ben?" asked one of the others. Ben turned to Peter.

"Look, we can travel faster than you. We'll paddle up to the pub. That's the nearest telephone. You stay here and keep everyone off. O.K.?"

"O.K."

"And right off. The police will curse us for trampling over so much as it is." He spoke to Doreen. "What about you? Better come with us. Get a cup of tea at the pub."

"I'm all right. I'll stay here."

"Come on, boys."

They jumped into their punt and cast loose. Ben called back. "Keep your eyes skinned for the police. They may get here first. And keep everyone else off. O.K.?"

The punt receded.

"Aren't they bossy?" She crinkled her nose.

"They're public schoolboys. Think everyone else is a gormless nit."

"Ordering us about. Anyone'd think they found it."

"Always take charge. Must always take charge."

The punt curled round a bend of the river.

"Did he say how . . . ?"

"Strangled. Her own stocking, looks like."

"Ooh." She felt her own neck. "One of those students says it often happens. The police call it accidentally drowned to save all the bother of finding out who did it."

"Don't you believe it."

"He says there's always some in the mortuary. One every week. It's where most sex-murders take place. On the river. That's what he said."

"Talking balls."

She turned away.

"Where you going?"

"Get my headscarf. I'm cold." The wind had dropped a little, but to the north the thickening clouds had lead-gray bottoms. There was one fitful gleam of sunlight on the Cumnor hills, but the landscape had gone gray, and the cirrus had developed into a high luminous veil spreading right over Oxford. Doreen came running back with her white headscarf on. "Fancy it being us," she said.

"Someone had to."

"Yes, but today." She seemed more excited than shocked. She sat down against a willow-tree, facing the river. A huge American bomber whined sluggishly overhead on its way to land. "I expect it was one of them," he said, looking up. "I bet she was one of those women you see round the Carfax."

He went back to the punt and poled it to where Doreen was. As he tied it up he asked her if she felt hungry.

"I couldn't."

"It'll take them half-an-hour to get there. And then some."

"I couldn't."

He rummaged about in the small shopping-basket they had brought, and began to eat. He was hungry, but he also wanted to show her it took more than a corpse to put him off his food. Other punts drifted past their mooring place.

She spoke from the bank. "Supposing they knew what we knew." He nodded. "I don't know how you can eat."

"Come on. Have a bite. Do you good."

"I couldn't."

"Have to go on living, you know."

She did not deign to answer this, and he didn't press the point. She looked very small and pale. Her nostrils had gone pink. "I wonder who she was."

"The police'll find out."

"How?"

"They can do it through the teeth. The fillings and things."

"How old d'you think she was?"

"Dunno. Not old."

"What I saw didn't look old." She shivered. "About my age."

He dabbled his hands in the river, then got out on the bank to see if there was any sign of the police. Then he turned and sat down beside her, putting his arm around her.

"Cold, Doreen?"

"Yes."

A moorhen scuttered across the river. He pressed her a little closer. "Ought to have brought a blanket."

"A rug. Blanket's for beds." She looked secretly at him, then away. "I wouldn't have missed it."

"That's a funny thing to say."

"I know. It's . . . it's like . . . I can't explain."

She stared at the opposite bank, and then down in front of them. There a thin tongue of reeds shivered in the wind, mournful, lonely, desolate against the cold gray water. She felt death everywhere; everywhere cemeteries, ambulances, tombs, people in black, moldering, decay; and waiting. "I'll remember this day to the day I die," she said. "It's what they call predestination. I read about it."

"How do you mean?"

"It was always going to happen—we being the ones who found her."

"If there hadn't been such a bloody wind we'd never have gone up there."

"But there was a wind. That's the point."

"It's not the point at all." He sounded too bluff, too Yorkshire commonsensical.

She stared out across the river. "It's easy for you. You know what to believe. I don't know what to believe."

"About what?" When he felt he couldn't answer her he resorted to analysis, as if by proving that she could not express her feeling he proved the feeling did not exist. He had played the trick before.

"About anything."

"Every second, someone's dying somewhere. But you got to go on living."

"I don't see why."

"Don't be daft." He patted her shoulder. He was afraid she might cry.

"What's the point of living when you end up like that."

"It's only one in a million do."

"There's other ways. It might have been me. Any girl."

"Except it isn't. It's her. Not you."

She had picked a veronica flower and was twizzling it slowly, watching the delicate blue corollas. "D'you believe in a life after death?"

"Course not."

"I used to. I don't think I do any more."

"All that spiritualist muck—it makes me sick."

"I don't see how you can ever *reely* know."

"You can have a damn good guess. When we're dead we're dead."

A petal fell off the flower and down through the interstices in the grass. She searched for it in vain. She stared again at the shivering reeds and the gray water. "I know someone says when we die we just start living again. So it's a sort of whatchermercallit."

"Vicious circle."

"That's why sometimes you think you've done something before just when you're doing it."

"They ought to be back by now." He strained round to look for the police, but there was no sign of them.

"It's because we've lived everything before."

"I'd remember this lot if I'd lived it all before."

"You might not."

He did not answer, and they sat for a time in silence.

"You forget what being dead means," she said. She saw death like some mysterious frayed rope's-end, existence suddenly unravelled and snapped short, a stub in space; her voice had lost its affectation.

He bent and kissed the side of her head. It was the first time he had ever kissed her in daylight. For a few moments she did not look at him, or move, and he thought he had offended her.

"Why did you do that?"

A punt came round the bend. He let go of her shoulder. "Here they are!"

"Why did you?"

"I don't know."

"I'm glad I was with you."

"You're being daft again."

She was so eager to tell him what she felt. He kept his eyes on the approaching punt. "I'm glad it was us that found her."

"Can't let someone be killed just so you can be glad." He sounded impatient, faintly shocked. He stood up.

"You don't understand, Peter," she said, trying to get his attention. But he was waving to the students in the punt.

It curved in and came to rest alongside their own. "Police on their way, should be here," panted the Jewish medical student.

Doreen said "There!" and pointed. A field away five figures, two in black, three in civilian clothes, could be seen making toward them.

The police-car dropped them at the top of Linden Road. The sky had completely clouded over, but the threatened rain had not come. It was simply dull. They walked in silence down the quiet brick street of detached Victorian houses, and up the steps to the front door of No. 29. Peter unlocked the door. Doreen's mother always went over to Cowley on Saturday afternoons, to a sister's. It was always cold supper, and she was never back before seven. The other two undergraduates were away in Bicester playing cricket. The house lay in silence.

Doreen went through to the kitchen, and after a hesitation, because the three students normally never went there, Peter followed her. She was staring out at the back garden, looking sapped, at a loss. A church clock chimed three, and then, after a few seconds' pause, the clock in the dining-room gave a genteel silvery echo; it was a house dense with gentility, but ordinarily saved, at least during the evenings, by the clatter of feet and the sound of radios. Now it waited, waited, waited.

"Here. I'll make you a cupper." He briskly put the kettle on. She sat slumped in a chair, watching him get cups and saucers ready, as she had sat in the police station while he made a brief statement for them both. He was very neat with small things; quick and methodical, all that he wasn't with words and people.

"Try a boiled egg?"

She nodded. He put a saucepanful of water on to boil.

"It was done for anyway," he said, looking out of the window at the leaden sky. "What a day. Eh?"

"What'll they do to her?"

"There'll be an autopsy."

"Will she be used by the students?"

"Now come on, Doreen. You're being too bloody morbid." He chucked her shoulder. "Come on, there's a good girl. It's over now."

She went to the dresser and got herself one of her mother's secret store of cigarettes. She rarely smoked and the ladylike way she held the cigarette and the tough way she exhaled smoke made him smile. She stood over by the window. He turned and made the tea and put the egg in the seething water.

"It all shrinks away, doesn't it? Till there's nothing but bones."

He answered with a spoon in his hand, jabbing with it. "Look, Doreen. The living expanded cells shrink, so they're like dust. Dead cells. But dead cells are still matter. Matter is atoms, and atoms are living things. This spoon, I know it doesn't look alive. But it's a mass of moving atoms, see. You put a corpse into earth and it turns into food. It's nature. That's what death is. Changing the physical structure."

There was a pause. She turned away again. "I don't know what you're trying to say."

"It's clear enough."

"You undergraduates."

"What about us?"

"I thought you were s'posed to be cleverer than us."

"Who's us?"

"People who leave school at sixteen." She surveyed him, breathing smoke through her nostrils.

He put the teapot on the table. "Your tea's ready." He felt odd serving her; quite often she brought the supper trays into the dining-room, though less since she had started going out with him.

"You don't understand what I feel." She took no notice of the tea. "At all." He gestured at the table. "And I suppose you think it doesn't matter anyway. What ordinary people feel. What I feel."

"Your tea's ready."

"I feel like . . . completely changed."

"It's been a shock."

"I mean like waking up."

"Sit down. There's a good lass. Have your tea."

"You're like all men. You won't listen."

He beat the spoon in sarcastic time to his words. "You feel changed. It's like waking up."

She surveyed him again, then moved toward the table. "Do you know the nicest thing you said today?" He shook his head. "It wasn't words. It was what you did on the bank. Kissing me like that. I thought for a moment you understood."

"I'd better stick to kissing then, hadn't I. And keep my bloody mouth shut."

"I wish you would sometimes." Her voice wasn't sour, but almost sad, and the sadness stung him more than sourness would have done.

She sat down, stubbing out the cigarette; then let a little sugar slip sideways from her spoon and stirred the brown tea. He silently put the egg before her. She buttered herself a piece of brown bread and sprinkled salt on the egg. Suddenly she was enjoying the egg, the moment, the salt, and the egg on the dipped-in strips of brown bread-and-butter. He sat on the other side of the table and watched her eat in her professionally dainty way.

"Stop watching me eat."

He got up and went to the window to look out, but after a moment turned. Every so often she looked up without expression at his silhouetted figure against the gray afternoon light. It was a dark kitchen, and she frequently complained to her mother about it. But she liked it then as it was; his standing and serving there and her mystifying him, troubling him; it had been mysterious, the whole day; exciting and mysterious. And the two of them in the empty house stirred in her unconscious certain repressed childhood experiences; secrets shared with little boys, the troubled communions of child with child and child with place. It was like being in a cupboard, hiding with someone; hiding and exploring. There was too a heavy feeling of the day's being unfinished, of anticlimax. They had no right to be back at this hour, in such a vacuum, such an eery doldrum. They had never before been together alone in the house. Their brief goodnight kisses were given on the porch, before they entered; then she always went to see her mother, while he clumped upstairs to his room.

The silence unnerved him after a while. "Hope they took the punt back," he said. The other students had offered to tow it back to the boathouses. But she refused to rise to the bait. He took her plate and the egg-cup and set them on the draining-board. When he turned she was staring at him. He smiled awkwardly. "How about the pictures? Or maybe there's something on the telly." She shook her head. "Take your mind off things a bit. Have a lie-down, then."

"Why should I lie down?"

"The shock and all."

The intensity with which the small face with its smudged eyebrows continued to regard him began to be alarming. He wondered whether it wasn't really a case of delayed shock. She would suddenly burst into tears, or faint.

"Well . . . what do you want to do then?"

"I don't know."

There was another silence. He felt increasingly awkward, but he was determined not to break it this time.

"Do you think she was—you know—first?'

"Usually are when it's like that."

"I expect she was taken there in a punt. After he did it."

"The police'll find out."

"They'll never find out what it was like for her." She picked up her tea-cup, and began to tilt it, watching the dregs. She didn't look up when she spoke. "Did you ever want to do that to me?"

"Do what?"

Between their words opened deep silences.

"Things you shouldn't."

"Course I have. I'm only human."

"I don't mean just kissing. Other things. Things you shouldn't do even if we were married."

"I don't know what you're getting at."

She put her cup down. Another American bomber went over. "It's all you want, isn't it? You boys. Take our clothes off."

"There's ways and ways of wanting." It was a stock expression of his father's.

"That's what I thought when you asked me to marry you. I thought, all he wants is to . . . get me into bed."

He was staring at the floor, at his shoes, holding the sides of his head in his palms. "What if I did?"

"You admit you did then." Once again her voice was unexpectedly not sour; but inquisitive.

"What's wrong with thinking about it?"

"There's ways and ways of thinking about it." She stood up abruptly. "Shan't be a sec."

He heard her go upstairs, the sound of the lavatory flushing. Five minutes passed. He remembered a new book on the transuranic elements that lay on his desk upstairs. In that world, he knew where he was, or if he didn't, how to find his way forward. He began to count up to one hundred. If she didn't come back, he would slip away to his room.

She reappeared in the doorway. "Like to come upstairs?"

He stood up, disconcerted. "Now?"

She smiled. "Well, not tomorrow."

"What about your Mum?"

It had been made plain to them all at the beginning that no student ever in any circumstances went to Doreen's room, or she to theirs.

"She won't be back yet."

He tried to see in her eyes what she meant. "D'you want me to?" She stood against the doorpost, picking at the jute matting with the toe of her left shoe; then nodded. "I thought you were fed up with me for being so stupid."

"Did you?" She gave him a swift look, and then she turned.

He went up the stairs after her, down the passage past her mother's closed door and to the open door of her own room. The curtains were drawn, but some light filtered through. He stood in the doorway, looking in at the penumbra. "Why've you got the curtains drawn then?"

"I felt like it. I often do it."

"Oh." He came forward into the room, staring around. She sat on a rep-covered divan, sorting through some records. He saw a shelf of glass animals; some photos of film-stars and royalty over the divan; a white dressing-table with brushes and things neatly laid out; a huge old wardrobe; a pink screen patterned with magnolia boughs in one corner, apparently hiding a wash-basin.

"Don't look at that wardrobe. I'm saving for a modern one."

"It's all right. Very nice." He indicated the whole room. She put on a trad jazz record, turning the volume down low, and patted the bed beside her, but as soon as he sat down she stood up.

"Which of my dresses do you like best?"

"Like them all, Doreen." He was very ill-at-ease.

"Doh!" she said in mock scorn. "I knew you'd say that."

"Well I do."

She danced a few steps on the other side of the room, by the mantelpiece, over which hung a framed reproduction of a Degas ballet scene, and posed for a moment in an arabesque position. She looked sideways at him. "You must like something best." She went to the wardrobe and opened it, looked in a moment, took a dress on its hanger out and held it in front of her matelot jersey and orange trousers. He nodded approvingly from where he was perched on the divan. Then she showed another dress, a skirt, a suit, her whole wardrobe. He nodded and nodded, conscious of his gaucheness, of his double nervousness, both sexual and situational; to try to counteract it he sat further back on the divan and leant against the wall. The record stopped. "They're all nice."

"Oh I forgot . . . wait." She flung the cotton dress she was holding over the dressing-table stool and ran out of the room. He had a curious feeling that she hadn't forgotten anything. All had been planned. She was away some minutes. He moved up the divan and looked through the records. Then she called through the door. "Shut your eyes."

"They're shut."

"Don't open till I say." He kept them shut, and heard her come in and open a drawer at the bottom of the wardrobe. "You can look."

She had on an indigo blue party dress and high-heeled shoes. She turned around like a model, exhibiting. There was an imitation red rose in the corsage. "D'you like it? It's my evening dress. I keep it in Mum's room."

"You look smashing."

"Reelly?" She looked at herself in the mirror, twisting and veering a little to get a better view. She pulled the alice band off and shook her hair loose. "Do you think blue suits me?"

"Yes. You look smashing." She came and stood close to him. He smelt perfume. He found it difficult to look up at her; at her bare shoulders and small white face. The palms of his hands were sweaty, and his heart was beating uncomfortably fast. He braced himself back against the wall again. She turned and, fluffing out the skirt, knelt on the divan beside him. Her shoes dropped off onto the carpet. She started to fiddle with the rose.

"D'you think the rose is fussy? I can never decide."

He felt she was making a fool of him in some way he could not fathom, and he reached sideways to take her in his arms. She pushed him back before he could get his lips near her face, but more as if he were interrupting the business with the rose than for any other reason. "Peter, please. Not now."

He flushed. "It's always not now."

"Don't you like being in my room?"

"Very much. But . . . ."

"But?" She had gone back to arranging her rose.

"It doesn't matter."

"I don't like it when you're rough." He banged his head back against the wall. There was a little silence. "You ever hear me playing my records at night sometimes?"

"You know I do. I told you I did."

"Ballet records? D'you know what I do?"

"No." He stared straight out past her, avoiding her looks.

"I dance. In proper tights. I used to have lessons. Not real ballet. No one knows I've got tights. Not even Mum. I keep them hidden. I put them on when I know she's gone to bed. I lock the door." She spoke in little sentences, busy with the rose, but watching him.

"Why's it got to be a secret?"

She shrugged. "It's silly. I can't dance. Not reelly dance."

"Nothing wrong with it." He sounded gruff.

"I bought them in a shop in London. I told them I was a student."

"Daft."

There was a pause. When she spoke it was in an almost hurt voice.

"I trust you. I've always trusted you."

"You were making out I was a bloody sex maniac just now. Down in the kitchen."

"I was only teasing. I said I always feel safe with you."

"I know. I'm your brother and all."

"I didn't mean that." She put a friendly hand on his leg and pushed herself off the divan, then went over to the mantelpiece and looked at the Degas print; then back at him. Her shoulders seemed very white in the dim light. "Would you like to see me dancing with my tights on?"

He leant forward. "Just for me?"

"If you'd like."

"Well I would. Very much, Doreen."

She went and moved the dressing-table stool, and stood on it and took a writing case from behind the top of the wardrobe; then searched for a key in a drawer of the dressing-table. He watched her unlock the case and take the black tights out.

"I won't be a min." Again she disappeared. And then she was standing in front of him, pirouetting with her arms outstretched, all in black, a ballerina.

"By gum. It's bloody wonderful. You look like the real thing." It was clear he was not pretending. She made a ballerina's curtsy.

"D'you mind if I lock the door? It feels funny when it's unlocked."

There was a shocked pause. "What if your Mum comes back early?"

"I've bolted the front door. She can't get in without ringing." She said it with a mixture of demure pertness and timid collusion, not looking at him.

"You cheeky devil."

She locked the door, turned and went to the record-player by the divan. "I'm not very good. I never had real lessons in a real ballet school."

"Doesn't matter. Go on. Let's see you."

"You're sure you want me to?"

"Go on." He made an inviting gesture with his hand, and leant forward elbows on knees. As she sorted through her records he looked at her body, at her back, her waist, her haunches, her small black buttocks.

She put on a record of excerpts from *Coppelia* and began to dance, with a kind of weird amalgam of classical ballet steps and poses and improvisations of her own. All that aspect of her he normally disliked, her over-conscious petiteness and daintiness, now was converted into an indefinable charm; in spite of her amateurishness, her occasional toppling inability to hold a pose, her losing time, there was a delicacy of a kind in the tenderly small black figure with the white hands, black limbs, white face, turning, flexing, bending, moving through the half-light; a kind of pathos, too, that he felt without being able to name. The record came to an end, but she went on dancing, using the mantelpiece as a *barre,* indicating with a quick flip of her hand that he was to turn to the other side; and she caught up the music again and went on. Gradually she seemed to forget he was there watching her, and her dancing improved, became more free, less attemptedly classical, more purely herself, her secret self when she danced in secret by herself.

As soon as she had danced the other side she went and chose another record. She did not look at him and he sensed that she didn't want him to speak. All that could be heard in the room was her breathing. Then the music of the Swan Lake began.

As he watched her, two feelings began to mount and struggle in him. The tights were a kind of black nakedness. At the same time he felt more and more shocked; he might think and daydream permissively, but he had been brought up in a Methodist house; perhaps it was that, perhaps it was some obscure yet allied scientist's fear of the uncontrolled experiment, but this change, this breaking of all past rules, this wild throwing away of normality seemed to him deeply blasphemous, and not only because of what had happened earlier. He felt locked in, trapped, endangered.

The music stopped and with a little run she sank, panting, flat on her back, onto the other end of the divan, and threw her feet across his thighs. For a long moment they looked at each other, and then without warning she covered her face with her hands, exactly as she had that morning when she saw the corpse. She twisted over on her side, toward the wall.

He got off the bed. "Doreen?"

She curled up her knees and lay in a fetal position.

"Doreen, you were wonderful."

Dismayed by this sudden collapse, he hesitated a moment, looked at the door, then knelt by the top of the divan and touched her shoulder. "You looked the real thing. I wouldn't know the difference."

She stretched out her legs and lay with her head half-buried in the cushions, her shoulders gently heaving as she breathed. He looked down over her prostrate body and patted her shoulder again. "What's wrong, Doreen?"

She began to cry. He tried to turn her to comfort her, but she kept pulling away, and he had to give up. After a time, she lay more still; she gave odd little shudders, little backwash sobs.

He stroked her arm. "You were lovely."

She turned. Her eyes and cheeks were wet. "I saw what you thought."

"I thought you were wonderful."

"No you didn't. I saw it in your eyes."

"You can't have. You danced . . . beautifully."

"You'll tell everyone."

"I shall not."

"You'll tell them I can't dance."

"You dance beautifully." He looked down. "It wasn't your dancing."

"What was it then?" She was almost fierce.

His voice sounded ashamed. "I can't explain."

They stayed there. Dimly, from an outer world, came the half-hour chime of the church at the end of the road; then of the clock downstairs.

"I feel all lonely," she said. "I've never felt so lonely as I felt when we came back this afternoon. Never in my whole life. If you hadn't stayed with me I'd have died." She gave him a timid look.

"You know what you said in the field. I thought it was all over between us."

"You wanted it to be."

"You were the one said no."

"You don't like me anyway."

They were both staring at her small hand, carmine fingernails, picking at the edge of the cushion.

"I do."

"Only one way then."

"What's that?"

"The way you were that night in the park."

He turned and sat on the floor, his back against the divan. There was just enough light for her to see the heavy blond eyelashes.

"I said I was sorry."

"It was so sudden. I was frightened." She let the silence run, nursing it, before she spoke again. "You just don't understand, you boys."

"Don't we?"

"*You* don't." She saw him give his lips a rueful press.

Then she reached out and pulled his head around toward her, and kissed him quickly and lightly first on the mouth and then on his right eye. "Come up on the divan and hold me. Just hold me."

She made him lie as she wanted, so that he had one arm round her and she could rest her head on his shoulder. Then she began to talk; not continuously, but with pauses, as the ideas came up out of her mind, and he understood that her talking was like her dancing, something strange she had decided he should be allowed to watch; he must not argue with her; but let her teach him her tempo.

"It's like everything's all come at once today. I mean for me. Locking the door and being a ballerina and never telling anyone because I was so afraid they'd laugh." He pressed her back. "And what you said about the way I speak. Like with those three students. I could hear it myself. I saw you looking."

"It's not your fault, love."

"And I told you a lie. I did tell Mum about you asking."

"What did she say?"

"She said about us being different in education."

"I've had a look at some of those bloody stuck-up geniuses in the women's colleges. And no thank you very much."

They were silent for a moment. He tried to turn to kiss her, but she stopped him. "Lie still. It's nice."

"Just one little kiss." She kissed him, then made him lie back.

"I've been thinking about Mum being dead. Me being alone."

"You've got your auntie."

"It's more than that. I mean no one I can be like I really am with."

"Like you've just been with me?"

"That's what I mean." Her voice sounded almost excited. "You know what it's like sometimes when you come out at the end of a film? You feel we're all nobodies; just a lot of nobodies they can do what they like in front of. We can never be like they are. D'you ever feel that?"

"Yes."

"It's like the way people treat you. You know, all bossy. And you get so's you believe it. So's you're ashamed of what you are half the time. All the time. If I feel like having you in my room and showing you my clothes and my dancing, I can, can't I?"

"Course you can."

She was silent a minute. "We're as free as they are." She turned and raised herself on her elbow for a moment, looking at his face, and then came close to him so that he could kiss her. For several moments they lay locked. And the house waited, waited.

She bent back her head. "I can't breathe."

He lay staring at her face, her closed eyes, her small cheekbones; so close, in the near-darkness of the corner of the room, she seemed strangely young. She opened her eyes and looked at him. He kissed her again wildly, forcing her on her back and moving half on top of her. She pushed him away, then reached up and took his head in her hands, as she had seen it done on the screen, and gently brought his face down to hers, slipping her tongue between his lips as their mouths met. For a few seconds he seemed to lose control of himself. Then without warning he muttered something, pulled roughly away, and swung his legs off the divan. She could only see his bowed back.

"Peter?" She leant up. "What's wrong?"

"Lying necking here like this."

"But you like it." She lay back. "I know you like it."

"Of course I like it."

"Well then."

"I want to do things." His voice sounded thick.

"I know."

He flashed a look at her as she lay staring at him.

"We can't. Not here."

"Why can't we?"

He turned away. "I haven't got any doodahs."

"You're frightened." He sat with bowed head. There was a silence between them. "Aren't you?" Still he would not answer, but sat with averted face.

"I'm frightened too," she said.

Then she said, "Shut your eyes, don't look."

He felt her get off the divan, heard her undress, a pause, and then the weight of her body again. He would not turn. She said his name, but he would not turn. She knelt and put her bare arms round his neck. Then at last he gave in and with his eyes desperately closed, flung himself beside her and began to caress.

After a moment she said, "Peter, I want you to look."

He opened his eyes. She was lying on her back. He saw her white face, the whiteness of her body. And then he stiffened with shock.

Round her neck, loosely knotted, was a nylon stocking. She said nothing; lay there, her eyes closed, with her bizarre long-ended scarf. He saw the foot, the dark thighband. It seemed to him a terrible thing to do, the most extraordinary and incomprehensible thing. She was not going to speak, he could see it by her mouth. Abruptly, roughly, he unknotted the stocking and threw it behind him. Then her eyes opened as if she was frightened by him, yet wanted to be. When he began to kiss her, she whispered in his ear, and he undressed.

His hands were at first very tentative, incredulous, and for a time she lay without responding in any way, trembling, but letting him touch her, kiss her, murmur to her.

"You're so lovely. You're so small." His hands touched her breasts.

It was for him as if a wall had suddenly disappeared; a wall made of fears, puritanities, scales of values in which facts, figures, analysis, verifiability were all and the flesh and the mystery nothing, mere amusement for after work; a wall gone, and over the rubble lay this warm young female thing in darkness, this ungraphable curve of flesh, this apple of a shoulder he could cup in the palm of his hand, this neck like silk, this hair he could put his fingers under; all darkness, shock, emotion, tenderness, force, possession, a flux of unverifiables.

"You're all changed," she whispered. "You're all gentle."

"It's you. It's because of you."

She let his words sink into her, impregnate her with the significance she craved, with the power of the thing she wanted.

For a moment she saw the revolutionary prespective of her room past his bare shoulders, his strange hanging face with its shut eyes; she saw or sensed the photographs on the wall around the head of the divan, the faces of film-stars and princesses, of *them,* the others, the supposedly free, and she knew, without having the words or the time to define it, that freedom was not what she had always thought it to be, but was this, this thrownback moment; was escaping, not being escaped; was an act, not a dream; a new life, not an old death. She saw her existence and all existence there, poised, for one second, like a glimpse through a thousand-times-passed locked door.

She saw the dead, white body in the reeds; and then imagined, out there, at that very moment, a grim cortege of men in uniforms and plainclothes moving away from the reeds, moving through the drizzle, the stretcher-bearers leading the way. They seemed to be walking in silence, almost like a party of surveyors, some boundary commission that had established one point and were walking to the next, as if all that could ever be done would be done by them, and by them alone, as if the earth and the sky and all else between it except them, and the shrouded thing they carried, did not exist, was irrelevant chaos.

She lay as still as death for a moment. In the old may-tree out in the garden a wood-pigeon began to purr. The she raised her arms and pulled him down, with violence, as if she were the man and he the woman.

Falling Off the Scaffold

Lyn Coffin

Dear Sir:

I am enrolling in your correspondence course. Yours is the only ad that doesn't take a "writer's cheerleader" approach—"You too can write a sentence that sells," etc. I feel that someone who advertises his services in such a curt, laconic, or at least a "no nonsense" way may have something to offer me.

I would appreciate your not sending me the customary 'credentials' sheet, incidentally. I'm sure your credentials are excellent; if not, I have enough for both of us.

My check and my first submission (*At the Museum*) are enclosed.

Very truly yours,

e. trace

At the Museum

At the museum, looking at the mummy,
I think about mortality.
I think about
The hieroglyphs
Slow time has inscribed
On my moving face.
How did you feel,
Egyptian man?
You had long fingers,
Did you play the harp,
Cast the sticks,
Or were you a card shark?
The bones tell no story.
The linen, dissolving,
Tells no story.

I don't want it this way,
All up to the imagination!
Couldn't you have left a letter,
A suicide note
(All letters, poems, are ultimately suicide notes)
Saying
I was a painter of pyramids.
I got careless.
One day I fell off the scaffold
And got a fungus
And that fungus
Ate me up. I just shriveled away and
Died. But before I died, I picked out my favorite
Pots and knives and beads and here I am.
That's how I died, that's the way you see me.
Well, that would make me feel much better,
I could even get into that painter's trip,
Feel the scaffold slip—
The sudden drop, the scream—
Perhaps I'd die
And wouldn't you wonder
Seeing me curled up next to the mummy
In my turtleneck and bell-bottoms?

Dear Mr. or Ms. Trace:

Welcome to the course! My salutation is not meant to offend you in any way—merely to point out that presently I exist in a state of unawareness as to your gender, if I may put it that way.

Taking your most interesting and intriguing letter point by point (which is something I believe very strongly in doing), I feel that I must in all honesty admit that it was not considerations of *verbal* economy alone which led me to make my ad short and sweet. I'm sure you know what I mean!

As for the matter of credentials, I believe you spoke of having credentials enough for both of us. Well, all I have to say to *that* is, you must have quite a few! Seriously, I would like to know something about you—your gender, of course, as I mentioned above—but that's just a beginning. The more I know about you, the more I can help you realize your own individual talent, and that's what we're both concerned with at this point, right?—Naturally, I don't expect you to tell me all the intimate details of your personal life—at least not yet!—as interesting as those details may be! But if you could tell me a little bit about the kind of education you've had, the kinds of things you're interested in writing about, etc., etc., I'd be in a much better position to advise you.

I'll bet you're wondering at this point just what I thought of *In The Museum*. Okay. Well, on the whole, I thought it was excellent. Really excellent. I just have a couple of points I'd like to make. First of all, I think you might be better off, if you're going to write poetry, to work within more or less traditional forms for a while. The poem as it is is too strung out, so to speak. I'm not sure that you have the poetic control (yet!) which one needs if one is going to write free verse. So that's one suggestion I'd like to make, that you try something in meter. Now, of course, *I* don't know (hint hint) what *you* know about matters of prosody. If you're interested, I can recommend several books on the subject, one of which I wrote myself!

Another thing. I think you run into a point-of-view problem at the end of the poem, when you address someone ("And wouldn't you be surprised") and the reader can't tell exactly who that someone is. Up to that point, remember, the poet-you has been speaking directly to the mummy (I think that's one of the best things about the poem, that use of direct address!), so when you (the poet) say, "And wouldn't *you* be surprised," I don't think you can complete the line as you do, by saying, "Seeing me curled up here next to the *mummy*."

As for the beginning, my honest feeling is that it should be cut! ("I think about mortality" is particularly bad. In poetry, especially, one has to "show—don't tell."*) I don't think you really hit your stride until the ninth or tenth line.

To sum it all up, I think you ought to try being less *casual,* less prosaic, as it were—assuming you still want to stick to poetry after all my discouraging comments!

I'm looking forward to your next submission and (one last reminder) to learning more about you.

Happy writing!

K. C. Jedenacht

*Ditto, the line about all poems and letters being suicide notes. You're perfectly right, of course, but being right is not at all the same as being poetic!

                                                          K. C. J.

Dear Prof. Jedenacht:

Thank you for your letter. I agree with everything you said about the poem. I disagree with everything else.

I am enclosing my poetic response to your poetic suggestions.

Very truly yours,

evelyn trace

THE CATCH

```
              I swam the long sea
         Down, a silver flash in deepest
       Leagues of green, lifted by the swell
   And surge, the strong, the sure, the slowly-rising
  Tide. Exposed to seizures by a sudden ebb, your bare
 Hands had me. I was cruelly beached. I dully thudded
   Out my life against your bones and body strand-was
      Cut, slit open by a most incisive blade. My Death
       Was spasmodic-I labored like a girl
            In frank breech birth.
```

Dear Ms. Trace:

Well, I must say that your second letter (?) intrigued me even more than the first! (And that's saying a lot!) As you will note by the salutation, I took your advice about trying to learn about you through your poems. Putting together some of the more obvious, shall we say, phrasings of your latest poem ("I was slit, cut open by your most incisive blade" and so on) with the name "Evelyn," I have come to the conclusion that you are a female-type person.

Also, judging from your address, you live in the suburbs. Going on the assumption that most women (your poems and letter are far too mature for a girl to have written them) who live in the suburbs are married and have a husband and children, I have concluded nothing less than that you are a married woman and a suburban mother! (How am I doing so far?)

As for the poem itself, I thought it was excellent, a real step up from the museum piece (if I may so phrase it)! *The Catch* shows a lot of thought and poetic craft. Still, it's not exactly the kind of thing I had in mind for you. The fish-shape, which (stupid me) I didn't see at first, represents an extremely ingenious bit of spatial engineering, of course, but I'm afraid emblem poems went out of style with Geo. Herbert and his bunch (c. the 1590s) and haven't come back in since! The line-raising ("rising") and lowering ("De$_{ath}$") sort of thing never was in! Seriously, I'm afraid you suffer, as so many others of us do, from what I call "the curse of cleverness."

And, again, it seems to me, the poem takes too long to get off the ground. (Metaphorically speaking, of course!)

One last thing: I seem to remember your using a phrase like "my moving face" in your *Museum* poem. In *Catch,* you have words like "seizures" and "incisive" and "frank" and phrases like "had me," all of which are, it seems to me, more or less in the nature of puns. Perhaps you pun unconsciously, perhaps not. (My mother was a great one for unconscious puns. I remember she told me once she ironed her under-wear because "I want my drawers to look neat.") Anyway, I think you ought to seriously consider how much, if at all, you want to use puns in a serious piece of writing.

To sum it all up, I would suggest your trying to write a more or less regular poem for your next submission, something I'm very much looking forward to reading.

Good luck,
"Sherlock" Jedenacht

Dear Sir:

Just a few items of possible interest: A) I agree with your criticisms of *The Catch;* B) "Evelyn" is a name which most authorities consider proper for either males *or* females; C) As so many other poets do, I "suffer from" a tendency to use *personae* in my work, a tendency which I should think you, as a detective if not as a fellow writer, would do well to keep in mind; D) George Herbert (1593–1633).

Enclosed is my latest submission. The puns are quite deliberate.

Very truly (and pseudonymously) yours,
e.d.t.

Presentation

Fluidly, they draw me out; I take it as it goes.
They wrap my genitals with white so nothing manly shows.
And in the padlock of my hands they place a waxy rose.
In covered wagons, peasant-like, they horse me to my room.

They let me down. I come to terms, assume a studied pose.
Like backward dogs, they shower dirt. They fill me in on doom.

Dear Evelyn,

Well, as you can see from the salutation, I still haven't given up on the idea that we can be friends (even if you do seem insistent upon regarding me from the "height of an unwritten book"!) Actually, I never really thought about you as a suburban housewife at all: I just said that as a kind of test. Even if I hadn't been sure before, the phrase "so nothing manly shows" would have clued me in as to the true state of things.

Anyway, about the poem itself. I think it's fairly good. Your rhymes are a trifle sophomoric, but perhaps that is a good thing, given the subject with which the poem attempts to deal. I really object to two things: your use of puns, about which I cautioned you in my last letter, and which I really feel you would do well to avoid; and, second, the nebulous nature of what you like to call the "persona" of your work.

Expressions like "draw me out," "take it as it goes," "let me down," "come to terms"—all of these plays on words seem to me unfortunately chosen. You said in your letter that all your puns were deliberate, however, so this may just be one of those things we're going to have to agree to disagree about!

As for the "persona"—Beyond the fact that the speaker of the poem is a dead man, the reader knows nothing about him. Also, with the one possible exception of the phrase "padlock of my hands" (the meaning of which I'm afraid escapes me), I see little or no *traces* (turn about and all that!) of a truly poetic sensibility in your work. You are obviously intelligent, well-read, sensitive, etc. But it seems to me (and I cannot stress too strongly that this is a purely personal opinion—in fact, not even an opinion so much as a gut feeling, if you will) that you would do better in the medium of prose. I think the broader scope of a novel, or even a short story, would help you to develop your personae and your extremely interesting ideas. This is something one of my creative writing teachers told *me* once, and I've always been grateful to him for his honesty.

If you want to continue with the poetry, of course, that's your prerogative. If you do decide to stick with it, though, then my advice would be to choose something other than death to write about. Of all the subjects about which to write poetry, it seems to me, death is apt to produce the worst writing. If you want my honest opinion, I don't think anybody's been able to come up with even a half-way decent poem about the thing, including Donne and Thomas and whomever else you wish to include. Frankly, I look at it this way—death is just something that happens. We make a big deal out of it because it terrifies the hell out of us; when one looks at it objectively, though, one finds it is a good subject for a writer (particularly a poet) to steer away from.

As a matter of fact, I can't think of a more boring topic—unless it's daffodils!

Looking forward to hearing from you, I remain

Sincerely yours,
Prof. "Casey" Jedenacht

Dear Prof. Jedenacht:

As you will see from the enclosed, I took your advice about trying to express myself (much as I hate that phrase) in prose. I *tried* to take your other major piece of advice and write about something relatively positive, but the latter attempt, as you will soon discover, utterly failed. I find myself unable to write about anything except death.

And yet, I am not completely without hope that "Lucite" will strike some small spark of interest in you: after all, the *persona's* attitude toward the thing is very largely the same as I take yours to be.

Very truly yours,
Evelyn

Lucite

My father died when I was thirteen years old. I remember because that was my year for lucite.

Perhaps a little background information would be of use here before I proceed.

I am—and if I am, I undoubtedly always was—a genius. I am also extremely wealthy. I am also what I suppose you would call "a cold fish"; as far as I'm concerned, that's the only rational way to be.

Oh, I know most people believe in love and friendship and emotions and all that; in fact, one of my earliest maxims was "The worse something is, the more people tend to believe in it."

I don't want to get into a discussion of Nazism or anything like that, not at this point. You want to hear about my father's death and I'm here to oblige you. About the love business, though: the two kinds of love which are most universally acclaimed are the parental-filial and the amo-rati. Allow me simply to point out that modern psychologists agree with me that the first is no more or less than a dependency bond. (As a person who could have survived by his own wits from an early age, I never really, or at least consciously, knew what it was to feel dependent.) As for romantic love, I shall exercise my well-known classical restraint and limit myself to pointing out that the concept of romantic love *qua* concept was invented as late as the thirteenth century by troubadours and minnesingers who probably dreamed it up as what we today would call "a promotion gimmick."

So much for love.

Now I know a lot of you are probably "feeling sorry" for me, and I can assure you there is no need. Perhaps you would not wish to grant me the right to use the term "happy." So be it. But I consider that my life is "blest," as a character in *Joseph Andrews* expressed it, since I continually "experience the falsehood of common assertions."

When my father died, I did not have any feelings of guilt or sadness. I hardly knew my father—as, indeed, I hardly knew, or know, anyone. He seemed pleasant enough, you understand, and I was glad (as opposed to grateful) not to have been born to a cruel or a stupid man. But that was all.

When mother came into my room, I was at work making a pair of lucite bookends. As most of my biographers have pointed out, my fame as an innovator in the field of crafts could have been predicted almost from the very beginning by anyone with a modicum of intelligence and sensitivity. Fortunately or unfortunately, I myself was the only such person then acquainted with my work.

I was always careful not to do *too* well in school, of course, since I knew all too well the resentment that would have stirred up in my peers and the annoying consequences I would have had to put up with.

Still, however, despite all my precautions on this score, I encountered a certain amount of residual hostility among my fellow students, particularly the boys.

It was partly in order to minimize this residual antipathy that I first began doing work with lucite. One boy of rather pronounced sadistic tendencies asked me to build him "a home for my guinea pig." The resulting cage was quite satisfactory. I built a number of cages for the pets (I privately referred to them as "the nameless horrors") of the other boys.

Then I began making book-ends. On the night my father died, I had just finished the well-known "Black-and-White Pony Book Ends" which I understand are the earliest pieces featured in the Smithsonian. It was the first time I had ever really carved the lucite, and the first time I had ever used a pictorial motif.

Anyway, when my mother told me my father had died—this may shock some of you—I was rather pleased. I had read all kinds of stories about children being made to kiss the lipsticked mouths of departed relatives and so on, and I suppose I hoped for something of the sort—anything, really, that would relieve the tedium of life in general.

Of course, nothing of the sort occurred. My father's casket was closed and the entire funeral service carried out in a quiet, dignified, and hence boring manner. To be sure, my mother cried a bit, but I had seen her cry as much when her mother's porcelain vegetable dish broke.

As it turned out, my father had left instructions that he be cremated: again, I had some expectations of drama—the casket sliding precipitously down into the roaring flames, and so on. Again, I was cheated. In fact, the family, at my mother's request, was not even present when the cremation took place.

A messenger brought us father's remains the following day. Mother didn't know what to do with them, she said, since father had left no instructions as to their disposal. She didn't want them walled up in some columbarium, with the other "cinery urns," she asserted. Nor did she "want the thing cluttering up the house and making people uncomfortable." I said I would be glad to keep the urn (it looked like a coffee can, I thought, for all that it had "R.I.P." engraved on the top). With only the slightest of hesitations, she agreed.

I think the rest is pretty well-known to you all. It took me only a few days to hit upon the idea of sifting the remains to get out the bone fragments and embedding a handful of the finest ash in a book-end. From there, it was only a small step to the whole line of "Loved Ones in Lucite" which first brought me fame and fortune.

Dear Evelyn,

To begin with, I'm delighted that you took my advice about trying out the short story form. I definitely feel that you're on the right track, although perhaps not quite yet at the station! *Calcite* seems to me very good for a first attempt. In fact, for a piece of its kind I think it's truly excellent; the only problem is, I think what you've written is not so much a story as it is a character portrait—the kind of thing Browning might have written if he'd written prose.

The main ingredient of a story is action, it seems to me, and not point-of-view, although, of course, point-of-view can be very important. What I'd suggest is that you try, in your next story, to develop a sequence of events—try to weave a narrative thread, as it were.

Also, if you must write about death, perhaps you could approach it from a more positive—at least a less morbid or off-beat—angle. If you could choose a more normal persona, I think you would appeal to a wider audience.

Keep up the good work.

Very truly yours,
Prof. K. C. Jedenacht

Dear Sir:

As usual, I agreed with the criticisms you made in your letter.

Enclosed please find my latest attempt to please you.

Sincerely yours,
evelyn trace

Catharsis

For purely personal reasons, I want to describe what she was like and how it happened.

She was so beautiful it almost hurt to look at her. She was very small and delicate, with skin so fair it seemed translucent. She had thick, dark hair that kind of swirled around, framing her little locket-face. I guess it was her high cheekbones and rather deep-set eyes that gave her a pathetically proud expression; she looked like a little girl facing her First Confession—not that that explains anything.

I suppose in her own way she was intelligent, but she got good grades mainly by virtue of her photographic memory. Being the kind of person who'd forget his head if it weren't attached, I really envied her that memory.

"God, school would be so much easier to take if I could only remember everything, like you do," I commented once. "It's not that I can remember," she said. "It's just that I can't forget."

Not only did she remember everything she read, heard or saw, however—unfortunately, she also tended to believe it. This uncritical acceptance of things prevented her from doing any real scholarship. Her papers always represented impressive but ultimately unsuccessful attempts to reconcile incompatible views.

Her term paper on Chamberlain was a perfect case in point. After skimming through it, I took her to task. "First, you side with those who think he was a schmuck, then you agree with the 'unsung hero' faction," I said. "Don't give me that 'hobgoblin of little minds' business, either. Just accept the fact that you can't have things both ways."

She mumbled something about black-and-white ponies and about light being both a particle and a wave; I didn't pay too much attention. After a few minutes, she smiled ruefully and said: "Well, I've heard that most student papers tend to throw out the baby with the bath. At least I don't do that—I just try to diaper the water."

Naturally, her penchant for accepting things at face value stood her in good stead socially. She came as close to being a real aristocrat as any midwestern Catholic can, but she never had that air of inaccessibility most people of her class exhibit. Average people felt at home with her.

There were widespread rumors to the effect that she was a little too accessible, particularly when it came to men, but when I heard things like that, I just shrugged them off. For one thing, she was pretty religious. More importantly, though, it was hard for me to imagine anyone's being promiscuous who was as uninterested in sex as she was. I say uninterested because although she never put me off or turned me down, not even during her periods, she never initiated anything either.

Unfortunately, her doctor had advised her not to take the pill. (Something to do with her having inherited a tendency to develop embolisms—it seems they can prove fatal if they travel to the heart—which meant birth control pills were dangerous for her.)

Anyway, what with her passivity and my having to wear a condom, sex wasn't all that satisfactory. . . .

It sounds funny, I guess, but the best times we had were spent in discussing rather sad and serious things. I had her read my thesis on the Aristotelian aspects of Euripides, since she had read most of his plays. Although she had read them while quite young, she remembered everything in them and more. . . . She started talking abut Medea's having cooked her children and served them up to their father, for example; I'm afraid I teased her unmercifully about that.

On the lighter side, she liked my collection of famous last words ("Puto deus fio") and treasured phrases from children's nursery rhymes.

Her favorite, which she claimed had something to do with a battle, was typical of the kind of thing she liked. It started innocently enough with reference to a garden full of seeds (weeds?). But it went on to talk about a lion at the door and ended by saying, "When your heart begins to bleed / You're dead, and dead, and dead, indeed."

She told me once her father used to feed her lines of gallows-humor ("Why is dying like going to the bathroom?"—"When you gotta go, you gotta go") while she drank her warm milk at bedtime. With a father like that, I suppose it's no wonder she had a morbid streak. For a time, in high school, she wanted to be a poet: she wrote hundreds of strange little poems, all of them morbid:

> Death moves toward me. I'm dancing—He cuts in
> The gay young blade—I'm now at his disposal.
> I get the point of Women's Lib,
> Accept his generous proposal.

I don't really think I can tell you much more about her. I'll just try to describe what happened as near as I can recall it.

I remember I had trouble unlocking the door. (I'd had a key made for myself, I'm not sure whether she really liked that or not, but she spent a lot of time in bed, the covers pulled up over her head, and I was afraid one time she wouldn't hear the buzzer.) I was carrying a pizza in one hand, a six-pack in the other.

I kicked the door shut behind me, turned off the t.v., and set out plates and napkins. I don't remember what was said, except that she called me "Ivan" (after her literary hero, Ivan Karamazov), which was usually a good sign.

I poured the beer too quickly and some of it foamed over onto the rug. I started dabbing at the wet spots with my napkin but she told me her mother, who had bought the rug for her, had said it was "'a good rug and good rugs don't show stains.'" So I stopped dabbing.

After a while, I realized she wasn't eating. Usually, she ate whatever I put in front of her. I asked her about it, and she said she didn't want any more.

"How can you not want *more* when you haven't had *any?*" I wanted to know. She mumbled something abut being a hunger artist, but bowed her head dutifully and began to eat.

She had told me a few weeks before that there was to be an important lecture-and-slide presentation on the Normandy invasion that evening, and I asked her what time it was suposed to start.

"8:00," she said. "But I don't think I'll go."

I was unpleasantly surprised: as far as I knew, she had never missed a single class or class-related event and now didn't seem the time to start.

"Why not?"

"I'm sick of having to brown-nose. Sick of educational insemination. Sick of being fed on the blood of gods. Sick of conceptual consumption, for Christ's sake!"

She rattled out the "k" sounds in a sort of rapid-fire machine-gun stutter and it struck me that I had never seen her show any sign of temper before.

In a way, I was encouraged. I had held off making love to her for a couple of weeks, hoping for once she'd be the one to make the overtures. I don't know—I suppose I connected temper with passion somehow. I'd had several beers by then, and the weeks of abstinence *had* left me sort of sexed-up.

At any rate, I remember thinking maybe she wanted to stay home so we could have a real night of it. I guess that was when I asked her if she'd been to confession. (The next day was the Feast of the Epiphany, a holy day of obligation.)

She said no, she hadn't, adding that she didn't want to take communion any more. Again, I asked her why. She said something about swallowing being for the birds and gagging not being a joke. I really didn't pay much attention; the fact that she wasn't planning to take communion sort of cinched things in my mind.

I'm not sure what I said or did next. I do remember carrying her to bed and making rather short work of the situation.

I must have fallen asleep right away, because I woke up about an hour later and I was still on top of her and still attached, so to speak. She was wide-awake, apparently had been the whole time. Her eyes had a funny kind of glazed look. Her fists were clenched. Her whole body was rigid.

Needless to say, I immediately withdrew. . . .

I vaguely remember making a few comments about the way she'd been acting the last couple of weeks. I finished by saying something like, "I don't know what's gotten into you lately."

She didn't say anything for a few minutes. Then she asked me where I bought the "Trojans" I kept in her bathroom cabinet. I told her and she nodded. "I thought so," she said.

Naturally, I didn't let it go at that. I kept after her until she revealed the following facts:

1. The pharmacy where I bought condoms had recently fired one of their employees;

2. The guy they fired was mentally ill; among other things, he amused himself by opening packages of condoms and making pin-prick holes in some of the tips;

3. She thought I must have purchased a batch which included some of these "punctured prophylactics";

4. She had missed her last period and although the rabbit-test "hadn't taken" (and was thus inconclusive), she was pretty sure she was pregnant;

5. That's what had 'gotten into her' lately.

Well, I was pretty upset by what she'd said, mostly because it made our whole relationship sound like something out of daytime t.v. But I told myself it was no good sitting around thinking about it. If she were pregnant, there would be time enough in the days ahead to decide what to do, and if she weren't, so much the better. It occurred to me that getting out and going to the lecture might be just the ticket in getting our minds off things. "At any rate, it can't hurt," I thought.

It was sleeting out, apparently had been for some time; ice had glassed over large stretches of the sidewalks. The winds seemed to be of gale force—"things too fierce to mention." I was wearing boots and a hooded parka, though, so I didn't mind too much.

We were a little late. The elevator didn't seem to be in operation so we went up the fire-stairs. I guess others had been that way before us; in any event, the fire-door had been propped open.

As we walked down the corridor, I noticed that all the office doors were shut and the air in the corridor was unusually close. I thought of going back and opening the window at the far end of the hall, but decided there wasn't time.

We got to the office where the talk was being given, and she opened the door.

Out of nowhere, there was an ear-splitting explosion. Dagger-like shards of glass flew past her and into the hall. Someone began to scream.

Instinctively, I pulled her back into the corridor. She was dry-eyed, but making strangled, mewing sounds; she seemed to be having some sort of convulsions.

Someone later tried to explain to me just what had happened. It seems the fire door being the ony thing open had set up a kind of air-trap. I don't know—the explanation was too scientific to mean very much to me. What I do know is that at the instant she opened the door to the lecture-room, the window imploded. (I also learned later that, despite the screaming, no one had been seriously hurt.)

Well, all I could think of then was that I had to get her out of there. Whatever had happened in the room was not her fault, and nothing whatever would be achieved by our hanging around. Besides, she was obviously in a state of shock.

I led her back to the apartment. When we arrived, I got her to drink some warm milk while I finished the six-pack. I gave her a tentative kiss, but there was a noticeable lack of response, so I turned in, advising her to do the same. ("Sleep knits up the ravelled sleeve of care" and all that.)

As I recall, she said she'd "be right there."

When I woke up the next morning, she wasn't in bed; one look at her pillow (in her sleep, she really mauled the thing) told me she hadn't been there at all.

I was heading for the study when I saw the note adhesive-taped to the bathroom door. In her curious, backhand scrawl, she had written: "I would be afraid of a less expressive death."

It's impossible to lock that door, but somehow she had managed to jam it shut. I forced it open, and peered in.

It was the most awful thing I've ever seen. (Luckily, I've pretty much managed to blot the sight out of my mind.) She had gotten into the bathtub—it was full—and cut her throat. There was blood every-where. . . .

Being somewhat of a classicist, I don't think tragedies can be ex-plained; I think they're to be felt rather than understood. . . . Describing what happened, reliving the pity and terror of it all, hasn't been easy, but I feel better for having done so.

Things have a way of working out.

Dear Evelyn,

Now you're really getting it together, as some of my other students like to say. I liked your story very much. I think this time you chose the right point-of-view and the subject is pretty much within the parameters of popular tastes. (What could be more normal than a guy getting his girl pregnant, right?)

The tissue of references and symbolic actions (spilling beer on the rug and all that) seems carefully, though perhaps a trifle too obtrusively (with an "r"!) elaborated. I haven't really had time to think about whether Euripides and the Latin ("I think I am making a god") and so on are truly *inevitable* in the story, but they sound good just on the surface of it, and I'm willing to take your word for the rest.

The only case which strikes me as a possible exception to the above is the girl's reference to a pony of some sort. Now I noticed horse references in a couple of your other things if I remember right, and I had trouble with the darn things then, too. . . . Probably ponies and horses and the like serve as some kind of private symbol for you—that's fine. But when you're writing a story, you have to make all your references at least potentially accessible to the reader. Not only that, but in this particular case, your private way of looking at horses—which I take to be almost completely asexual—directly conflicts with the standard (Freudian, neo-Freudian, psychoanalytic, whatever) way of looking at them. I suggest that you leave this particular warhorse (my puns are deliberate, too!) to the authorities and choose something else to be private about!

Enough of the harangue, already! Just one more point: although I think *Catharsis* is far and away the best thing you've written, it—like your other pieces—takes much too long to get going. Your beginining is more or less just deadwood, just straight exposition. I would suggest that the next time you do as Hemingway used to do: write your story, then go back and cut the first paragraph or two. (He used to cut the endings off as well, I believe, but I think your work is quite all right in that department.)

Incidentally, may I take this opportunity to remind you that additional coursework, according to the terms of that ad you liked so much, necessitates another financial remission on your part. How time does fly, eh?

Well, with that word to the wise, I remain

Yours truly,
"Casey" Jedenacht

Dear Sir:

Enclosed please find my latest and last submission. I am aware that it is not strictly covered by the terms of our agreement; I sent it to you as a kind of "thank you," in the hope you will find it enjoyable—or at least edifying.

Happy criticizing!
evelyn trace
N.B. I am a woman.

Famous Last Words

She had not wanted a lingering death; she had wanted to "go out like a light," as her husband, a well-known journalist, had put it. That was how he had gone—a stroke in his sleep.

But turning misfortunes into their opposite had always been her strong point. This lingering death (her death), seen positively, represented a chance to get even, somehow. (With whom, for what, she didn't know.)

"Life imitates art," her husband had been fond of saying. She was experiencing the truth of that now.

As a girl, millennia ago, she had wanted to be a writer. She had written a story called "Famous Last Words" about an unbelievably old woman, lying on her deathbed, who was determined to go out with a flourish, if not a bang.

Now she herself was unbelievably old. . . . If she could just remember the story and follow it, she would be acting the lead in her own play. She could die in the service of her own creation. She could be the artist of her own destruction.

The trouble was, she couldn't remember how the story ended. . . . She remembered that her first thought had been to have the old woman choke to death in the middle of a tantalizing sentence: "The only thing that really matters is—" But even in her youth, she had had enough sense to reject that idea. "Dime-novel stuff," her husband would have called it.

Another possibility she'd considered was that of having the old woman be successful—say just what she wanted to say—and then die happy. The problem with that approach, apart from the fact that most people nowadays didn't believe one could 'die happy,' was that it wasn't playing fair with the public not to tell them what those last words were. And if one elected to play it straight, what words could one put in the story-woman's mouth that would be meaningful but mysterious, etc., that would justify all the narrative build-up?

Of course, one could play the thing for laughs: have the old woman come out with a kind of vaudeville routine—"I'm goin' fast, but 'fore I go, I got one thing to say: 'I'm goin' fast.'"

But she had rejected that idea, too. It was too much like masturbating. (Her husband had said mastrubation was "carried out in frustration, and concluded in defeat." "Even when it's good, it's bad," he had remarked.)

She had considered other endings and rejected them in turn: having the old bat's "famous last words" turn out to be gibberish ("The moon is an eagle") or something somebody else had already said ("More light") or a variation on it ("Less light," even "More life"), but all those endings were cheap, they were cop-outs, and she had never been one in favor of copping out.

A more attractive possibility had been having the old woman do something (give her grand-daughter a rose or a shiny new quarter) rather than trying to speak. But a story like that wouldn't be much more than a moralistic cliché (her husband had called such pronouncements "profundisms"), like "Life must go on" or even (God forbid) "Actions speak louder than words."

She had also considered an epilogue-ending: the old woman would say something personally meaningful (like "Rosebud"), then there would be a significant space, then a sentence like "The doctor put away his stethoscope and, turning to the husband (son? father?), said: 'You can be thankful it was a stroke—she never knew what hit her.'"

All those endings and others had been rejected: she remembered that. But she couldn't remember, she simply could not remember, how she *had* ended the story. Maybe she hadn't finished it at all, in fact; maybe that was it.

Even if it had never been finished, though, she knew it had been a good story. Thinking too much about endings, after all, was a mistake: you have an idea; you write a story. The story ends whenever you stop writing.

Dear Evelyn:

Famous Lost Words was excellent. I'm only sorry you chose not to go on with me. As one of my sidelines, I publish a small journal. With a little polishing, your story might well have proved suitable for publication.

If you should change your mind, you know where I am! Until then, I remain,

Very truly yours,
Kathy Christine Jedenacht

Harmony of the World

Charles Baxter

I

In the small Ohio town where I grew up, many homes had parlors that contained pianos, sideboards, and sofas, heavy objects signifying gentility. These pianos were rarely tuned. They went flat in summer around the fourth of July and sharp in winter at Christmas. Ours was a Story and Clark. On its music stand were copies of Stephen Foster and Ethelbert Nevin favorites, along with one Chopin prelude that my mother would practice for twenty minutes every three years. She had no patience, but since she thought Ohio—all of it, every scrap—made sense, she was happy and did not need to practice anything. Happiness is not infectious, but somehow her happiness infected my father, a pharmacist, and then spread through the rest of the household. My whole family was obstinately cheerful. I think of my two sisters, my brother, and my parents as having artificial pasted-on smiles, like circus clowns. They apparently thought cheer and good Christian words were universals, respected everywhere. The pianos were part of this cheer. They played for celebrations and moments of pleasant pain. Or rather: someone played them, but not too well, since excellent playing would have been faintly antisocial. "Chopin," my mother said, shaking her head as she stumbled through the prelude. "Why is he famous?"

When I was six, I received my first standing ovation. On the stage of the community auditorium, where the temperature was about 94°, sweat fell from my forehead onto the piano keys, making their ivory surfaces slippery. At the conclusion of the piece, when everyone stood up to applaud, I thought they were just being nice. My playing had been mediocre; only my sweating had been extraordinary. Two years later, they stood up again. When I was eleven, they cheered. By that time I was astonishing these small-town audiences with Chopin and Rachmaninoff recital chestnuts. I thought I was a genius and read biographies of Einstein. Already the townspeople were saying that I was the best thing Parkersville had ever seen, *that I would put the place on the map.* Mothers would send their children by to watch me practice. The kids sat with their mouths open while I polished off another classic.

Like many musicians, I cannot remember ever playing badly, in the sense of not knowing what I was doing. In high school, my identity was being sealed shut: my classmates called me "el señor longhair," even though I wore a crewcut, this being the 1950s. Whenever the town needed a demonstration of local genius, it called upon me. There were newspaper articles detailing my accomplishments, and I must have heard the phrase "future concert career" at least two hundred times. My parents smiled and smiled as I collected applause. My senior year, I gave a solo recital and was hired for umpteen weddings and funerals. I was good luck. On the fourth of July the townspeople brought out a piano to the city square so that I could improvise music between explosions at the fireworks display. Just before I left for college, I noticed that our neighbors wanted to come up to me, ostensibly for small talk, but actually to touch me.

In college I made a shocking discovery: other people existed in the world who were as talented as I was. If I sat down to play a Debussy etude, they would sit down and play Beethoven, only louder and faster than I had. I felt their breath on my neck. Apparently there were other small towns. In each one of these small towns there was a genius. Perhaps some geniuses were not actually geniuses. I practiced constantly and began to specialize in the non-Germanic piano repertoire. I kept my eye out for students younger than I was, who might have flashier technique. At my senior recital I played Mozart, Chopin, Ravel, and Debussy, with encore pieces by Scriabin and Thomson. I managed to get the audience to stand up for the last time.

I was accepted into a large midwestern music school, famous for its high standards. Once there, I discovered that genius, to say nothing of talent, was a common commodity. Since I was only a middling composer, with no interesting musical ideas as such, I would have to make my career as a performer or teacher. But I didn't want to teach, and as a performer I lacked pizzazz. For the first time, it occurred to me that my life might be evolving into something unpleasant, something with the taste of stale bread.

I was beginining to meet performers with more confidence than I had, young musicians to whom doubt was as alien as proper etiquette. Often these people dressed like tramps, smelled, smoked constantly, were gay or sadistic. Whatever their imbalances, they were not genteel. *They did not represent small towns.* I was struck by their eyes. Their eyes seemed to proclaim, "The universe believes in me. It always has."

My piano teacher was a man I will call Luther Stecker. Every year he taught at the music school for six months. For the following six months he toured. He turned me away from the repertoire with which I was familiar and demanded that I learn several pieces by composers whom I had not often played, including Bach, Brahms, and Liszt. Each one of these composers discovered a weak point in me: I had trouble keeping up the consistent frenzy required by Liszt, the mathematical precision required by Bach, the unpianistic fingerings of Brahms.

I saw Stecker every week. While I played, he would doze off. When he woke, he would mumble some inaudible comment. He also coached a trio I participated in, and he spoke no more audibly then than he did during my private lesson.

I couldn't understand why, apart from his reputation, the school had hired him. Then I learned that in every Stecker-student's life, the time came when the Master collected his thoughts, became blunt, and told the student exactly what his future would be. For me, the moment arrived on the third of November, 1966. I was playing sections of the Brahms Paganini Variations, a fiendish piece on which I had spent many hours. When I finished, I saw him sit up.

"Very good," he said, squinting at me. "You have talents."

There was a pause. I waited. "Thank you," I said.

"You have a nice house?" he asked.

"A nice house? No."

"You should get a nice house somewhere," he said, taking his hand-kerchief out of his pocket and waving it at me. "With windows. Windows with a view."

I didn't like the drift of his remarks. "I can't afford a house," I said.

"You will. A nice house. For you and your family."

I resolved to get to the heart of this. "Professor," I asked, "what did you think of my playing?"

"Excellent," he said. "That piece is very difficult."

"Thank you."

"Yes, technically excellent," he said, and my heart began to pound. "Intelligent phrasing. Not much for me to say. Yes. That piece has many notes," he added, enjoying the *non sequitur.*

I nodded. "Many notes."

"And you hit all of them accurately. Good pedal and good discipline. I like how you hit the notes."

I was dangling on his string, a little puppet.

"Thousands of notes, I suppose," he said, staring at my forehead, which was beginning to get damp, "and you hit all of them. You only forgot one thing."

"What?"

"The passion!" he roared. "You forgot the passion! You always forget it! Where is it? Did you leave it at home? You never bring it with you! Never! I listen to you and think of a robot playing! A smart robot, but a robot! No passion! Never ever ever!" He stopped shouting long enough to sneeze. "You *should* buy a house. You know why?"

"Why?"

"Because the only way you will ever praise God is with a family, that's why! Not with this piano! You are a fine student," he wound up, "but you make me sick! Why do you make me sick?"

He waited for me to answer.

"*Why do you make me sick?*" he shouted. "Answer me!"

"How can I possibly answer you?"

"By articulating words in English! Be courageous! Offer a suggestion! Why do you make me sick?"

I waited for a minute, the longest minute my life has seen or will ever see. "Passion," I said at last. "You said there wasn't enough passion. I thought there was. Perhaps not."

He nodded. "No. You are right. No passion. A corruption of music itself. Your playing is too gentle, too much good taste. To play the piano like a genius, you must have a bit of the fanatic. Just a bit. But it is essential. You have stubbornness and talent but no fanaticism. You don't have the salt on the rice. Without salt, the rice is inedible, no matter what its quality otherwise." He stood up. "I tell you this because sooner or later someone else will. You will have a life of disappointments if you stay in music. You may find a teacher who likes you. Good, good. *But you will never be taken up! Never!* You should buy a house, young man. With a beautiful view. Move to it. Don't stay here. You are close to success, but it is the difference between leaping the chasm and falling into it, one inch short. You are an inch short. You could come back for more lessons. You could graduate from here. But if you are truly intelligent, you will say goodbye. Goodbye." He looked down at the floor and did not offer me his hand.

I stood up and walked out of the room.

Becalmed, I drifted down and up the hallways of the building for half an hour. Then a friend of mine, a student of conducting from Bolivia, a Marxist named Juan Valparaiso, approached, and, ignoring my shallow breathing and cold sweat, started talking at once.

"Terrible, furious day!" he said.

"Yes."

"I am conducting *Benvenuto Cellini* overture this morning! All is going well until difficult flute entry. I instruct, with force, flutists. Soon all woodwinds are ignoring me." He raised his eyebrows and stroked his huge gaucho mustache. "Always! Always there are fascists in the woodwinds!"

"Fascists everywhere," I said.

"Horns bad, woodwinds worse. Demands of breath made for insanes. Pedro," he said, "you are appearing irresoluted. Sick?"

"Yes," I nodded. "Sick. I just came from Stecker. My playing makes *him* sick."

"He said that? That you are making him sick?"

"That's right. I play like a robot, he says."

"What will you do?" Juan asked me. "Kill him?"

"No." And then I knew. "I'm leaving the school."

"What? Is impossible!" Tears leaped instantly into Juan's eyes. "Cannot, Pedro. After one whipping? No! Disappointments everywhere here. Also outside in world. Must stick to it." He grabbed me by the shoulders. "Fascists put here on earth to break our hearts! Must live through. You cannot go." He looked around wildly. "Where could you go anyway?"

"I'm not sure," I said. "He said I would never amount to anything. I think he's right. But I could do something else." To prove that I could imagine options, I said, "I could work for a newspaper. You know, music criticism."

"Caterpillars!" Juan shouted, his tears falling onto my shirt. "Failures! Pathetic lives! Cannot, cannot! Who would hire you?"

I couldn't tell him for six months, until I was given a job in Knoxville on a part-time trial basis. But by then I was no longer writing letters to my musician friends. I had become anonymous. I worked in Knoxville for two years, then in Louisville—a great city for music—until I moved here, to this city I shall never name, in the middle of New York state, where I bought a house with a beautiful view.

In my home town, they still wonder what happened to me, but my smiling parents refuse to reveal my whereabouts.

II

Every newspaper has a command structure. Within that command structure, editors assign certain stories, but the writers must be given some freedom to snoop around and discover newsworthy material themselves. In this anonymous city, I was hired to review all the concerts of the symphony orchestra and to provide some hype articles during the week to boost the ticket sales for Friday's program. Since the owner of the paper was on the symphony board of trustees, writing about the orchestra and its programs was necessarily part of good journalistic citizenship. On my own, though, I initiated certain projects, wrote book reviews for the Sunday section, interviewed famous visiting musicians—some of them my ex-classmates—and during the summer I could fill in on all sorts of assignments, as long as I cleared what I did with the feature editor, Morris Cascadilla.

"You're the first serious musician we've ever had on the staff here," he announced to me when I arrived, suspicion and hope fighting for control on his face. "Just remember this: be clear and concise. Assume they've got intelligence but no information. After that, you're on your own, except you should clear dicey stuff with me. And never forget the Maple Street angle."

The Maple Street angle was Cascadilla's equivalent to the Nixon Administration's "How will it play in Peoria?" No matter what subject I wrote about, I was expected to make it relevant to Maple Street, the newspaper's mythical locus of middle-class values. I could write about electronic, aleatory, or post-Boulez music *if* I suggested that the city's daughters might be corrupted by it. Sometimes I found the Maple Street angle, and sometimes I couldn't. When I failed, Cascadilla would call me in, scowl at my copy and mutter, "All the Juilliard graduates in town will love this." Nevertheless, the Maple Street angle was a spiritual exercise in humility, and I did my best to find it week after week.

When I first learned that the orchestra was scheduled to play Paul

Hindemith's *Harmony of the World* symphony, I didn't think of Hindemith, but of Maple Street, that mythically harmonious place where I
actually grew up.

III

Working on the paper left me some time for other activities. Unfortunately, there was nothing I knew how to do except play the piano and
write reviews.

Certain musicians are very practical. Trumpet players (who love
valves) tend to be good mechanics, and I have met a few composers who
fly airplanes and can restore automobiles. Most performing violinists and
pianists, however, are drained by the demands of their instruments and
seldom learn how to do anything besides play. In daily life they are
helpless and stricken. In midlife the smart ones force themselves to
find hobbies. But the less fortunate come home to solitary apartments
without pictures or other decorations, warm up their dinners in silence,
read whatever books happen to be on the dinner table, and then go go
bed.

I am speaking of myself here, of course. As time passed, and the
vacuum of my life made it harder to breathe, I required more work. I
fancied I was a tree, putting out additional leaves. I let it be known that
I would play as an accompanist for voice students and other recitalists,
if their schedules didn't interfere with my commitments for the paper.

One day I received a call at my desk. A quietly controlled female
voice asked, "Is this Peter Jenkins?"

"Yes."

"Well," she said, pausing, as if she'd forgotten what she meant to
tell me, "this is Karen Jensen. That's almost like Jenkins, isn't it?" I
waited. "I'm a singer," she said, after a moment. "A soprano. I've just
lost my accompanist and I'm planning on giving a recital in three
months. They said you were available. Are you? What do you charge?"

I told her.

"Isn't that kind of steep? That's kind of steep. Well, I suppose . . . I
can use somebody else until just before, and then I can use you. They say
you're good. And I've read your reviews. I really admire the way you write!"

"Thank you."

"You get so much information into your reviews! Sometimes, when
I read you, I imagine what you look like. Sometimes a person can make

a mental picture. I just wish the paper would publish a photo or something of you."

"They want to," I said, "but I asked them to please don't."

"Even your voice sounds like your writing!" she said excitedly. "I
can see you in front of me now. Can you play Fauré and Schubert? I
mean, is there any composer or style you don't like and won't play?"

"No," I said. "I play anything."

"That's *wonderful!*" she said, as if I had confessed to a remarkable
tolerance. "Some accompanists are so picky. 'I won't do this, I won't
do that.' Well, *one* I know is like that. Anyhow, could we meet soon?
Do you sightread? Can we meet at the music school downtown? In a
practice room? When are you free?"

I set up an appointment.

She was almost beautiful. Her deep eyes were accented by depressive
bowls in quarter-moon shadow under them. Though she was only in
her late twenties, she seemed slightly scorched by anxiety. She couldn't
keep still. Her hands fluttered as they fixed her hair; she scratched nervously at her cheeks; and her eyes jumped every few seconds. Soon,
however, she calmed down and began to look me in the eye, evaluating
me. Then *I* turned away.

She wanted to test me out and had brought along her recital numbers, mostly standard fare: a Handel aria, Mozart, Schubert, and Fauré.
The last set of songs, *Nine Epitaphs,* by an American composer I had
never heard of, Theodore Chanler, was the only novelty.

"Who is this Chanler?" I asked, looking through the sheet music.

"I . . . I found it in the music library," she said. "I looked him up.
He was born in Boston and died in 1961. There's a recording by Phyllis
Curtin. Virgil Thomson says these are maybe the best American art
songs ever written."

"Oh."

"They're kind of, you know, lugubrious. I mean they're all epitaphs
written supposedly on tombstones, set to music. They're like portraits.
I love them. Is it all right? Do you mind?"

"No, I don't mind."

We started through her program, beginning with Handel's "Un
sospiretto d'un labbro pallido" from *Il Pastor fido.* I could immediately
see why she was still in central New York state and why she would
always be a student. She had a fine voice, clear and distinct, somewhat

styled after Victoria de los Angeles (I thought), and her articulation was superb. If these achievements had been the whole story, she might have been a professional. But her pitch wobbled on sustained notes in a maddening way; the effect was not comic and would probably have gone unnoticed by most non-musicians, but to me the result was harrowing. She could sing perfectly for several measures and then she would miss a note by a semitone, which drove an invisible fingernail into my scalp. It was as though a gypsy's curse descended every five or six seconds, throwing her off pitch; then she was allowed to be a great singer until the curse descended again. Her loss of pitch was so regularized that I could see it coming and squirmed in anticipation. I felt as though I were in the presence of one of God's more complicated pranks.

Her choice of songs highlighted her failings. Their delicate textures were constantly broken by her lapses. When we arrived at the Chanler pieces, I thought I was accustomed to her, but I found I wasn't. The first song begins with the following verse, written by Walter de la Mare, who had crafted all the poems in archaic epitaph style:

> Here lyeth our infant, Alice Rodd;
>   She were so small,
>   Scarce aught at all,
> But a mere breath of Sweetness sent from God.

The vocal line for "She were so small" consists of four notes, the last two rising a half-step from the two before them. To work, the passage requires a dead-eye accuracy of pitch:

Singing this line, Karen Jensen hit the D-sharp but missed the E and skidded up uncontrollably to F-sharp, which would sound all right to anyone who didn't have the music in front of his nose, as I did. Only a fellow-musician could be offended.

Infuriated, I began to feel that I could *not* participate in a recital with this woman. It would be humiliating to perform such lovely songs in this excruciating manner. I stopped playing, turned to her to tell her that I could not continue after all, and then I saw her bracelet.

I am not, on the whole, especially observant, a failing that probably accounts for my having missed the bracelet when we first met. But I saw it now: five silver canaries dangled down quietly from it, and as it slipped back and forth, I saw her wrist and what I suddenly realized *would* be there: the parallel lines of her madness, etched in scar tissue.

The epitaphs finished, she asked me to work with her, and I agreed. When we shook hands, the canaries shook in tiny vibrations, as if pleased with my dutiful kindness, my charity, toward their mad mistress.

IV

Though Paul Hindemith's reputation once equalled Stravinsky's and Bartok's, it suffered after his death in 1963 an almost complete collapse. Only two of his orchestral works, the *Symphonic Metamorphoses on Themes of Weber* and the *Mathis der Maler* symphony, are played with any frequency, thanks in part to their use of borrowed tunes. One hears his woodwind quintets and choral pieces now and again, but the works of which he was most proud—the ballet *Nobilissima Visione, Das Marien-leben* (a song cycle), and the opera *Harmonie die Welt*—have fallen into total obscurity.

The reason for Hindemith's sudden loss of reputation was a mystery to me; I had always considered his craftsmanship if not his inspiration to be first-rate. When I saw that the *Harmony of the World* symphony, almost never played, would be performed in our anonymous city, I told Cascadilla that I wanted to write a story for that week on how fame was gained and lost in the world of music. He thought that subject might be racy enough to interest the tone-deaf citizens of leafy and peaceful Maple Street, where no one is famous, if I made sure the story contained "the human element."

I read up on Hindemith, played his piano music, and listened to the recordings. I slowly found the music to be technically astute but emo-tionally arid, as if some problem of purely local interest kept the com-poser's gaze safely below the horizon. Technocratic and oddly timid, his work reminded me of a model train chugging through a tiny town where only models of people actually lived. In fact, Hindemith did have a lifelong obsession with train sets: in Berlin, his took up three rooms, and the composer wrote elaborate timetables so that the toys wouldn't collide.

But if Hindemith had a technocrat's intelligence, he also believed in the necessity of universal participation in musical activities. Listening was not enough. Even nonmusical citizens could learn to sing and play, and he wrote music expressly for this purpose. He seems to have known that passive, drugged listening was a side-effect of totalitarian environments and that elitist composers such as Schoenberg were engaged in antisocial Faustian projects that would bewilder and infuriate most audiences, leaving them isolated and thus eager to be drugged by a musical superman.

As the foremost anti-Nietzschean German composer of his day, therefore, Hindemith left Germany when his works could not be performed, thanks to the Third Reich; wrote textbooks with simple exercises; composed a requiem in memory of Franklin Roosevelt, set to words by Walt Whitman; and taught students, not all of them talented, in Ankara, New Haven, and Buffalo ("this caricature of a town"). As he passed through late middle age, he turned to a project he had contemplated all his life, an opera based on the career of the German astronomer Johannes Kepler, author of *De Harmonice Mundi*. This opera, a summary of Hindemith's ideas, would be called *Harmony of the World*. Hindemith worked out the themes first in a symphony, which bore the same title as the opera, and completed it in 1951. The more I thought about this project, the more it seemed anachronistic. Who believed in world harmony in 1951? Or thereafter? Such a symphony would have to pass beyond technical sophistication into divine inspiration, which Hindemith had never shown any evidence of possessing.

It occurred to me that Hindemith's lifelong sanity had perhaps given way in this case, toppled not by despair (as is conventional) but by faith in harmony.

V

For the next rehearsal, I drove to Karen Jensen's apartment, where there was, she said, a piano. I'd become curious about the styles of her insanity: I imagined a hamster cage in the kitchen, a doll-head mobile in the living room, and mottos written with different colored inks on memo pads tacked up everywhere on the walls.

She greeted me at the door without her bracelet. When I looked at her wrist, she said, "Hmmm. I see that you noticed. A memento of adolescent despair." She sighed. "But it does frighten people off. Once you've tried to do something like that, people don't really trust you. I don't know why exactly. Don't want your blood on their hands or something. Well, come on in."

I was struck first by her forthrightness and secondly by her tiny apartment. Its style was much like the style in my house. She owned an attractive but worn-down sofa, a sideboard that supported an antique clock, one chair, a glass-top dinner table, and one nondescript poster on the wall. Trying to keep my advantage, I looked hard for tell-tale signs of insanity but found none. The piano was off in the corner, almost hidden, unlike those in the parlors back home.

"Very nice," I said.

"Well, thanks," she said. "It's not much. I'd like something bigger, but . . . where I work, I'm an administrative assistant, and they don't pay me very much. So that's why I live like a snail here. It's hardly big enough to move around in, right?" She wasn't looking at me. "I mean, I could almost pick it up and carry it away."

I nodded. "You just don't think like a rich person," I said, trying to be hearty. "They like to expand. They need room. Big houses, big cars, fat bodies."

"Oh, I know!" she said, laughing. "My uncle . . . would *you* like to stay for dinner? You look like you need a good meal. I mean, after the rehearsal. You're just skin and bones, Pet—. . . may I call you Peter?"

"Sure." I sat down on the sofa and tried to think up an excuse. "I really can't stay, Miss Jensen. I have another rehearsal to go to later tonight. I wish I could."

"That's not it, is it?" she asked suddenly, looking down at me. "I don't believe you. I bet it's something else. I bet you're afraid of me."

"Why should I be afraid of you?"

She smiled and shrugged. "That's all right. You don't have to say anything. I know how it goes." She laughed once more, faintly. "I never found a man who could handle it. They want to show you *their* scars, you know? They don't want to see any on you, and if they discover any, they just run." She slapped her right hand into her forehead and then ran her fingers through her hair. "Well, shit. I didn't mean to do this *at all!* I mean, I admire you so much and everything, and here I am, running on like this. I guess we should get down to business, right? Since I'm paying you by the hour."

I smiled professionally and went to her piano.

Beneath the high culture atmosphere that surrounds them, art songs have one subject: love. The permutations of love (lust, solitude, and loss) are present in abundance, of course, but for the most part they are simple vehicles for the expression of that one emotion. I was reminded of this as I played through the piano parts. As much as I concentrated on the music in front of me, I couldn't help but notice that my employer stood next to the piano, singing the words sometimes toward me, sometimes away. She was rather courageously forcing eye-contact on me. She kept this up for an hour and a half until we came to the Chanler settings, when at last she turned slightly, singing to the walls.

As before, her voice broke out of control every five seconds, giving isolated words all the wrong shadings. The only way to endure it, I discovered, was to think of her singing as a postmodern phenomenon with its own conventions and rules. As the victim of necessity rather than accident, Karen Jensen was tolerable.

> Here sleep I,
> Susannah Fry,
> No one near me,
> No one nigh:
> Alone, alone
> Under my stone,
> Dreaming on,
> Still dreaming on:
> Grass for my valance
> And coverlid,
> Dreaming on
> As I always did.
> 'Weak in the head?'
> Maybe. Who knows?
> Susannah Fry
> Under the rose.

There she was, facing away from me, burying Susannah Frey, and probably her own past and career into the bargain.

When we were done, she asked, "Sure you won't stay?"

"No, I don't think so."

"You really haven't another engagement, do you?"

"No," I admitted.

"I didn't think so. You were scared of me the moment you walked in the door. You thought I'd be crazy." She waited. "After all, only ugly girls live alone, right? And I'm not ugly."

"No, you aren't," I said. "You're quite attractive."

"Do you think so?" she asked, brightening. "It's so nice to hear that from you, even if you're just paying a compliment. I mean, it still means *something*." Then she surprised me. As I stood in the doorway, she got down on her knees in front of me and bowed her head in the style of one of her songs. "Please stay," she asked. Immediately she stood and laughed. "But don't feel obliged to."

"Oh, no," I said, returning to her living room, "I've just changed my mind. Dinner sounds like a good idea."

After she had served and we had started to eat, she looked up at me and said, "You know, I'm not completely good." She paused. "At singing."

"What?" I stopped chewing. "Yes, you are. You're all right."

"Don't lie. I know I'm not. You know I'm not. Come on: let's at least be honest. I think I have certain qualities of musicality, but my pitch is . . . you know. Uneven. You probably think it's awfully vain of me to put on these recitals. With nobody but friends and family coming."

"No, I don't."

"Well, I don't care what you say. It's . . . hmm, I don't know. People encourage me. And it's a discipline. Music's finally a discipline that rewards you. Privately, though. Well, that's what my mother says."

Carefully, I said, "She may be right."

"Who cares if she is?" she laughed, her mouth full of food. "I enjoy doing it. Like I enjoy doing this. Listen, I don't want to seem forward or anything, but are you married?"

"No."

"I didn't think so." She picked up a string bean and eyed it suspiciously. "Why aren't you? You're not ugly. In fact you're all right looking. You obviously haven't been crazy. Are you gay or something?"

"No."

"No," she agreed, "you don't look gay. You don't even look very happy. You don't look very anything. Why is that?"

"I should be offended by this line of questioning."

"But you're not. You know why? Because I'm interested in you. I hardly know you, but I like you, what I can see. Don't you have any trust?"

"Yes," I said, finally.

"So answer my question. Why don't you look very anything?"

"Do you want to hear what my piano teacher once said?" I asked. "He said I wasn't enough of a fanatic. He said that to be one of the great ones you have to be a tiny bit crazy. Touched. And he said I wasn't. And when he said it, I knew all along he was right. I was waiting for someone to say what I already knew, and he was the one. I was too much a good citizen, he said. I wasn't possessed."

She rose, walked around the table to where I was sitting, and stood in front of me, looking down at my face. I knew that whatever she was going to do had been picked up, in attitude, from one of her songs. She touched the back of my arm with two fingers on her right hand. "Well," she said, "maybe you aren't possessed, but what would you think of me as another possession?"

VI

In 1618 at the age of seventy, Katherine Kepler, the mother of Johannes Kepler, was put on trial for witchcraft. The records indicate that her personality was so deranged, so deeply offensive to all, that if she were alive today she would *still* be called a witch. One of Kepler's biographers, Angus Armitage, notes that she was "evil-tempered" and possessed an interest in unnamed "outlandish things." Her trial lasted, on and off, for three years; by 1621, when she was acquitted, her personality had disintegrated completely. She died the following year.

At the age of six, Kepler's son Frederick died of smallpox. A few months later, Kepler's wife, Barbara, died of typhus. Two other children, Henry and Susanna, had died in infancy.

Like many another of his age, Kepler spent much of his adult life cultivating favor from the nobility. He was habitually penniless and was often reduced, as his correspondence shows, to begging for handouts. He was the victim of religious persecution, though luckier in this regard than some.

After he married for a second time, three more children died in infancy, a statistic that in theory carries less emotional weight than one might think, given the accepted levels of infant mortality for that era.

In 1619, despite the facts cited above, Kepler published *De Har-*

monice Mundi, a text in which he set out to establish the correspondence between the laws of harmony and the disposition of planets in motion. In brief, Kepler argued that certain intervals, such as the octave, major and minor sixths, and major and minor thirds, were pleasurable, while other intervals were not. History indicated that mankind had always regarded certain intervals as unpleasant. Feeling that this set of universal tastes pointed to immutable laws, Kepler sought to map out the pleasurable intervals geometrically, and then to transfer that geometrical pattern to the order of the planets. The velocity of the planets, rather than their strict placement, constituted the harmony of the spheres. This velocity provided each planet with a note, what Armitage calls a "term in a mathematically determined relation."

> In fact, each planet performed a short musical scale, set down by Kepler in staff notation. The length of the scale depended upon the eccentricity of the orbit; and its limiting notes could generally be shown to form a concord (except for Venus and the Earth with their nearly circular orbits, whose scales were of very constricted range). . . . at the Creation . . . complete concord prevailed and the morning stars sang together.

VII

We began to eat dinner together. Accustomed to solitude, we did not always engage in conversation. I would read the newspaper or ink in letters on my geometrically patterned crossword puzzles at my end of the table, while Karen would read detective novels or *Time* at hers. If she had cooked, I would clear and wash the dishes; if I had cooked, she did the cleaning. Experience and disappointments had made us methodical. She told me that she had once despised structured experiences governed by timetables, but that after several manic-depressive episodes, she had learned to love regularity. This regularity included taking lithium at the same time—to the minute—each day.

The season being summer, we would pack towels and swimming suits after dinner and drive out to one of several public beaches, where we would swim until darkness came on. On calm evenings, Karen would drop her finger in the water and watch the waves lap outward. I favored immature splashing, or grabbing her by the arm and whirling her around me until I released her and she would spin back and fall into the water, laughing as she sank. One evening, we found a private beach, two hundred feet of sand all to ourselves, on a lake thirty miles out of town. Framed on both sides by woods and well-hidden from the highway, this beach had the additional advantage of being unpatrolled. We had no bathhouse in which to change, however, so Karen instructed me not to look as she walked about fifty feet away to a spot where she undressed and put on her suit.

Though we had been intimate for at least a week, I had still not seen her naked: like a good Victorian, she demanded the shades be drawn, the lights out, and the covers pulled discreetly over us. But now, with the same methodical thoroughness, she wanted me to see her, so I looked, despite her warnings. She was bent over, under the tree boughs, the evening light breaking through the leaves and casting broken gold bands on her body. Her arms were delicate, the arms of a schoolgirl, I thought, an impression heightened by the paleness of her skin, but her breasts were full, at first making me think of Rubens's women, then of Renoir's, then of nothing at all. Slowly, knowing I was watching her, she pinned her hair up. Not her breasts or arms, but that expression of vague contentment as she looked out toward the water away from me: *that* made me feel a tingling below my heart, somewhere in an emotional center near my stomach. I wanted to pick her up and carry her somewhere, but with my knees wobbly it was all I could do to make my way over to where she stood and take her in my arms before she cried out. "Jesus," she said, shivering, "you gave me a surprise." I kissed her, waiting for inspiration to direct me on what to do next: pick her up? Carry her? Make love to her on the sand? Wade into the water with her and swim out to the center of the bay, where we would drown together in a Lawrentian love-grip? But then we broke the kiss; she put on her swimsuit like a good citizen, and we swam for our usual fifteen minutes in silence. Afterwards, we changed back into our clothes and drove home, muttering small talk. Behavior inspired by and demonstrating love embarassed both of us. When I told her that she was beautiful and that I loved her, she patted me on the cheek and said, "Aw, how nice. You always try to say the right thing."

VIII

The Maple Street angle for *Harmony of the World* ran as follows: SYMPHONY OF FAITH IN A FAITHLESS AGE. Hindemith, I said, wished to confound the skeptics by composing a monument of faith. In an age of organized disharmony, of political chaos, he stood at the barricades defending tonality and traditional musical form. I carefully avoided any specific discussion of the musical materials of the symphony, which in the Schott orchestral score looked over-complex and melodically ugly. From what I could tell without hearing the piece, Hindemith had employed stunning technique in order to disguise his lack of inspiration, though I did not say so in print. Instead, I wrote that the symphony's failure to win public support was probably the result of Hindemith's refusal to use musical gimmicks on the one hand and sticky sweet melodies on the other. I wrote that he had not been dismayed by the bad reviews *Harmony of the World* had received, which was untrue. I said he was a man of integrity. I did not say that men of integrity are often unable to express joy when the occasion demands. Cascadilla liked my article. "This guy sounds like me," he said, reading my copy. "I respect him." The article ran five days before the concert and was two pages away from the religion-and-faith section. Not long after, the symphony ticket office called me to say that my piece had caused a rush of ticket orders from ordinary folk, nonconcert types, who wanted to hear this "religious symphony." The woman from the business office thanked me for my trouble. "Let's hope they like it," I said.

"Of course they will," she assured me. "You've told them to."

But they didn't. Despite all the oratory in the symphony, it was spiritually as dead as a lampshade. I could see why Hindemith had been shocked by the public reaction. Our audience applauded politely in discouragement, and then I heard an unusual sound for this anonymous city: one man, full of fun and conviction, booing loudly from the balcony. Booing the harmony of the world! He must be a Satanist! Don't intentions mean anything? So what if the harmony and joy were all counterfeit? The conductor came out for a bow, smiled at the booing man, and very soon the applause died away. I left the hall, feeling responsible. Arriving at the paper, I wrote a review of crushing dullness that reeked of bad faith. Goddamn Hindemith! Here he was, claiming to have seen God's workings, and they sounded like the workings of a steam engine or a trolley car. A fake symphony, with optimism the composer did not feel! I decided (but did not write) that *Harmony of the World* was just possibly the largest, most misconceived fiasco in modern music's history. It was a symphony that historically could not be written by a man who was constitutionally not equipped to write it. In my review, I kept a civil pen: I said that the performance lacked "luster," "a certain necessary glow."

IX

"I'm worried about the recital tomorrow."

"Aw, don't worry. Here, kiss me. Right here."

"Aren't you listening? I'm worried."

"I'm singing. You're just accompanying me. Nobody's going to notice you. Move over a little, would you? Yeah, there. That pillow was forcing my head against the wall."

"Why aren't you worried?"

"Why should I be worried? I don't want to worry. I want to make love. Isn't that better than worrying?"

"Not if I'm worried."

"People won't notice *you*. By the way, have you noticed that when I kiss you on the stomach, you get goosebumps?"

"Yes. I think you're taking this pretty lightly. I mean, it's almost unprofessional."

"That's because I'm an amateur. A 100% amateur. Always and totally. Even at this. But that doesn't mean I don't have my moments. Mmmmmm. That's better."

"I thought it would maybe help. But listen. I'm still worried."

"Uhhhn. Oh, wait a minute. Wait a minute. Oh, I get it."

"What?"

"I get it. You aren't worried about yourself. You're worried about me."

X

Forty people attended her recital, which was sponsored by the city university's music school, in which Karen was a sometime student. Somehow we made our way through the program, but when we came to the Chanler settings, I suddenly wanted Karen to sing them perfectly. I wanted an angel to descend and to take away the gypsy's curse. But she sang as she always had—off pitch—and when she came to "Ann Poverty," I found myself in that odd region between rage and pity.

Stranger, here lies
Ann Poverty;

Such was her name
   And such was she.
May Jesu pity
   Poverty.

But I was losing my capacity for pity.

In the green room, her forty friends came back to congratulate her.
I met them. They were all very nice. She smiled and laughed: there
would be a party in an hour. Would I go? I declined. When we were
alone, I said I was going back to my place.

"Why?" she asked. "Shouldn't you come to my party? You're my
lover after all. That *is* the word."

"Yes. But I don't want to go with you."

"Why?"

"Because of tonight's concert, that's why."

"What about it?"

"It wasn't very good, was it? I mean, it just wasn't."

"I thought it was all right. A few slips. It was pretty much what I
was capable of. All those people said they liked it."

"Those people don't matter!" I said, my eyes watering with anger.
"Only the music matters. Only the music is betrayed, they aren't. They
don't know about pitch, most of them, I mean, Jesus, they aren't genuine musicians, so how would they know? Do you really think what we
did tonight was good? It wasn't! It was a travesty! We ruined those
songs! How can you stand to do that?"

"I don't ruin them. I sing them adequately. I project feeling. People
get pleasure from them. That's enough."

"It's awful," I said, feeling the ecstatic lift-off into rage. "You're so
close to being good, but you *aren't* good. Who cares what those ignora-
muses think? They don't know what notes you're *supposed* to hit. It's
that goddamn slippery pitch of yours. You're killing those songs. You
just *drop* them like watermelons on the stage! It makes me sick! I couldn't
have gone on for another day listening to you and your warbling! I'd die
first."

She looked at me and nodded, her mouth set in a half-moue, half-
smile of non-surprise. There may have been tears in her eyes, but I didn't
see them. She looked at me as if she were listening hard to a long-
distance call. "You're tired of me," she said.

"I'm not tired of you. I'm tired of hearing you sing! Your voice makes my flesh crawl! Do you know why? Can you tell me why you make me sick? Why do you make me sick? Never mind. I'm just glad this is over."

"You don't look glad. You look angry."

"And you look smug. Listen, why don't you go off to your party? Maybe there'll be a talent scout there. Or roses flung riotously at you. But don't give a recital like this again, please, okay? It's a public disgrace. It offends music. It offends *me*."

I turned my back on her and walked out to my car.

XI

After the failure of *Harmony of the World,* Hindemith went on a strenuous tour that included Scandinavia. In Oslo, he was rehearsing the Philharmonic when he blinked his bright blue eyes twice, turned to the concertmaster, and said, "I don't know where I am." They took him away to a hospital; he had suffered a nervous breakdown.

XII

I slept until noon, having nothing to do at the paper and no reason to get up. At last, unable to sleep longer, I rose and walked to the kitchen to make coffee. I then took my cup to the picture window and looked down the hill to the trees of the conservation area, the view Stecker had once told me I should have.

The figure of a woman was hanging from one of the trees, a noose around her neck. I dropped my coffee cup and the hot coffee spilled out over my feet.

I ran out the back door in my pajamas and sprinted painfully down the hill's tall grass toward the tree. I was fifty feet away when I saw that it wasn't Karen, wasn't in fact a woman at all, but an effigy of sorts, with one of Karen's hats, a pillow head, and a dress hanging over a broomstick skeleton. Attached to the effigy was a note:

In the old days, this might have been me. Not anymore. Still, I thought it'd make you think. And I'm not giving up singing, either. By the way, what your playing lacks is not fanaticism, but concentration. You can't seem to keep your mind on one thing for more than a minute at a time. *I* notice things, too. You aren't the only reviewer around here. Take good care of this doll, okay?

XXXXX,
Karen

I took the doll up and dropped it in the clothes closet, where it has remained to this hour.

Hindemith's biographer, Geoffrey Skelton, writes, "[On the stage] the episodic scenes from Kepler's life fail to achieve immediate dramatic coherence, and the basic theme remains obscure. . . . "

She won't of course see me again. She won't talk to me on the phone, and she doesn't answer my letters. I am quite lucidly aware of what I have done. And I go on seeing doubles and reflections and wave motion everywhere. There is symmetry, harmony, after all. I suppose I should have been nice to her. That, too, is a discipline. I always tried to be nice to everyone else.

On his deathbed, Hindemith has Kepler sing:

Und muss sehn am End:
 Die grosse Harmonie, das is der Tod.
 Absterben ist, sie zu bewirken, not.
 Im Leben hat sie keine Statte.

Now, at the end, I see it:
the great harmony: it is death.
To find it, we must die.
In life it has no place.

XIII

Hindemith's words may be correct. But Dante says that the residents of limbo, having never been baptised, will not see the face of God. This despite their having committed no sin, no active fault. In their fated locale, they sigh, which keeps the air "forever trembling." No harmony for them, these guiltless souls. Through eternity, the residents of limbo—where one can imagine oneself if one cannot stand to imagine any part of hell—experience one of the most shocking of all the emotions that Dante names: "duol senza martíri," grief without torment. These sighs are rather like the sounds one hears drifting from front porches in small towns on soft summer nights.

The Woman Who Knew Judo

Mary Gaitskill

I met Jean Taylor when I was five years old. She was the tallest woman I had ever seen, and she walked slowly, with her head up and her shoulders back, her hips moving like the hips of a slender cat. She wore black slacks and she had big feet which seemed to me very graceful, especially when she wore her straw sandals with the artificial cherries on them.

She started coming to our house to take my mother to the "Y" where she taught my mother how to swim. When they returned from the lesson, their hair wet and sleek against their heads, they'd hang their swim suits on the backs of kitchen chairs to dry in front of the stove while they sat with their feet up and talked. I used to sit in the kitchen and draw when Jean visited my mother. I loved to show my completed drawings to Jean. She made me feel as if I'd discovered an elemental truth, or shown her something vital. Once, when I handed her a picture I'd done of a yellow lion with spindly legs and huge round eyes, she looked at it with consideration and said, "You know, it doesn't look like a real lion. But I think you've caught the spirit of a lion here, and that's a lot more important. This lion has lion-ness."

My father liked Jean too. When he heard her come in, he would hurry to the living room to greet her. He looked at her warmly, especially when she walked, and he teased her about "that little black bathing suit" of hers. He called her "good old Jean" and he always wanted her to sit down and have a beer and listen to his opera records. Jean would sit and listen in his black leather chair, her auburn hair piled into a loose twist on her head, her slender face resting on her long hand, her cat-eye glasses tilted to one side. I thought she looked like she knew everything. I thought she was beautiful.

I was nine when we began visiting the Taylors regularly. My brother David and I became friends with Jean's daughter, Julie, a tiny, nervous child two years younger than I, and we often went to the Taylors' house to play with her. Jean's husband, Tom, was a scientist, so the house was full of exotic creatures and things. There was a stuffed wildcat with green glass eyes crouching and snarling from the top of a bookcase, jars with rocks and fungus in them, flat dishes with invisible animals growing in them, and microscopes sitting in the window sills. There was a human skull on the desk in the guest room where I would sleep with Julie when I spent the night. We could see the skull from where we lay in bed even when the lights were out. It could've been scary to sleep in a room with a skull in it, but at the Taylors' house, the skull was as benign as Frankenstein on TV in the afternoon, or dinosaur bones in a museum. I liked to touch it, and to think what it would be like if it came floating through the air one night chattering its teeth.

Mr. Taylor worked a lot, and he was very shy, so we didn't see him very often. Sometimes he brought home cages of hamsters or white rats with pink noses and put them in the basement. I had the feeling he tortured them in the name of science, and I knew some of them wound up as frozen bodies in the Taylors' freezer, so for awhile I didn't like him. But once, when I spent the night at the Taylors', I came downstairs early and saw Mr. Taylor eating breakfast in the dining room by himself. He was eating eggs and raisin toast, and he was letting the two house cats sit on the table and lick egg off his plate. I had never seen an adult let animals eat from his plate before. I stared, fascinated. He looked at me, smiled shyly and said, "Hello Freckles," even though I had no freckles. Then he stroked the cat. At the time I could not understand how a person could put one little animal in the freezer to be dissected, and then let another eat off his plate, but I couldn't help liking Mr. Taylor better.

In the summer, we visited the Taylors on the weekends. My mother and father would sit in the back yard in green and white lawn chairs drinking iced tea or beer, and Julie, David, and I would run around the yard acting out scenes from "Combat!" or "The Outer Limits." When we ate lunch there, Jean would bring out a small beige card-table for us to sit around, and put cheese sandwiches cut up into little squares on it, along with sliced carrots and celery and chocolate milk. When we sat there eating our sandwiches and carrots, I would listen to our parents' discussions with interest and satisfaction. They seemed to gather in the back yard to set right the wrong in life, and to make it all clear and understood, in its right place.

Jean would sit back in her chair in a relaxed attitude, her head cocked to one side, her loosely pinned-up hair falling on her shoulders and her long, thin legs folded like a griffin's wings. I remember her talking about her job. She was a counselor at a high school that was notorious for race riots and gang fights. When she'd first started, she'd had trouble getting accepted by the teachers and counselors, who didn't think she'd be able to handle the kids. Then, one day, a kid showed up in the office drunk and armed with a broken bottle. It was lunch hour and nobody was in the office but Jean and two secretaries.

"I'm telling you, it was the most frightening experience I ever had. All my impulses told me to run away, or to do anything that kid said to do. But I knew I had to stand my ground and not give in. When you're dealing with somebody like that, it's a lot like facing down an animal. You have to get a psychological edge."

"When I was in the army it was the same way," said my father approvingly. "Right from the start you had to stand up for yourself. If you didn't, there were bullies who'd just run you right over."

"That's right," said my mother. "I tell the kids the same thing. If anybody at school gives them a hard time, they've got to make it clear they won't put up with it."

They sat quietly in their lawn chairs, looking out into the yard, vigilant and inviolate. Then Jean would continue her story.

"I heard all this carrying on, and when I came out of my office, there was this lurching six-foot kid with a broken bottle demanding to see the principal. The secretaries were both standing up against the wall looking petrified. In fact, I guess maybe one of the reasons I was able to be so calm was that they were so panicked. I've noticed that seeing other people get scared tends to bring out the leader in you, or something. Whatever it was, I just ignored the fact that my knees were going like silly putty and I went up to him like I was going to have a conversation with him—"

"That probably surprised him," said my mother. "He probably expected you to collapse against the wall."

"I think that's right, and I think that's what saved me. My walking up to him like that unnerved him because he wasn't expecting it. Not only was I not afraid of him, I was acting like I expected him to be decent. That's something I learned a long time ago. If you act like you expect somebody to be decent, then nine times out of ten, he will. If you act like you expect somebody to be a bastard, that's just what he'll do. You really do have a lot of control."

"Well, if you've got some sonofabitch who wants to shoot you and take your money, it doesn't matter what you expect," said my father. "He's gonna do whatever he damn well pleases."

"Well, yeah." Jean held her long hand out in the air. "You can only exert your will to a point in a situation where somebody bigger and stronger is threatening you. If somebody's determined to hurt you, then he can. I'm just saying you do have some power in how you choose to react."

"That's true," agreed my father, nodding. "There's a lot of subtle factors involved."

"So anyway, I said to this kid, well, if you want to see the principal, you can come in and wait for him and act like a human being. He's out with everybody else for a conference at Jefferson and I'm not going to call him and tell him you want to speak to him immediately, no matter how many times you shake that thing at me. Then I turned my back to him and walked to the nearest chair and sat down."

"Boy, that was taking a risk," said my mother.

"I didn't even think about how dangerous it was at the time, or I wouldn't have been able to do it. Now that I think back on it, he probably didn't want to hit me to begin with. Besides, I think I really put him off the track by responding so calmly."

"And even if he'd tried anything, you could've thrown him. Right?" My father said this because Jean had been taking judo classes two times a week at the "Y." Whenever he said anything to her about it, he'd raise his eyebrows and tilt his head back speculatively, as if he didn't really believe that judo could help Jean throw large, drunken boys around, but that he wasn't sure.

But Jean said, "Right," and went on to tell about how she succeeded in rendering the boy civil and embarrassed by the time the principal arrived.

On Saturdays, Jean and my mother would go to the A&P in Jean's station wagon, sometimes with the three of us in the back seat. Jean's legs were long and tanned in her bermuda shorts, and she was regal behind her shopping cart. She always lingered in the fruit and vegetable area, and she bought a lot of round yellow grapefruit. Sometimes she bought a pineapple or mangoes, things my mother never got. She chose the fruit carefully and deliberately, and her long earrings would dangle wonderfully as she leaned forward to examine the avocados and cantaloupes. When she wore her yellow shorts and straw sandals, she looked as if she might gather the fruit up in a big straw hat and wear it on her head like an island lady.

My mother became vivacious when they shopped, and she and Jean would talk about books, art exhibits, soap operas and gossip. Sometimes they would talk about our fathers, particularly if they thought we weren't listening. They had a long talk about the time my father yelled at my mother because she wanted to watch Mitch Miller on TV instead of listening to his new opera record.

"Well, that's marriage for you," said Jean. "They want you to bring them their tea in bed and then sit there and admire them while they drink it. Then they want you to listen to them while they talk about it. Didn't you know that?"

"Well, no, I didn't. But I'm learning fast."

"Don't you learn, make sure he unlearns. Get it straight now. If he wants to listen to opera, fine. You want to listen to Mitch Miller, however awful Mitch Miler may be."

"That's right dammit. I have the right to be an uncultured slob in my own home. I'll sing along with Mitch if I want to!"

She and Jean laughed and a lady with puffy blond hair and round pink earrings stared at them.

"Tom and I started out on the right foot partially because I always had my own job," continued Jean as they pushed their carts down the aisle. "He always understood that I wanted to have my own life as well as sharing his. He always understood it was my house as well as his. When I told him I did not want a tarantula in a cage in the basement, there was no tarantula in the basement."

They walked along silently for a time, staring thoughtfully at the packaged food on either side of them. Then Jean said, apparently out of nowhere, "You know, you're going to think this is terrible, but I think any woman who lets her husband beat her deserves it. It sounds harsh, but I really think you have to take responsibility for your own life."

"Well, it is harsh, but I think you're basically right," said my mother. "I think women who put up with that kind of crap must like it in some way."

"That's right," said Jean, nodding her head. "They've got to be getting something out of it, or they wouldn't remain in that position. The thing is, what are they getting?" They moved down the aisle, meditative and quiet.

I was discomfited by that exchange, partially because I sensed that Jean and my mother weren't comfortable about it either. It had come up so suddenly, as if it were connected in their minds with the conversation that had gone on before. Their hard words, which were uncharacteristic of both of them, seemed to mask some great uneasiness, but I wasn't sure what it was.

Shortly after I overheard this conversation, I was beaten up by a boy in the fifth grade, a grade higher than me. Jimmy Race had followed me home from school one day yelling that he'd beaten my brother David in field hockey and that I had a nose like a pig. David wasn't there because he was a safety boy and had to stay after school. After about two blocks of this, I threw my books down and told Jimmy Race to shut up or I'd flatten him. He pulled my hair and yelled, "oink nose!" I scratched his face and kicked his shins like my mother told me to do if boys picked on me. He knocked me down and gave me a bloody nose.

The next day, David beat up Jimmy Race on the playground, but I was still too embarrassed to go to school for two days. My mother let me stay home and sulk because my nose looked awful. The second day I was home, Jean came to visit my mother during her lunch break. She understood why I didn't want to go to school, but she thought I should face down Jimmy Race.

"You did your best, so there's nothing to be ashamed of," she said. "Everybody loses sometimes, even tough people. It's part of being a person to lose and be embarrassed sometimes. The most important thing is not to quit. Be tough enough to go back and look that snotty kid in the eye." She put her arms around me. "Besides, you can learn to take care of yourself. Why don't you sign up for a judo class at the "Y"? They're starting them for kids in the summer, and I can teach you a few things before then."

I became obsessed with judo. When Jean taught me how to tuck my head in and roll forward on my shoulder and land on my feet, I practiced every day. I would practice anywhere. Sometimes I would be walking through the living room while everybody was watching TV, and I'd roll across the floor and land on my feet right in front of the screen.

"Has Jean Taylor taught you how to throw anybody yet, Sweet Pea?" asked my father one night at dinner.

"No," I said. "I'm just learning how to roll so that if anybody throws me, I can land and not hurt myself."

"Do you think you could learn how to throw me?" asked my father, pausing with his fork in the air.

"I dunno."

"Jean could probably throw you," said my mother. "She's been taking judo for a year."

"Well, Jean Taylor's a good woman," said my father. "She's smarter than hell. But if she tried to throw me, it would be a mistake. I haven't had four years in the army for nothing."

I thought Jean could throw my father very easily if she wanted to, but I didn't say anything. I remembered the time Jean once said, "Well, you just can't argue with that old male ego. When they get that way, you just have to rub them under their chins and let them think they're the greatest. Of course, you go on knowing you could do it just as good." I sat quiet and watched my father eat his dinner.

A few weeks later, we visited Jean and Julie for hot dogs and potato chips. Mr. Taylor was out of town for a convention, so Jean barbecued the hot dogs while my mother helped in the kitchen. My father sat in a lawn chair and talked to Jean as she stood over the grill in her bermuda shorts poking at the sweating dogs with a long metal prong. I don't remember what they were talking about, but what he said seemed to please Jean, and they were both smiling and laughing and looking at each other out of the corners of their eyes, as if what they were saying had some hidden meaning.

When my mother walked out of the house with a basket of potato chips and a tray of packaged cupcakes, Jean clapped her hands for us to gather round the little card-table. We all sat down and began picking the icing off the cupcakes. Our parents sat in their lawn chairs and held their hot dogs on paper plates on their laps. They began to talk about a Civil Rights march in the South which had been ambushed by the Ku Klux Klan. Three black people had been killed, including a sixteen-year-old girl.

"Well, those sons of bitches are sick, that's all there is to it," said my father. "When they find the one that shot that colored girl, I hope they hang him."

"They'll find him all right," said my mother. "You can't go around murdering women and kids and get away with it."

"But the thing is, those maniacs have been killing women and kids for years," said Jean. "Sometimes I wonder if the police are on their side. Doesn't it seem like they could've stopped them by now if they'd wanted to? Sometimes it seems like they just don't care."

"Aw, now, you can't say that," said my father. "Those Klanners are an isolated group of nuts. Nobody supports people who kill innocent kids."

"But whether people support them or not, they're getting away with it. I just can't tell you how much it upsets me to hear about things like this going on, with nobody doing anything to stop it. It makes me think Negroes should form groups to fight back if the law can't protect them."

My father looked annoyed. "That's a silly idea," he said. "That's vigilante justice. Suppose everybody decided to fight back every time they thought somebody'd done something wrong to them instead of going to the law? That's a nasty world you're making for yourself."

"I agree with you in general," answered Jean. "But what if you went to the law for protection and it didn't do a damn thing? You'd have no choice."

My father tightened his mouth with annoyance and looked away from Jean. Then he looked back at her, started to speak, changed his mind and looked away again. My parents and Jean chewed their hot dogs rapidly and quietly.

"Say Becky," said Jean. "How's judo coming? Are you practicing your rolls?"

"I can roll twelve times in a row in a circle around the yard," I said.

"That's impressive," said Jean. "Sounds like you're ready for the throws themselves."

"Yeah!" I said. "Any time."

"Why don't you show her something now?" said my mother. "So we can see some judo."

"How about it, champ?" said Jean.

"I'm ready any time you are," I said happily.

Jean stood before the circle of lawn chairs. I went to her, feeling shy and proud. My father was looking at me as if he was seeing a new and very surprising facet of my character, and wasn't sure what he thought of it.

Jean and I stood facing each other. She grabbed my wrist while telling me how to break her hold, turn my back to her and hoist her into the air. "Get your hip into me," she said as she loomed over me. "It's called 'the big hip.' You've got to use your hip." I planted my feet, thrust my hip into Jean's body, and tried to pull her onto my back. "No, that's not right," said Jean. "Turn your body and bend your knees. Squat." I panted. We were so close I could smell her faint scent of soap and perspiration. I was bent completely over and Jean was pulled half-way across my back, her breasts crushed against me, her feet barely on the ground. I shifted every which way, trying to figure out how to throw her on the ground before I collapsed, while she gave instructions. Suddenly, her weight seemed to shift and become lighter. "Now," she said. I yanked her arm, thrust my hip, and long, big Jean rolled forward over my body and onto the ground before me. I stood and stared at her, awed by what I'd done. Jean rolled elegantly to her feet and adjusted her glasses.

"Hey, there you go," said my father.

"That's some trick," said my mother.

"It's fake," said David. "You couldn't do that in a real fight. It took too long."

"That's because it was her first time," said my mother in an exasperated tone. "Don't rain on her parade."

"It's not that slow in a real situation," said Jean, tucking wisps of hair behind her ears. "Once you've been practicing for years, you get fast. An experienced person could do it to an attacker before he had time to figure out what was happening to him. It's a question of balance. If you get a person off balance, it doesn't matter how big he is."

"Why don't you show us?" said my father. "Why don't I pretend to be an attacker and you can throw me?"

Jean didn't say anything.

"Maybe you're afraid you can't do it to an old army man," said my father.

"Throw him, Jean," I said. "I want to see what it looks like."

"I can understand if you don't want to," said my father. "I'm not like those 'Y' people you're used to working with."

"Jean!" I looked at her imploringly.

Jean looked at me and then at my mother. "Okay, let's go," she said, shrugging lightly.

They stood in the same spot that Jean and I had stood. I came close and smiled, wanting Jean to throw my father. You could tell by looking at him that he didn't think she could.

"Now," he said, "this is how real people attack." He jumped forward, spun Jean around and grabbed her, holding her arms down tightly and pressing his body against her. Jean bent her knees and threw her hip out just the way she should. But my father didn't loosen his grip; he moved with her instead. Jean looked annoyed. She threw her hip to the other side. He moved with her. "What are you gonna do now?" he said panting a little.

Suddenly Jean squatted and swept one of her feet backward and then forward. She hooked my father's ankle and threw her body to one side. A startled look flashed across my father's face. He lost his balance, and he and Jean fell to the ground. He lost his hold on her in the fall, but when she started to get up, he grabbed her again. They rolled around, elbows and legs flying.

David and Julie got up and came closer. Julie looked scared.

My father rolled on top of Jean and tried to grab her. She got his head in the crook of her arm and violently thrust her pelvis into the air. My father's body rocked with her thrusting, but he held on.

"What are they doing?" asked David.

"He's hurting my mama," said Julie in a quiet, timorous voice.

"But she threw him," I said. "She's winning."

Julie's lip quivered.

I looked at my mother. Her face was flushed and she looked like she wanted to be somewhere else.

My father flipped Jean on her stomach and pinned her.

"See?" he panted, "See?" Jean struggled, but he held her. "Judo doesn't work with me," he panted.

Then he began to spank Jean. I had never seen an adult do something like that to another adult before. He spanked her very lightly, and it couldn't have hurt. But he was spanking her.

Jean's head was turned sideways, and she smiled at my mother as if to say that she was really in complete control of the game, and that my father was being very silly. My father continued to spank her.

Julie could stand it no longer. "He's spanking my mama!" she screamed. "He's spanking my mama!" She ran toward her mother, and began to cry in high-pitched squeals.

My father let go of Jean and sat up, staring at Julie with surprise and pity. "Oh no, little girl, we were only playing. I'm not hurting your mama, don't worry." He stood and put his hand on Julie's shoulder.

"That's right honey," said Jean, sitting up. "We were only playing."

Julie stared at Jean, her wide blue eyes full of tears, and her face pink. She did not believe her mother.

I stared at Jean and my father. My face was flushed too, and my heart was thumping dully. I turned away from the group and walked toward the house.

That evening, when my father came to my bedroom to say goodnight, as he always did, I didn't look at him. I felt curiously unable to tell him how angry and hurt I was about what he had done. I wanted to pretend that nothing was wrong, that I didn't care about what had gone on between him and Jean Taylor. In fact, I wanted to pretend that I didn't know what had happened. But I did know, and he knew it.

He came in and sat on my bed and said, "Well, are we ready to climb the Magic Mountain?"

I turned my head away from him and didn't answer.

He was quiet for a minute, and then he began to sing, "Up the Magic Mountain, one, two, three. Up the Magic Mountain, yessiree," in a low, soft voice, like he used to do when I was Julie's age.

I didn't sing with him.

He stopped singing after a few seconds and sat in silence. Then he said, "Well, we had a nice time at old Jean Taylor's, didn't we?"

I waited a minute before I finally whispered, "Yes."

He sat silently on my bed for a long time. I stared at the wall until I couldn't tell what it was any more.

Then he said, in a strange, low voice, "Do you know how much your old daddy loves his little girl?"

My father had never said anything like this to me before. It scared me. It made me feel that something serious and irreversible was happening right at that moment, and that there was nothing I could do about it. I almost turned and looked at him. I suddenly felt that I had to look at him or I would lose him forever. Then I thought about Jean Taylor, and how she had looked when he was spanking her.

My father reached down and put his hand on mine. A strange sensation darted through my stomach, and I jerked my hand away from him as if he'd bitten it.

I felt him stiffen. He only sat on my bed for a few seconds more. Then he left the room without a word.

I turned my head away from the wall. I lay on my back and stared into space while tears formed in my eyes and rolled down my face. I knew I wasn't going to sign up for that class at the "Y."

Mutilated Woman

Joyce Carol Oates

At the Hendon School for Girls in Princeton, New Jersey, many years
ago, one of the instructors, a young woman who taught French and
Spanish, told Constance Shea that she was one of those people who,
without desiring it, without evidently encouraging it, exact homage
from others throughout life. Such people, perversely, often doubt their
own self-worth. In fact they may secretly loathe themselves. They may
toy with the idea of suicide, or self-mutilation, almost in mockery of the
world's high estimation of them. But in general they tend to be strangely
unconscious of their effect upon others, the woman said, with an air of
subtle accusation.

"Why are you telling me these things?" Constance said. "I think
you're crazy—you're lying."

And she walked out of the woman's classroom, trembling with
rage.

But time passed. Decades passed. And Constance came gradually
to see—sometimes in anger, sometimes in bewilderment, sometimes
with an inchoate pride—that the woman's words were fairly accurate.
She never thought of suicide and certainly never of self-mutilation, but
it was true that people fell in love with her. It was Constance Shea's
misfortune that people, unbidden, fell in love with her.

The most recent was the young Lindenthal girl with the wild kinky
black hair and the hectic, melancholy manner—though Mira was not
that young, twenty-seven to Constance's fifty-two. She was a playwright whose first play had been successfully produced in a tiny theater
on Bleecker Street; she had acted in it herself, and though Constance had
not seen the play—she never went to experimental plays, on or off
Broadway—colleagues of hers whose judgment she respected informed
her that it was really quite good, surprisingly good; and that Mira had
acquitted herself well as an actress. But then that sort of play, highly
energetic and "iconoclastic," a sort of satirical blend of Brecht, Ionesco,

and Pinter, was difficult to assess. At any rate it had been warmly received by critics, and Mira had been written up last spring in the Sunday *Times* as one of the most promising of the younger woman dramatists. Constance remembered studying the young woman's photograph, touched by something raw and arrogant and hopeful in her strained smile, though of course she had not known Mira at the time. She had no idea of Mira, at the time.

Now it was October and Mira Lindenthal was visiting dramatist for one year at Elyria College, where Constance taught literature and a workshop in creative writing; and she went about the little college town of Fairfax, Maryland, speaking of Constance Shea in the most embarrassing terms. A beautiful woman, an extraordinary person, a writer of genius. The most remarkable person Mira had ever met, except possibly for Lillian Hellman, another of Mira's idols. (Lillian Hellman had helped Mira find a good director for her play, and had even given her some advice about revision.) Hidden away here in Fairfax, living almost in seclusion, a writer whose novels are obviously too exquisite and demanding for most of her students to appreciate—what a weird situation! But how fortunate for Elyria College! And for Mira most of all. "I consider it a great honor just to be on the same faculty as Constance Shea," Mira was reported to have said when the chairman of the Drama Department interviewed her. Her adulation must have been genuine, since she accepted the offer of a job, with noisy enthusiasm, before she was even told what her salary would be.

"Have you heard what Mira Lindenthal is saying about you?" Constance's colleagues inquired. "Evidently she worships you—did you know?"

"But I did nothing to encourage her," Constance said quickly.

A beautiful woman, a writer of genius. An extraordinary person.

All of which, Constance thought, might be true to some degree. (For though she was outwardly modest, and fairly shy in social situations, she never, in private, doubted her own high worth as a novelist.) But such histrionic claims, such exuberant bullying exclamations, were in very bad taste, and would have the effect—in Mira's mouth—of being merely embarrassing. "If only she were more restrained," Constance said with a wan smile. "If only she would leave me alone. . . ."

In recent years Constance had come to value quiet and privacy and near-anonymity. She supposed she was "famous" enough in the literary community though she had done nothing to pursue fame except write her novels, publishing only five during a thirty-year period; certainly she had the high esteem of her fellow writers, and was quite content with her position. A number of other colleges and universities had made her offers over the years, but she perferred to stay at Elyria, with its high tuition, its genteel pastoral tradition, and its fairly good students—all undergraduates, no graduate students, which was a relief; the president of the college respected her immensely, and the chairman of her department treated her with an urbane friendly caution she found distinctly gratifying. And then she was, in Fairfax, within an easy drive of Princeton and Hopewell and Pennington, where she had friends; and it was no problem to take the train to New York City for one of her infrequent visits with her publishers. Fairfax was hardly more than a village, a hamlet; it had no industry; no slums; no racial problems. The surrounding countryside was mainly farmland, hilly and remarkably attractive. Constance liked nothing so much as to drive out and go for long hikes, by herself, on warm autumn days. Coming to Elyria College had been a retreat of sorts but it had been absolutely correct. Constance thought with satisfaction that she was now settling into middle-age and that she would enjoy it, would take pleasure in it, as she had only infrequently enjoyed her young adulthood. In fact she often thought with a pang of excitement that she had slipped through relatively unscathed—she was now finished with all *that*.

At the age of thirty-six she had had her left breast removed, and in the months that followed that brutal—and, she thought, needless—operation she had undergone, rather too swiftly, a series of profound changes. At first she had felt, of course, sheer terror: a dizzying sense of panic: she had had to stop herself from clutching at the doctor's hands, as he told her his diagnosis, as he outlined the steps that must be taken at once. A biopsy, and if the growth is malignant, then the breast should be removed; even if the lymph glands are not affected the breast should be removed; so the doctor told her, and so she agreed. Afterward she wondered if she had acquiesced too readily. But then it was too late. But *then* . . . shouldn't she be grateful that the cancer had evidently been stopped, that the operation, radical as it was, had been a success . . . ? Yet, for a while, she felt anger; even fury. She could not determine if she loathed the doctor who had cut away her breast, or if she loathed herself, for being now so unwhole and unclean; a mutilated woman. She had not done it to herself but still she was mutilated and in time everyone would know. . . . Have you considered an operation to restore the breast, someone said, hesitantly, they have all sorts of miraculous techniques these days, the sister of a friend of mine was telling me that she flew to Texas for the operation and that it turned out beautifully. . . . Then, seeing Constance's rigid expression, the woman had gone silent.

At that time in her life Constance had been seeing a man, an old friend, really, in his fifties, who was newly divorced, and she was sickened at the prospect of his revulsion when he saw her hideous scarred chest. Though she had told him about the surgery—indeed, he'd known from the very first, even before her family, she had called him in tears from the doctor's office—and though he had been warmly sympathetic, she could not believe, she could not *really* believe, that he would not be disgusted. "I don't want to live," she had said tonelessly, calling from the doctor's office. "Where are you?" he said. "I'll come pick you up in a cab. Just stay there."

After the operation she refused to look at herself in mirrors, even when she was dressed. It was such a fraud, her image—such a blatant lie. Constance Shea from the outside was an attractive woman, somewhat tall, with dark blond hair neatly brushed back from her face to show her high, strong forehead, and to give prominence to her faint widow's peak which, she had been told as a child, is a sign of beauty. Her frank gray eyes had a customary quizzical expression. She was not pretty, had never been pretty, had long ago given up trying. Consequently the compliments of others surprised her; she did not *think* they were deliberately lying to her, or mocking her. Even after the operation she continued to look healthy, with her good coloring, her quick, graceful, almost lithe manner; and of course she told no one beyond her family and a few intimate friends about the operation. But her outward appearance was such a lie, she wanted at times to tear off her clothing, angrily, to undeceive her admirers. And what was she to do about her friend Perry, who continued to insist that he wanted to see her despite the mutilation. . . .

It was some time before Constance realized that she was not apprehensive of her friend's disgust; she was hoping for it. Because love—romantic, sexual, "companionable"—no longer interested her. It depended too much upon emotion, upon the subjective whims of the other; it was something she had outgrown. In a sense, Constance thought, it was a novel she herself had written, and had consequently outgrown.

During her first year at Elyria College a young English instructor named Thornton fell in love with her, quite openly. He was in his late twenties; he had published a few poems in literary journals, and was working on his first book. Constance was fond of him in her detached way, and offered to read his poetry, which he pressed upon her eagerly. His reverence for Constance Shea and his initial shyness in her presence were touching, when Constance did not find them ludicrous.

In the course of their peculiar eighteen months' friendship they were rarely alone together—he drove her up to Princeton one fine autumn day, to lunch at the Nassau Inn; he often escorted her to parties and college events. So far as Constance knew they touched only once, and then by accident—it was raining, Thornton was holding a large black umbrella over them both, Constance lost her footing on a slippery stone step and seized his arm to stop from falling. At once he squeezed her hand tight. But a moment later he released it, and neither alluded to the incident afterward.

Thornton was a burly, good-natured, soft-spoken young man with gingery curls and somewhat self-conscious mannerisms. Some of his students imitated him behind his back, others liked him immensely; he seemed frank, simple, open, unpretentious. His generosity surprised Constance, and began to annoy her as time passed: he gave her a six-ounce bottle of French perfume, a potted rose tree for the terrace of her little rented house, a signed first edition of Katherine Anne Porter's *Flowering Judas,* and a small carved ivory figurine from Malaysia which represented the goddess of "light and wisdom" rather than fecundity, and which possessed, despite its flat, near-featureless face and elongated body, an eerie sort of beauty. She had tried to refuse the ivory figurine, arguing that it was too costly; but Thornton had seemed genuinely upset and in the end she relented. "But no more presents, please," she said.

About his poetry: she suspected that it was too timid, too mannered and fastidiously crafted for the seventies, but it *was* promising, and she was reasonably sure that the young man did have talent. She even offered to write a letter to an acquaintance, an editor at a New York publishing house, to accompany Thornton's manuscript. From the very first he was boyishly grateful and could speak of nothing other than her "fantastic generosity." Constance told him that he must not exaggerate her influence, but he brushed her remarks aside. "You're just modest, Constance," he said, his voice rising. "Everyone knows you're absurdly modest."

But as Constance feared the manuscript was eventually returned, after a disgraceful delay of eight months, and her relationship with

Thornton was immediately altered. At first he pretended not to care—the rejection letter was, after all, a kindly one, filled with apologetic reasons for declining the book. Then, as the weeks passed, he became quite odd: he stopped her in the corridor of the English Department, or in the library, or in the parking lot, asking with a queer strained smile if she had "heard anything more" from her friend in New York. Constance tried to explain that the editor was not a friend; a casual acquaintance at best; but Thornton seemed not to listen. At a party, before curious witnesses, he told Constance in a whining voice that the least she could do was try again. "You know dozens of editors," he said with a plaintive smile. "You have innumerable connections. After all, Constance, you're a famous writer. . . . "

She refused him curtly. And awaited his apology. (For he was, after all, a sensible, sane person; there was nothing to indicate that he was aggressive or opportunistic, or emotionally unbalanced.) But days passed and he did not apologize and Constance began to hear from colleagues that Thornton was speaking angrily of her, of her "betrayal"; he was planning to "expose" her. Eventually he sent her several long poems dedicated to her. They were unlike his earlier work: crudely done, spiced with obscenities and exclamations, quite vicious. Constance read them in disbelief, trembling. Such hatred! Such rage! A "Constance Shea" emerged who was selfish, cold, arrogant, vain, sterile, ugly, bodiless, loveless. In the nastiest poem, typed out in the shape of a highly stylized vagina, Thornton fantasized raping and killing the "famous authoress" with the sharp point of an umbrella.

Everyone at Elyria was sympathetic with Constance. They told her that Thornton was notoriously unstable; confronted with a student's complaint, his first semester at the college, he had actually burst into tears in the chairman's office. His two-year contract was a terminable one and would not, of course, be renewed: which he had known from the first, but now he was agitating to be rehired, writing letters, making speeches to his classes. Constance was, they assured her, only one of his campaigns. He was bitter, fantastical, perhaps even dangerous. He experimented with drugs, his landlord was very unhappy with the condition of his apartment. . . . "But why didn't any of you tell me before all this happened," Constance cried in exasperation. "Well, you seemed so fond of each other," they said. "You got along so well, and Thornton was so obviously infatuated with you. . . . "

Because of that unhappy young man Constance came dismayingly close to being expelled from her little paradise. But in the end Thornton was the one, of course, to leave; she need not have worried.

"What has happened to your former courtier?" people asked, the following year, as if it were all a joke, and there had never been any danger. As if Constance had not been deeply wounded. Thornton left no forwarding address; he simply vanished. Buffoonish and ungainly and childlike in his egotism, he was remembered as an unpopular teacher, an untalented poet. He was no longer frightening; he was merely silly. Anecdotes could be invented at his expense. "You see, Constance, there's a considerable risk in being too kindly, too attractive, for an unmarried woman," people said. Constance half-thought they were blaming her, for being unmarried: she *should* have had a man to protect her from misfits like Thornton.

Then again they flattered her, indirectly. She was made to feel as if she were a temptress of some sort, a seductive woman. "Your poor hapless admirer," they said, smiling, "whatever became of him—do you know?"

"Of course I don't know," Constance said irritably.

Now, this autumn, there was Mira Lindenthal.

Of course she was no Thornton. She was successful and talented and popular with her students; she was even on excellent terms with her former husband, a black musician who still helped her with her career. She was wonderfully ebullient: monkeyish, flamboyant, a tireless talker. Her first week in Fairfax, she approached Constance boldly on Main Street in her soiled blue jeans and near-transparent shirt, and seized both Constance's hands in hers, and leaned close, and told her that she had begun reading her novels when she was thirteen years old and that they meant more to her than anything—that Constance's work had saved her life, perhaps—though, as she said with an anxious smile, she didn't want to exaggerate—but she hoped Constance would understand.

Constance did not, and the girl's brash bullying admiration was disconcerting, but she managed to thank her, and to make a few courteous inquiries about Mira's impressions of the college and Fairfax. But it was hopeless: Mira with her dark shining eyes, her olive complexion that fairly glowed with life, her bitten nails, compulsive winks and grins, her long untidy frizzy hair, her bare toes wriggling inside filthy sandals, her unstoppable *essence,* was not to be diverted from her subject, which was Constance Shea, Constance Shea's novels, and what they had meant to the adolescent Mira Lindenthal. So Constance stood quiet; Constance endured ten or fifteen minutes of praise. Her face burned, her eyes misted over. The girl was, despite her slovenliness, despite her disturbing intensity, really quite attractive: almost beautiful.

As if reading Constance's thoughts she took hold of Constance's hands once again, in parting, and stammered: "You're even more lovely, Constance, than your photographs. . . . "

That was in September. By mid-October Mira had talked Constance into attending a "house-warming party" in her small, cluttered apartment (a noisy frantic unpleasant evening filled with too many people, most of them from New York City), and a rehearsal of *Mother Courage* which Mira was directing for the Drama Department (during which Mira shocked—and rather impressed—Constance with her strident voice, her unashamed temper, her frankness and exuberance and profanity: and Constance could see that the student actors, though frequently crushed by the young woman's criticism, were in awe of her), and, most inexplicable of all, a photography session in the Millstone River Arboretum that lasted for several exhausting hours. (Mira had been quite serious about her disapproval of Constance's dust-jacket pictures. So she arranged for a young black woman to come down from New York City, "a very gifted photographer, an artist really," and take Constance's picture one sultry afternoon. The girl was bigbodied, taciturn, not particularly friendly; she frowned a great deal; *she* did not flatter Constance. And after the long session, after Mira's excited promises, nothing at all came of it—no prints, no photographs. Evidently they did not turn out. The black girl did not care for them. Or perhaps she had not troubled to develop them. Or something had come up, some complication in her life. Mira never satisfactorily explained, and since she seemed embarrassed about the episode, Constance did not question her further. Word had gotten out of the photographing in the Arboretum, and Constance dreaded people at Elyria gossiping about her: her newfound vanity: her wish for a publicity photo that would do her beauty justice.)

And then, at the Dean's Christmas party in mid-December, Mira made a fool of herself so openly, so noisily, that Constance rebuffed her, and left the gathering. Mira had been drinking a great deal of the Dean's inexpensive sweet California wine, and jabbering about how much she loved Elyria, what a change it was from the heavy neurotic atmosphere of New York: what an honor it was to be on the same faculty with a genius like Constance Shea. She had even sat on the floor, at Constance's feet, and forced everyone in the room to drink a toast to Constance and the success of her new novel (which would not be published for several months), and somewhere in the midst of the girl's gay drunken speech Constance arose and said, "Stop. Please. This is intolerable. This is asinine," and got her coat and walked out. Her heart pounded so violently she was afraid she would lose consciousness on the street.

Mira hurried after her to apologize; and telephoned the next morning, insisting that she meant no harm, she hadn't realized that her remarks were upsetting Constance, she had no *idea* Constance was distressed. "I wouldn't embarrass you for anything in the world," she said timidly.

But there was speculation. There was gossip. A friend told Constance that odd anecdotes were making the rounds: there had been a quarrel in public, a sort of lover's quarrel, and Constance had stalked out, and Mira had run after her. . . . Constance was sickened as much by the mere fact of the rumors as by the substance of the rumors themselves. And then, it was intolerable that she could not control them. They constituted a kind of story, an elaborate ungainly buffoonish fiction, not of her own invention.

Mira disappeared over the mid-winter break, and Constance's life resettled. She began to think of the young woman as merely imprudent; certainly she was good-natured, and generous, and appeared to be highly talented—so students said, and they were not easily impressed. So when Mira telephoned Constance in late January, asking if she might drop by, Constance hesitated only a moment before agreeing.

Mira brought with her a belated Christmas present—a three-foot high clay pot in a peculiar triangular shape, done by a friend of hers in the Village, a "very gifted" young Iranian artist. At the sight of the thing Constance's heart sank but she accepted it with a smile of polite gratitude. In a khaki windbreaker with sheepskin lining, and a jaunty crimson beret, and rather handsome leather boots, and her usual blue jeans, Mira was both penitent and exuberant; she was flushed as if from extreme cold, though the January evening was surprisingly mild.

Constance offered her a drink but Mira refused—"I want to cut down on that sort of thing," she said nervously.

She looked about Constance's attractive living room, and made appropriate comments, and seemed distinctly uneasy. Constance, sipping sherry, could not decide if she wanted the young woman to leave, or if she halfway hoped she would stay. There was plenty of food in the refrigerator, it would be no trouble to make dinner for the two of them. . . . But Mira kept jumping to her feet, pretending to be interested in one thing or another: Constance's cherrywood bookcase, Constance's books, Constance's emerald and gold Turkish rug, a gift from an old admirer. After thirty minutes of this Constance said curtly: "Did you have any particular reason for stopping by, Mira?"

It was the first time she had used the young woman's name, and Mira turned to her, startled and pleased. She had not really heard Constance's question; she had only heard her own name. She sat at the edge of a chintz-covered chair and said shyly that she'd thought of very little since the Christmas party except the misunderstanding between them: it had been a terrible surprise to her, but maybe, "in the long run," it would come to seem a good thing. "I need awakening," Mira said, brushing her hair out of her eyes. "I mean, constant awakening. My husband, my former husband, he says I'm catatonic inside all my energy. . . . I don't really *see,* I don't really *listen.* . . . The sort of thing friends do for each other, you know. . . . Not just politeness, and hypocrisy, but genuine truth: standing up the way you did, that night, and picking my fingers off your skirt, and saying, what did you say, Constance?—you wouldn't tolerate anything more from me—you thought my behavior was asinine—And so you told me, and walked out; and I can't stop thinking about it. I mean, it was so *honest.* It was so *direct.* Friends who are genuinely fond of each other must tell the truth at all times, otherwise there's a kind of anarchy . . . and it's terrifying, you know, to be unable to determine truth from lies."

Constance, blushing, murmured something appropriate. She was relieved, she said, that Mira hadn't been hurt. . . .

"Oh I was hurt! I was hurt," Mira laughed. "I was crushed. But then I went away, to this friend of mine in Miami Beach, and brooded over it, and bored everyone out of their skulls, and came to the realization that it was exactly what I required . . . that sort of abrupt awakening, you know. Like a slap in the face. And since then I've been able to work again. Revising my new play, the one the Drama Department is supposed to put on this spring, you know, I was rather depressed about it for a while . . . but now it's coming along, I'm not totally ashamed of it. . . . "

Constance asked her about the play, hoping to divert her from the original topic; but she spoke of it perfunctorily, saying that "that side" of her could take care of itself. "What I really came here to talk about, Constance," she said, grinning uneasily, "is . . . is something very different. I suppose you would call it abstract, theoretical. The sort of thing people never talk about. In a marriage you don't talk about it, and in most friendships. . . . It's too primitive, I think. Or too exalted."

"Yes?" Constance said.

"Maybe I will have some sherry," Mira said.

And then, swallowing a large mouthful, she crossed one long leg over her knee and waggled her booted foot and told Constance, who was staring at her in dismay, that she wasn't certain about her existence.

"I don't understand," Constance said. "Your existence at the college . . . ? Or as a playwright . . . ?"

"My existence as a human being," Mira laughed forlornly. "Not even as a woman, a female. By that point you're pretty well specialized, and I'm not at that point, I'm somewhere far below. My mind drifts about on the level of protoplasm. Maybe algae. Do you know what I mean?" she said, fumbling in the khaki jacket for her cigarettes. "Sometimes I wake up in the morning and I just lie there, wondering who the hell I am, what the hell I'm required to do. The night's dreams, far from helping me, are a hopeless jumble: a ragbag: half appear to be the dreams of other people, strangers. Does any of this sound familiar to you?"

Constance remembered, but not clearly, a fictional character of hers, a young woman, long ago, in retreat from a bad marriage, enduring a winter in Colorado, alone; and this fictional character, of whom Constance had been quite fond at the time, had also doubted her existence; and had been quite eloquent about it. But she frowned now, and set down her sherry glass, and said nothing.

"Oh I realize I'm taking up your time, you certainly want to be working," Mira said. "I imagine half the misfits in Fairfax take you aside, and beg you for wisdom. . . . It's because, Constance, you seem to radiate such certainty. And knowledge. I mean," she said quickly, blushing, taking note of Constance's expression of displeasure, "I mean you're just such a fine calm fulfilled individual. You're centered—do you know the term?—no?—it's a sort of Eastern concept—or maybe it's just a fashionable Western concept now—Being centered means that your center of gravity is in *you;* in your own soul. Most people, you know, people like me, everyone I know, our centers of gravity are outside us—we're always running around getting reflections of ourselves from other people, or hoping to read about ourselves in the paper, we may be intelligent enough to know that it's ridiculous—it's hell—our "delirious profession"—but we can't change our behavior; it's just the way we are. But you're very different, Constance."

Constance poured the young woman more sherry. She said lightly, "But my dear, aren't you simply telling me that I'm much older than you and your friends? After all I will be fifty-three in April—"

"*No.* Shit, no," Mira said. "People your age are the worst. I mean, the ones I know. The women, the men. . . . No, it has nothing to do with age, it's something in your character."

"But really. . . . " Constance said uneasily.

"Character. Like bone structure. Like the body's frame," Mira said emphatically. "It must be in the chromosomes. Determined. Biology is destiny, Freud said, but I mean something even more primordial than that. . . . Christ, am I embarrassing you again?"

Constance tried to smile. "I really don't get much pleasure, Mira, out of talking about myself. I don't imagine most people do."

"Most people—! Oh the hell with most people," Mira laughed. "They talk about nothing else. They see and hear and know only themselves. They're like Beckett's talking heads, stuck in jars. Oh they go on and on and it's amazing. . . . But you really are different, Constance," she said, lowering her voice. She fixed her dark shiny doggish eyes on Constance and was silent for a moment. "Somehow I knew you would be, before we met. I knew, from your writing. From your picture, even though it doesn't do your eyes—your marvelous eyes— justice. I *knew.* I've been telling everyone how we were fated to meet, it had to happen, there've been these queer dreams of mine for the past year, they have to do with turning thirty, will I survive or not—am I going to make it or not—Certain people I know haven't made it, and the ones who have might be better off dead: but I won't go into that. I'm certainly not going to bore you with my depressing life, and my crazy depressing friends. The thing is. . . . The thing is," she said vaguely, her gaze still fixed on Constance as if, for a moment, she had lost the train of her own thought, "some people are born beautiful and perfect. Their faces mirror their souls. Or their souls mirror their faces. Whatever Plato said. . . . "

"You exaggerate, Mira," Constance said softly.

But Mira did not hear. She went on to speak of the fact that some people *existed* more substantially than others. It might sound bizarre but

it was nevertheless true. She spoke quickly, as if intoxicated, her cigarette burning forgotten in an ashtray, her long narrow foot wriggling
with the intensity of her voice. An odd young woman! An endearing
but most exasperating young woman, Constance thought. She was waiting now for her to leave; she would not suggest dinner after all. Mira
Lindenthal's mere presence was exhausting, as if Constance's spirit were
being drained from her though she did little more than listen.

Chatter about acquaintances in Soho, and the loneliness of Fairfax,
Maryland, and Shakespeare's *Winter's Tale* (what relevance this had Constance did not catch), and one of Constance's early novels, and the fact
that she, Mira, had hours of work awaiting her back in her ugly apartment, and could barely force herself to leave. . . . Constance prudently
offered her no more sherry. Yet she remained seated, running a hand
through her stiff hair, smiling and winking and squinting. "You won't
tell anyone about our conversation, will you," she said.

"Of course not," Constance said.

"Because I wouldn't want certain things to get around. . . . This
uncanny feeling that I don't exactly exist, or that the existence I find
myself in isn't quite the correct one: I wonder if anyone shares it? But
of course if anyone did, he might not confess, he might not want to
confess," Mira said slyly. She waited, but Constance did not reply. "I
don't *think* I'm going crazy. I mean, I've gone a little off my head in the
past, two or three times, but it didn't feel like this: it was primarily
emotion and this is all intellect. The question of one's existence is theoretical, isn't it . . . ? By thinking of our own position aren't we also
thinking of everyone's . . . ?"

"I don't know," Constance said gently, glancing at her watch.

Mira rose to leave. But then lingered. Her khaki jacket half-
buttoned, her crimson beret dangling from a pocket. She apologized for
having taken up so much of Constance's time—"I know, I know, your
time is precious: I feel like a vandal, wasting it"—but still she dawdled,
talking of the college, her most promising students, the over-priced food
store in town, her need to get away to New York soon. And then,
inexplicably, she was talking once again of Constance Shea: and staring
at Constance in that peculiar hungry way. "I think what I really want
to know," she said, nearly whispering, "is . . . how does it feel to be *you?*
To stand where you are standing, to look out upon the world from your
point of view, to know what you know, to have accomplished what
you've accomplished. . . . You are such an extraordinary person, Con-

stance," she said, her eyes shining, "you might almost forget the fact, now and then. And so someone must remind you."

A wave of sheer anger passed over Constance. She rose, her cheeks burning unpleasantly. "Exactly what do you mean by that, Mira?" she asked.

"Mean? Mean by what?"

"The hyperbolic things you've been saying."

"What things? That you're beautiful, that you're extraordinary?"

"And perfect too? I believe you said—perfect too?"

"Everyone knows it—"

"But how am I beautiful? How am I perfect?"

"By just—just *being* the person you are!" Mira laughed.

"Do you think so? Really? It's that simple?"

"I—I don't suppose it's necessarily *simple,*" Mira said, taking an involuntary half-step backward.

Constance's pulses rang strongly. The sherry had done her good, she thought. It gave her courage, it gave her an uncharacteristic sense of righteousness. She stared without smiling at the young woman who had ruined her evening, and began slowly, quite deliberately, to unbutton her blouse. She noted with pleasure that Mira was now alarmed. Really alarmed. Was she so slapdash and daring after all, was she so flamboyant as she pretended . . . ? Merely a pale, frightened girl, staring as Constance Shea unbuttoned her blouse, and slid her slip and brassiere straps off her left shoulder. She thinks I have gone mad, Constance thought.

Constance faced her, defiantly. "Well. Do you see? Do you see, and do you understand? All those lies about perfection—Beauty and perfection—"

A pale, frightened girl. Now stammering an incoherent apology. Now backing away. Constance wanted to taunt her—why are you suddenly so tongue-tied, when you've been jabbering away for hours?—for weeks? But she said only: "Goodnight, Mira."

The girl fled.

It had been a dramatic moment, a wonderfully theatrical moment. But Constance, standing alone in her living room, her scarred breast exposed, her flesh gathering itself into tiny goose bumps, felt only a sense of exhaustion. And bitterness. And hatred: for certainly she hated Mira Lindenthal, for having seduced her into behaving so crazily: for having behaved as Constance Shea never behaved.

"The impertinent little bitch," Constance whispered.

It was over. The relationship—it was not of course a friendship—was over.

And so Constance was appalled to receive a letter from the young woman two days later as if nothing were ended; as if Constance's contemptuous act had not been one of dismissal. She was so upset, she could barely force herself to read the poorly typewritten words: *My love for you has deepened.... The evidence of your suffering.... Your profound message.... Beyond words, the gesture of sheer mute anguish.... An intimate bond forged between us.... Between two women.... The sort of knowledge in the flesh that no man could comprehend....*

As she tore up the letter Constance began to cry.

She began to hear wild tales about Mira Lindenthal. A drinking bout in Baltimore with a student, one of the actors in Mira's play; trouble with the police; classes missed. Evidently the young woman spent an inordinate amount of time in a tavern out on the highway, where she made a fool of herself with her long impassioned monologues, and was gaining a reputation as a whore (crudely put, but then it was a crude, clumsy situation) since she brought back to her apartment not only male students from Elyria but men from the area—truck drivers, handymen, construction workers, even a highway patrolman. When she taught her classes and when she showed up for rehearsals of her play she was evidently in control of herself: she was brusque and confident and bullying as always: and she had a small, highly vocal circle of supporters in the Drama School. But she was out of place at Elyria. She should never have accepted the offer from Elyria. Had she told Constance what was troubling her?—had she confided in Constance at all?

No, Constance said, she had not.

She was relieved to learn that Mira was no longer talking about her; at any rate, tales no longer wound their way back to her. Perhaps, Constance thought, she has found someone else to idolize. A man, a lover. A legitimate lover.

When Mira disappeared from Fairfax on the day before her play was scheduled to open Constance was one of the first people contacted: but of course she knew nothing. "You might try her husband, in New York. Her former husband," Constance said. During the three days Mira was missing—the play did open on schedule, and was well-received; and Mira did turn up, refusing sullenly to explain herself—Constance slept poorly, and had no appetite, and was forced to dismiss her classes after half an hour or so, since she felt not only her own apprehension over the young woman but her students'; and she felt, too, how they blamed her.

She wanted to address them. And her colleagues. She wanted to reason calmly with them. She would *not* be emotional, she was *not* like Mira. She would explain to them that she had nothing to do with Mira Lindenthal and that Mira Lindenthal had nothing to do with her. It was all exaggerated, histrionic. Constance was not to blame. How was she to blame? One must reject the sentimental drivel that insists we are all to blame for everything—we share in Hitler's guilt—that sort of thing—nonsense—dangerous nonsense. Absurd. "I did not deliberately attract Mira Lindenthal," Constance would tell them. Just as she had not deliberately attracted Thornton, or the others. The nameless others. And so she would *not* accept responsibility, no matter how they judged her. "You have no right to judge me," she would say, her voice rising.

But Mira did return. She simply showed up for her first class on Monday morning, and refused to explain herself, and of course she refused to apologize. It was said that she looked sickly and dishevelled: her clothes looked as if she had slept in them. Your play was quite successful, people told her. We missed you. . . . But she would not talk about it, she seemed really indifferent, she murmured something about the play being a failure.

The actors came to see her, the assistant director came to see her, even the chairman of her department—but she would not talk about it.

But aren't you even going to see it performed, they asked.

She shrugged her shoulders and smirked.

I don't like that kind of theater, she was reported to say. I really prefer Chekhov. So why the hell should I sit through two hours of *that . . . ?*

Constance dreaded her call. Or perhaps Mira would come over, uninvited. I am not to blame for whatever you do to yourself, Constance would say. You should never have come here: you are out of place here. You must leave, go back to New York, go anywhere, and leave me alone. . . . She walked about her rented house, bringing her fists lightly together, whispering to herself. How dare people blame her for Mira Lindenthal! How dare people gossip about her, and tell grotesque lies!

Mira did not telephone, nor did she come to Constance's door. She sent another letter, as poorly typed as the first but much briefer. Constance did no more than scan it, holding it at arm's length; her hand trembled badly.

Why didn't you reply to my letter, Mira wanted to know.

Constance crumpled the sheet of paper and let it fall.

Some days later while she was having lunch with two of her colleagues in the faculty dining room, Mira Lindenthal appeared out of nowhere, pale and hulking and mockingly deferential. "May I have an audience with you, Miss Shea?" she asked. "It would only take up a few minutes of your time."

Constance stared at her. She felt that she had known Mira Lindenthal all her life, and that she had been fleeing her all her life.

"I realize your time is highly valuable," Mira said, licking her lips, smiling a queer wide smile. She seemed unaware of Constance's companions. "Perhaps I could pay you for your time. As one professional to another."

Constance felt suddenly that her body was slipping from her. That she had lost, or had left, her body; there was no weight to her any longer, only a frightening dizziness, an airiness that could not be controlled. A pulse rang in her head. Someone was speaking to her mockingly, someone was accusing her, but she could not protest—she could not get her words clear.

Yet she must have said something. She must have said *No,* politely and curtly. For the ungainly wild-haired young woman retreated, and everything was calm again. Except for Constance's panicky sense of having lost her body everything was calm again.

You did right to refuse her, Constance's friends said. It was the only thing you could do.

Or perhaps they did not say those particular words: perhaps Constance imagined them, afterward.

Mira left Elyria three weeks before the end of the spring semester, without contacting Constance again. She sent no farewell note, she made no attempt to call. One night, very late, she turned up on Constance's doorstep—laughing drunkenly, trying the doorknob and pounding the door—raving in a man's voice—but Constance lay in bed, rigid beneath the covers, and did not allow herself to become terrified, and within a few minutes the disturbance faded. She did not telephone the police. There was no need, she was not really frightened. She simply lay in her bed, in the dark, her arms pressed tightly against her sides, until the convulsive shivering stopped.

You did right to refuse her, people whispered.

Still, her life at Elyria was over.

She had to leave, she was expelled, there were too many rumors, too many fanciful lies. In public she could not mistake certain glances, certain intonations. It would do no good to protest: to point out that the young woman was clearly fated to destroy herself within a few years: and that it had nothing to do with Constance. They would listen, would pretend to sympathize; but secretly they blamed her.

And so Constance Shea resigned. And the president of Elyria College, who so much admired her, accepted her resignation with little more than a token protest.

Her life was over. She was expelled. It took her days to pack, to sort through her papers and letters—ah, she had accumulated so many letters!—and most of them had no value—had to be thrown out. The labor of sorting and packing exhausted her. A pulse beat oddly in her temple, her heart lurched, she was dizzy almost constantly, and found it difficult to keep her balance. Bodiless, weightless: like a ghost: drifting about the box-filled unfamiliar rooms like a ghost.

She did manage, however, to throw away useless things. And there were many of them. Letters, papers, parts of manuscripts, books given as gifts, books inscribed by fellow writers, outworn clothing, furniture with tiny scratches, soiled cushions and pillows, soiled curtains. It was too much trouble to have her carpets cleaned, she might as well throw them away. And snapshots kept untidily in manila envelopes, years of accumulation, years of clutter. She had meant to arrange the snapshots neatly in an album but there had never been any time, and now it was too late.

Despite the dizziness and weakness that buzzed close about her like a cloud of gnats Constance took distinct pleasure in certain chores. Like throwing away that Malaysian statue. It had been a gift from someone, from an admirer. A fairly recent gift. But she could not remember, for a space of several minutes, which one of them had given her the ugly thing.

Bees: A Story to Be Spoken

Arthur Miller

It was high summer and the days were long. The baby crawling around on the rattan carpet suddenly let out a cry and we both looked down and shushed him. The setting sun's orange rays crossed his little quizzical face as he looked intently at the back of his hand and now screamed again, but hysterically this time and I saw the bee walking on his finger and rushed to knock it away. His mother picked him up, still screaming in pain. It was infuriating that he was stung. Then I saw three or four more bees moving around on the carpet where he had been sitting, and then further away a few more, making a total of a dozen or so. Then I saw that even more were crawling up the tan sackcloth drape next to the slider through which the dying sunlight was pouring into the room. Where were they coming from? But they were moving slowly, feeling around rather than darting here and there, disoriented somehow, a slight reassurance.

We examined the baby's bedroom before putting him to bed and shutting his door. But of course bees could get under a door, so we kept looking in on him through half the night until we were too tired to stay awake, and we slept in exhaustion.

In the morning there was no sign of bees in the living room or anywhere else. It seemed strange. The house was screened, how had they gotten in?

After breakfast I went outside to fix a hole in the vegetable garden fence. A perfect clear day and a faultless blue sky. After I had gone a few yards a small dark shadow passed across the grass in front of me, a black shadow about the size of a desk when there wasn't a cloud in the sky. And then I realized I was hearing a roaring over my head and looked up. About fifteen feet up in the air thousands of bees were swarming in a compact, football-sized black mass which was moving coherently at about a walking pace toward the edge of the lawn where the whole hovering lump elevated higher and higher and seemed to settle in the

branches of a tall oak which stood at the border of the woodline a
hundred yards from where I stood watching. I learned later from a bee
man that a new queen had been hatched and crowned, which started the
swarming and the beginning of a new hive. It was wonderful because
our bees had gone from us in a sort of natural good-will way.

But the next evening when we turned on the lamps to read they
appeared on the light bulbs, moving tentatively in that same hypnotized
way, and then we saw some stumbling on the light tan carpet again.
And now I saw one coming out of the wall.

Next to the fireplace was a section of tongue-and-groove pine wall.
I stood quietly watching and presently could see a bee squeezing himself
through a tiny separation in the joint between two boards. Then I heard
the thrumming inside the wall. This was alarming. There had to be
hundreds, maybe thousands of bees behind the wood to make so solid
and continuous a bass sound and when I laid my hand on the wall I could
feel a faint vibration.

This was a long time ago and there were farmers all around here
then, in fact I was the only non-farmer in the area long before it became
a suburb, a time when you could get little more in the store than cheddar
cheese, bacon, ketchup and white Wonder Bread. I went over to see
Jerome Hale about the bees but he only made milk and knew about
cows, he said, but had never bothered with bees and didn't know anybody who kept them although his grandfather had but he was dead and
gone. I tried Phillip Cole who had gone through high school and had a
twin brother, a lawyer, but he could only repeat, "Yeah, I guess they'll
get in anywhere."

This was only a few years after the War and nobody thought anything about using chemicals and they were selling pure full-strength
DDT in steel, khaki-colored pressurized canisters about the size of an
elongated grapefruit. In fact, the Army had been spraying it directly on
people in Germany and France just after the War to keep down the lice
and typhus, soldiers would board trains and shoot the stuff right into
passengers' hair and down their backs inside their clothes. It was the new
postwar world where with a squirt you were suddenly able to kill anything that crawled and people were very excited about this. I bought a
canister in the hardware store and drilled a quarter-inch hole between the
boards where I had seen the bee emerging, and just opened the valve into
it and let them have it. Inside the wall an uproar broke out, a panic, and
I could hear them whamming themselves against the pine boards. But

they had hurt my son and I was angry at them and besides it was my house and they had thousands of acres around here to live in. Gradually the uproar died down in there. After all, DDT pure was deadly, especially in a sealed area like they were in. I just hoped their corpses wouldn't smell up the living room. I would wait a day or two till the last one had died and then pull a board off the wall and clean them out.

We were reading in the living room again next evening and the baby was sitting on the floor and crawling around when I heard the drumming. I went over to the wall and listened. No doubt about it, they were alive in there, maybe not as many as before but enough, hundreds is what it sounded like and it was unbelievable. I went to the store next morning and brought back two more canisters of DDT, but this time I took a keyhole saw and cut a hole about two inches square at the base of what I had figured out was a bay between studs, and stuck the nozzle into it and let them have it, but straight up this time, right into the hive. When the first canister was empty I hit them with the second until liquid DDT started dripping out of the hole. They were roaring in rage in there but I had them now. I could tell because they went silent much more quickly this time and that had to be the end of them.

Next evening, the living room smelling of DDT, we turned the reading lamps on after dinner and sat down to read. I opened my newspaper under the light and in less than a minute two bees landed on it. The craving in their little bodies tingled my spine. Creatures that wanted anything so much could finally take over the world, certainly this house. And of course I had to wonder whether these insects might somehow remember what I had tried to do to them. When I looked over to the pine wall at the end of the room it looked like a broad chest with some kind of stern statement hidden in it.

Next morning I went around the house and inspected the clapboard wall inside which the bees were living. It was really quite simple, what I had to do, for bees were crawling in and out of a space they had worn away between the clapboard and the fieldstone chimney. It was amazing how they totally ignored my presence; I was standing only a couple of yards from their entry and to get to it they were making a ninety degree turn in mid-air hardly a foot in front of my face, they might have been rounding the corner of an invisible building. The solution was clear.

I mixed a little plaster of Paris and filled the entry crack next to the chimney. That afternoon when I returned to inspect my work the plaster was all but gone. So I mixed a little Portland cement and forced that into the opening and then nailed a board over it to protect it while it dried. Standing by for a few minutes to observe, I saw a traffic jam of bees piling up at this blockage and I decided to get out of the way before it occurred to their minds who had done it. At the crack of dawn next morning I came out for a look and found that the cement had indeed hardened, but they had managed to wear away enough of the wood around it to pass through. By the nature of our contest I saw that the candid violence of their determination was something I could never equal and that if I were to continue living here I would have to use deceptions and subterfuges and it was all getting slightly ignoble.

Next night we turned on our reading lamps but now it was impossible to concentrate as we waited for the first landing to be made. Meanwhile, we could no longer leave the baby to wander the floor without supervison at every single moment. Our lives were narrowing, our eyes noticing every dark spot on a chair or table and we couldn't help waiting to see if they moved. We were growing conscious of a new presence in the house, like an uninvited occupant.

There had to be a solution. The drumming in the wall was gradually returning to its old loudness but it seemed vengeful now and it was unnerving. I phoned Leonard Crown, our County Agent, and he stopped by one afternoon and thought that maybe a sulfur candle would do the trick. I bought a couple, and after enlarging the square hole I had cut, carefully inserted one vertically, and lit it. Its vapors rose into the bay behind the boards. A roar of panic resounded in there. But now I would have to sit and keep watch against a fire starting. With great pleasure at first, and later with some pity and remorse, I saw bodies of bees piling up around the candle as they dropped out of the hive above. In a while they were so deep they threatened to smother the flame. But in an hour or so the bay went silent.

Carefully I pried out the bottom of a board and with a flashlight peered behind it. I had a DDT canister ready to go an arm's length away in case a thousand of them came pouring out at me—they might have quieted down to trick me. But as I pulled out more of the nails and the board came down no sound rose from within. Finally, I pulled it completely away and there I saw a solid mass of beeswax that filled the entire bay, a hive about six feet in height and two feet wide. At the bottom on the horizontal two-by-four lay dead bees eight or ten inches deep. It was terrible. I cursed them for damned fools, and swept them into cardboard boxes and a couple of bushel baskets. Their honey and wax was poisoned, of course.

Then I chipped away at the hive and removed it in long, beautifully wrought shards. It was like wrecking some ancient church. I made sure no scrap of anything remained to attract some new colony, and to make absolutely certain painted the interior of the bay with asphalt tar to kill any odor that might attract them.

Then we divorced and I sold the house.

But I bought another one about half a mile up the road, and five or six years later I was having my lunch with another wife when a man I had never seen before appeared at the kitchen door and asked if he could come in and I said of course and he introduced himself as Mr. Peet who had recently bought the house on the corner which he was given to understand I had once owned.

Yes, I said, I had indeed owned that house, and he said, "Did you ever have any trouble with bees there?"

And I said, are they in the living room?

And he said, yes. He said that when he and his wife turned on the lights at night to read in the living room they seemed to come out of somewhere and landed on the light bulbs and the pages of their books.

And I said, they are most probably coming out of the wall next to the fireplace, and then I told him all the things I had done to defeat these creatures so many years ago now, and I realized that I was enjoying being able to talk with authority about something I really knew to be true, it was a good feeling that drew me strangely closer to my former enemies. I said that he could try what I had and maybe they would leave him in peace for a while but that if he wanted my advice he would be better off selling the house. Whether he should divorce his wife too was something I couldn't advise him about but the house, I thought, definitely had to go because it belonged, quite obviously, to the bees.

Six: Eighteen Poems

Ode to the Alien

Diane Ackerman

Beast, I've known you
in all love's countries, in a baby's face
   knotted like walnut-meat,
         in the crippled obbligato
of a polio-stricken friend,
in my father's eyes
     pouchy as two marsupials,
          in the grizzly radiance
of a winter sunset, in my lover's arm
   veined like the blue-ridge mountains.
To me, you are beautiful
       until proven ugly.

   Anyway, I'm no cosmic royalty
either; I'm a bastard of matter
   descended from countless rapes
         and invasions
of cell upon cell upon cell.
I crawled out of slime;
    I swung through the jungles
      of Madagascar;
I drew wildebeest on the caves at Lascaux;
    I lived a grim life
    hunting peccary and maize
in some godforsaken mudhole in the veldt.

   I may squeal
  from the pointy terror of a wasp,
or shun the breezy rhetoric
     of a fire;
but, whatever your form, gait, or healing,

you are no beast to me,
I who am less than a heart-flutter
  from the brute,
        I who have been beastly so long.
Like me, you are that pool
            of quicksilver in the mist,
  fluid, shimmery, fleeing, called life.

    And life, full of pratfall and poise,
  life where a bit of frost
one morning can turn barbed wire
            into a string of stars,
  life aromatic with red-hot pizzazz
drumming ha-cha-cha
            through every blurt, nub, sag,
    pang, twitch, war, bloom of it,
life as unlikely as a pelican, or a thunderclap,
  life's our tour of duty
        on our far-flung planets,
        our cage, our dole, our reverie.

    Have you arts?
  Do waves dash over your brain
        like tide-rip along a rocky coast?
Does your moon slide
    into the night's back pocket,
            just full when it begins to wane,
so that all joy seems interim?
        Are you flummoxed by that millpond,
deep within the atom, rippling out to every star?
        Even if your blood is quarried,
I pray you well,
    and hope my prayer your tonic.

    I sit at my desk now
            like a tiny proprietor,
a cottage industry in every cell.
  Diversity is my middle name.
My blood runs laps;
        I doubt yours does,

but we share an abstract fever
called thought,
a common swelter of a sun.
So, Beast, pause a moment,
you are welcome here.
I am life, and life loves life.

Lofty Calling

A. R. Ammons

Chimney-top, aerial- or cherry-tree top,
Bob Shorter's mockingbird
splits daybreak to air-light glint glass,
chips slabs superfine, bubbles and pops

blisters, chisels light to pane-flint floats:
he wangles crescendos up from
cedar roots and sprays improvisations
into as many song-tips as cedar tips;

then with stark repetition
hacks a few cedars down:
he works at it—air's tilled over Bob's
place, tone-farmed: and then

at times, as if restless with stodgy air,
Shorter's mockingbird gets
the leaps and leaps on song swells
and settles down again as if into

buoys of his own music:
line and formation apprise the air;
invention on invention piled up
figure the invisible invisibly.

Wake Up

Raymond Carver

In June, in the Kyborg Castle, in the canton
of Zurich, in the late afternoon, in the room
underneath the chapel, in the dungeon,
the executioner's block hunches on the floor next
to the Iron Maiden in her iron gown. Her serene features
are engraved with a little noncommittal smile. If
you ever once slipped inside her she closed her spiked
interior on you like a demon, like one
possessed. Embrace—that word on the card next to
the phrase "no escape from."
       Over in a corner stands the rack, a dream-like
contrivance that did all it was called on to do, and more,
no questions asked. And if the victim passed out
too soon from pain, as his bones were being broken
one by one, the torturers simply threw a bucket of water
on him and woke him up. Woke him again
later, if necessary. They were thorough. They knew
what they were doing.
       The bucket is gone, but there's an old cherrywood
crucifix up on the wall in a corner of the room:
Christ hanging on his cross, of course, what else?
The torturers were human after all, yes? and, who
knows?—at the last minute their victim might see
the light, some chink of understanding, even acceptance of
his fate might break, might pour into his nearly molten
heart. *Jesu Christo, my Savior.*
       I stare at the block. Why not? Why not indeed?
Who hasn't ever wanted to stick his neck out without fear
of consequence? Who hasn't wanted to lay his life on the line,
then draw back at the last minute?

Who, secretly, doesn't lust after every experience?
It's late. There's nobody else in the dungeon but us,
she and me, the North Pole and the South. I drop down
to my knees on the stone floor, grasp my hands behind
my back, and lay my head on the block. Inch it forward
into the pulse-filled groove until my throat fits the shallow
depression. I close my eyes, draw a breath. A deep breath.
The air thicker somehow, as if I can almost taste it.
For a moment, calm now, I feel I could almost drift off.
        Wake up, she says, and I do, turn my head over to see
her standing above me with her arms raised. I see the axe too,
the one she pretends to hold, so heavy it's all she
can do to hold it up over her shoulder. Only kidding,
she says, and lowers her arms, and the idea-of-axe, then
grins. I'm not finished yet, I say. A minute later, when I
do it again, put my head back down on the block, in
the same polished groove, eyes closed, heart racing
a little now, there's no time for the prayer forming in my
throat. It drops unfinished from my lips as I hear her
sudden movement. Feel flesh against my flesh as the sharp
wedge of her hand comes down unswervingly to the base of
my skull and I tilt, nose over chin into the last
of sight, of whatever sheen or rapture I can grasp to take
with me, wherever I'm bound.
        You can get up now, she says, and
I do. I push myself up off my knees, and I look at her,
neither of us smiling, just shaky
and not ourselves. Then her smile and my arm going
around her hips as we walk into the next corridor
needing the light. And outside then, in the open, needing more.

A Prospect of Swans

Dorothy Donnelly

We came out through the high doors, our heads
full of Daumiers and Delacroix's, and still
elated, descended the marble steps,
and across the water a swan moved toward us,
noble, and slow as the slowest pavane.

As if she had a year and a day,
she delayed, as if she knew admirers
stood on the stair before her, that the rose
of the sunset opened behind her—alone,
illumined, afloat on an acre of lake.

And while we watched, approving the poise
and the pose, she suddenly dove, turned up-
side down like any goose, submerging
her head, like a moose after lily pads
or lily roots—a working bird

like others. Here was no opera swan,
nor emblematical, but animal,
her sinuous alabaster figure
proof enough that a thing of beauty
turns the eye, and will forever.

At an early age, with love at first sight,
seated on a hard black oval-backed chair
under a gas-globe light in a room
with more past than my own, I saw through the two
glass eyes of the stereopticon

my first swan, on a pond under ostrich-
tail palms, molded, so it seemed, of porcelain
or snow. That was long ago. I still

see swans, not dreamed-up like Sindbad's roc
but real as wrens. The swan is *not*

an ivory tower type—the poet's
pet—but a bird preferred by the people.
She is everywhere: in Plato's prose,
adrift on the Avon, wan in watermarks,
flashing in neon. Though symbolists

and kings have claimed her, she refuses
to be exclusive, to be looked at only
by some presumptive royal eye,
but is visible to any idler or boy,
saunterer in parks or gazer at the zoo.

Any day, soundless, gliding as on glass,
she may come into view on some lagoon
the green of celadon, framed
in the willow's fronds, clothed like the curved
camellia, whiter than winter's moons.

Arrow

Rita Dove

The eminent scholar "took the bull by the horns,"
substituting urban black speech for the voice
of an illiterate cop in Aristophanes' *Thesmophoriazusae*.
And we sat there.
Dana's purple eyes deepened, Becky
twitched to her hairtips
and Janice in her red shoes
scribbled *he's an arschloch; do you want
to leave? He's a model product of his
education*; I scribbled back, *we can learn from this.*

So we sat through the applause
and my chest flashed hot, a void
sucking at my guts until I was all
flamed surface. I would have to speak up.
Then the scholar progressed

to his prize-winning translations of
the Italian Nobel Laureate. He explained the poet
to us: immense difficulty
with human relationships; sensitive;
women were a scrim through which he could see
heaven.
We sat through it. Quite lovely, these poems.
We could learn from them although they were saying
you women are nothing, nothing at all.

When the moment came I raised my hand,
phrased my question as I had to: sardonic,
eminently civil my condemnation
phrased in the language of fathers—
felt the room freeze behind me.

And the answer came as it had to:
humanity—celebrate our differences—
the virility of ethnicity. My students
sat there already devising

their different ways of coping:
Dana knowing it best to have
the migraine at once, get the poison out quickly
Becky holding it back for five hours   and Janice
making it to the evening reading and
party afterwards
in black pants and tunic with silver mirrors
her shoes pointed and studded, wicked witch shoes:
Janice who will wear red for three days or
yellow brighter
than her hair so she can't be
seen   at all

Hardware

Alice Fulton

I don't know how this silk-screened memory
expansion board—its soldered subdivisions
exposed yet unembarrassed as a city seen from air—
holds a million bytes that flame
to words when touched, but it does.

It sits on my desk like a skull
or a phone, another sculpted composure.
I like a phone because I can hold it
and join the circumference
of radial cables that bind
the earth's hot core with voice.
And I know a touch that sends it
on a global search to snare the line
I need, immediately.
Technology is something

to rely on when your clothes catch fire,
as mine did all last year.
I don't know how the everyday selvage
from my closet became a conflagration,
but what a spectacle I made
in my candescent dress!
Trying to run from what consumed me
only urged it on.

When my friend said, "Hold still,
I'll help you out," I was distracted
by a hundred molten buttons.
Wrapped in that emphatic shift,
I lacked self-discipline.

Besides, even a fiery daywear covers
nakedness. Only love can disembarrass one
to strip. When I did
I kept undressing
long after all the clothes were gone.
My skin felt like brimstone,
so I thought I'd take it off.

I don't know if the comforts of others—
the man who visits fabric stores to play
with bolts of silk that ask for nothing
when he's estranged,
the woman who test-drives cars
she'll never buy to feel
the anointed engine fire—
apply to those who don't know how to live or die.

Still, my friend has given me a memory
expansion board of turquoise pools
and resilient springs,
a thing outside myself to hold
whatever sharp endowments
I choose. And I choose the trees

harboring little pneumatic drills
outside my window, trees infested
with the fricative fuss of small soft birds
along Le Forge. "Le Forge Road—
Isn't that where people go
to dump old stoves?" a man asked at a party.
Yes, and where they come for frication
in the front seats of foreign cars,
their drunken consonance
riding on the wind to me.

I don't know if drivers in those lively confines—
where windows rise electrically,
wipers wave at misplaced knees,
and rear defrosters sap the battery—
find ease, a soft exchange

that's more than fabrication, but I like to think
they might: those drivers who remove their synthetic
permanent press suits
to remove their suits of fire.

Crystal

Thom Gunn

He arrives, and makes deliveries, after 3:00,
Then strolls to a ramp that leads up from the dance,
And sits apart, quiet, hands clasped round a knee,
Smelling the fresh-sawed planks, no doubt. Not tense
—Fixed, merely. While he watches us, his face
Is almost readable, his recessed shape
Gleams like a friendly visitor's from space.
As in a sense it is, now. To escape
The sheer impurity of the other lives,
He has always been extreme, he puts his soul
Into each role in turn, where he survives
Till it is incarnation more than role.
Now it is Dealer. 52, tall, scarred,
His looks get nobler every year, I find,
Almost heroic.
                 I once saw in the yard
A half-grown foxglove that he brings to mind
Here, so magnificently self-enwrapped.
Its outer leaves were toothed and all alike.
With a rough symmetry they overlapped
Circling around the budded central spike,
Still green. Dense with its destiny, it waited
Till it might fling itself up into flower.

Now he sits similarly concentrated,
And edged, and similarly charged with power,
Certain of that potential, which his mood
Fairly feeds on, but which is still contained.

The foxglove flowers in its damp solitude
Before its energy fades, and in the end

The chemical in the man will fade as well.
Meanwhile he watches how the dancing feet
Move to the rhythms of the fresh wood-smell;
And in the crowded night he feels complete.

Paul Laurence Dunbar

(for Herbert Martin)

Robert Hayden

We lay red roses on his grave,
speak sorrowfully of him
as if he were but newly dead.

And so it seems to us
this raw spring day, though years
before we two were born he was
a young poet dead.

Poet of our youth—
his cri du coeur our own,
his verses "in a broken tongue"

beguiling as an elder
brother's antic lore.
Their sad blackface lilt and croon
survive him like

the happy look (subliminal
of victim, dying man)
a summer's tintypes hold.

The roses flutter in the wind;
we weight their stems
with stones, then drive away.

The Skate-Boards

Frances Minturn Howard

They surf the pavement, cresting asphalt waves;
Over their heads the green elm-combers break.
Struck to stone
They stand in accidental grace—
Feet turned like ballet-dancers.
The sloping Mall rolls undulant beneath
Their cunning turns, near spills, recoveries.
A dear, precarious balance struck with wood
Keeps them upright; leaners on wind,
They lurch downhill, drinking in speed like wine.

Their chirring skates scrape music from the stones
All the warm day. Men mop their faces; women limp, tight-shoed,
Dreaming of home and long, slow drinks,
Yet these remain, at twilight
Charmed, still sweeping down
Still trudging up the long hot hill, still sailing down again.

O praise, O sudden praise
For all irrelevant grace!
Wanton and irresponsible as paper figures
Blowing before their minds' own vagrant breeze
The skate-boards voyage, tranced, impervious—
As young men, beautiful and grave and transient
Played their long games in China, Greece, and Rome,
Keeping alive each age, from man to boy,
Through all the frivolous thunder of our wars,
The serious business of joy.

On the United States,
Considered as a Landscape

Richard Howard

TO THE PAINTERS:

Not a building, this earth, not a cage,
   these waters: the country is
a body, to be treated so: when
   the weather is mild, think
of the past, when the weather is mean,
   think of the future. Men do
thus, and evolve a metropolis
   from litter: leaves, straw, floating
bottles and boxes, a mainland which,
   like anything else, cannot
be made all at once to drop its rags,
   suddenly to stand naked,
fully disclosed. Time—it has taken
   time to collect in wide pools
even the beginnings, skeleton
   and cartilage, arteries
and bladder: if our Sublime cannot
   rise above such things as beer
cans and plastic picnic forks, it is
   not all we say, it cannot
really be the God in which we trust.

Who creates by transforming, until
   we know the joy of having

This poem was commissioned by the U.S. Department of the Interior for an exhibition of landscape paintings by American artists to commemorate the nation's Bicentennial.

ourselves—the Master of Qualified
   Assertion puts it this way—
having ourselves been created by
   whatever has been endured
and mastered in the past: agreement
   with reality is not
necessarily agreeable,
   but there may be in the world
around us things (is a beach a thing?
   a river between red bluffs?)
which solace as well as any ruin
   could, or the funeral rites
of Phocion, say, in the distance . . .
   Maybe there is no difference,
among us, between the God and his
   Temple—that would be success,
the undemeaned American thing
   our Master of Dogmatic
Doubt calls the bravery to be new.

We have another Master, hear him—
   he is neither qualified
nor dogmatic, he is a man there,
   on the scene: "A good day here,
amid the sand and salt, a steady
   breeze setting in from the sea,
the sun shining, the sedge odor, noise
   of the surf, a mixture of
hissing and booming, the milk-white crests
   curling over. Leisurely
I bathed and had a naked ramble
   as of old on the warm gray
shore, my companions off in a boat
   in deeper water (I hailed
my friends with Jupiter's menaces
   against the gods, from Homer)."
Even Walt requires a god—requires
   Homer, Pope's Homer! to make

the moment more than facts that harass
  like flies, buzz but do not sing.
Have we said yet what we had to say?

Are we at home here, have we made this
  our place? Following the lines
between the States, a plane gave Gertrude
  Stein her vision, "made it right
that I had always been with cubism and
  everything that came after."
Straight lines ("compare them to the others,
  the ones that go all over,
nothing neat and clean like the maps of
  America") and Indian names
no one knows, only recognizes,
  Latin names who remembers?
Looking back we do not remember
  ourselves but the neighborhoods
we lived in and the things there we knew
  (is a marsh a thing? and what
the sun makes of western windows, pane
  after pane igniting?). How
much we belong to the past we learn
  only when we have labored
to survive and prevail without it.

Keeping up with the body, then, till
  it falls where it may, we know
what our exertions teach: everyone
  who makes something new does harm
to something old. Inside what we make,
  or what we have made, inside
our work is another work trying
  to get out. We help it out,
doing harm, for we are not at home
  in this literal climate,
terrain without metaphor, without
  reference to preference:
the leaves are too green and the rocks
  too red, the sea around us

is a sea of silent blasphemies.
 It is all too new for us,
and somehow too old as well: we are
 not safe here, and we know it.
Our knowledge is our hope, as we look
 out the window and over
the cliff . . . We change and, ourselves changing,
 change what we see: this beloved,
defiled and continuing body.

Sand Nigger

Lawrence Joseph

In the house in Detroit
in a room of shadows
when grandma reads her Arabic newspaper
it is difficult for me to follow her
word by word from right to left
and I do not understand
why she smiles about the Jews
who won't do business in Beirut
"because the Lebanese
are more Jew than Jew,"
or whether to believe her
that if I pray
to the holy card of Our Lady of Lebanon
I will share the miracle.
Lebanon is everywhere
in the house: in the kitchen
of steaming pots, leg of lamb
in the oven, plates of kousa,
hushwee rolled in cabbage,
dishes of olives, tomatoes, onions,
roasted chicken, and sweets;
at the card table in the sunroom
where grandpa teaches me
to wish the dice across the backgammon board
to the number I want;
Lebanon of mountains and sea,
of pine and almond trees,
of cedars in the service
of Solomon, Lebanon
of Babylonians, Phoenicians, Arabs, Turks

and Byzantines, of the one-eyed
monk, Saint Maron,
in whose rite I am baptized;
Lebanon of my mother
warning my father not to let
the children hear,
of my brother who hears
and from whose silence
I know there is something
I will never know; Lebanon
of grandpa giving me my first coin
secretly, secretly
holding my face in his hands,
kissing me and promising me
the whole world.
My father's vocal cords bleed;
he shouts too much
at his brother, his partner,
in the grocery store that fails.
I hide money in my drawer, I have
the talent to make myself heard.
I am admonished to learn,
never to dirty my hands
with sawdust and meat.
At dinner, a cousin
describes his niece's head
severed with bullets, in Beirut,
in civil war. "More than
an eye for an eye," he demands,
breaks down, and cries.
My uncle tells me to recognize
my duty, to use my mind,
to bargain, to succeed.
He turns the diamond ring
on his finger, asks if
I know what asbestosis is,
"the lungs become like this,"
he says, holding up a fist;
he is proud to practice

law which "distributes
money to compensate flesh."
Outside the house my practice
is not to respond to remarks
about my nose or the color of my skin.
"Sand nigger," I'm called,
and the name fits: I am
the light-skinned nigger
with black eyes and the look
difficult to figure—a look
of indifference, a look to kill—
a Levantine nigger
in the city on the strait
between the great lakes Erie and St. Clair
which has a reputation
for violence, an enthusiastically
bad-tempered sand nigger
who waves his hands, nice enough
to pass, Lebanese enough
to be against his brother,
with his brother against his cousin,
with cousin and brother
against the stranger.

Final Meeting

Carolyn Kizer

Old friend, I dressed in my very best,
Wore the furs I never wear,
Hair done at Bloomingdales,
Even a manicure; splashed on the good perfume
Before I rode the bus up Madison
To the rear entrance of the hospital;
Traversed for miles the corridors underground
Where orderlies in green wheeled metal carts
Piled with soiled linen, bottles pans and tubes.

Then, elevators found, I followed a colored line
To the proper nurses' station,
Embraced your wife: pale, having wept for weeks,
Worn out with your care.
She led me to your bedside. I swept in with an air,
Wrapped you in fur, censed you with my perfume.
Jaunty and thin, with the fine eyes and pursy lips
Of one of Holbein's Unknown Gentlemen,
You could not speak
Except for some unintelligible grunts
Through the hole they had made in your throat;
Impatient with your wife
Who, after years of understanding
Could not understand.

Months of practice with my dying father
(shamed by his memory lost, he refused to speak,
Like Ezra Pound at the last) taught me a monologue:
Of our days in Roethke's room so long ago
Far off across a continent in Seattle:
One day when the bell had rung

We stood by the stairs in shabby Parrington Hall
As the hordes rushed past us to their classes.
"Oh Carolyn," you said in such a grieving tone,
"Beautiful women will never love me."
And I replied, "One day
you're going to be a famous poet,
And you'll be pursued by lovely women."
"There! Wasn't I right?" I now say,
And you look up sweetly at the lovely woman
Who stands on the other side of your bed.

Dear one, back then you were so plain!
A pudgy face, a button nose, with a little wen
Right at the tip.
But we all knew, from the moment you spoke
On the first day in class, you were our genius.
Now pain has made you beautiful.
And the black satin domino
To shade your eyes when you nap,
Pushed back on your head, looks like a mandarin's cap.
With your shapely thin grey beard
you are phenomenally like Li Po,
A poet you adored.

"Well, dear, there's no Ohio left—except in poems";
I keep up a stream of jokes and reminiscences.
You scribble notes on your yellow pad,
Nod your mandarin nod.
Grief is not permitted till it's over,
And I'm outside, stunned, standing on Fifth Avenue
In the fierce cold of January.
Then I say what I could not say upstairs in your room:
A last goodbye. And thank you for the poems
You wrote to me when we were young.
                    Now go in peace, my friend,
Even as I go
Along the soiled pavement of the Avenue
Banked in the gutters with old snow.

Annus Mirabilis

Philip Larkin

Sexual intercourse began
In nineteen sixty-three
(Which was rather late for me)—
Between the end of the *Chatterley* ban
And the Beatles' first LP.

Up to then there'd only been
A sort of bargaining,
A wrangle for a ring,
A shame that started at sixteen
And spread to everything.

Then all at once the quarrel sank:
Everyone felt the same,
And every life became
A brilliant breaking of the bank,
A quite unlosable game.

So life was never better than
In nineteen sixty-three
(Though just too late for me)—
Between the end of the *Chatterley* ban
And the Beatles' first LP.

The Well

Denise Levertov

At sixteen I believed the moonlight
could change me if it would.
              I moved my head
on the pillow, even moved my bed
as the moon slowly
crossed the open lattice.

I wanted beauty, a dangerous
gleam of steel, my body thinner,
my pale face paler.
                 I moonbathed
diligently, as others sunbathe.
But the moon's unsmiling stare
kept me awake. Mornings,
I was flushed and cross.

It was on dark nights of deep sleep
that I dreamed the most, sunk in the well,
and woke rested, and if not beautiful,
filled with some other power.

My Grave

Philip Levine

Just outside Malaga, California,
lost among the cluster of truckstops
there is a little untended plot
of ground and weeds and a stone
that bears my name, misspelled,
and under the stone is dirt, hardpan,
more dirt, rocks, then one hundred
and one different elements
embracing each other in every way
they can imagine so that at times
they remind me of those photographs
I saw as a boy and which I was assured
were expensive and stimulating
and meant nothing. There are also
over a thousand beer bottle caps
one of my sons was saving until
he calculated that he would never
reach a million and so quit. (Quit
saving, not drinking.) One document
is here, ceremoniously labeled
"My Last Will & Testament." My sister
so hated it she threw it into
the bare hole and asked that it be
shovelled under. Not one foolish hope
of mine is here, for none was real
and hard, the hope that the poor
stalked from their cardboard houses
to transform our leaders, that our flags
wept colored tears until they became
nothing but flags of surrender.

I hoped also to see my mother
a long distance runner, my brother
give his money to the kids of Chicago
and take to the roads, carless, hatless,
in search of a task that befits a man.
I dreamed my friends quit lying
and their breath took on the perfume
of new-mown grass, and that I came
to be a man walking carelessly
through rain, my hair tangled, my one
answer the full belly laugh I saved
for my meeting with God, a laugh I
no longer need. Not one nightmare
is here, nor are my eyes which saw
you rise at night, barefoot and quiet,
and leave my side, and my ears which heard
you return suddenly, your mouth tasting
of cold water. Even my forehead
is not here, behind which I plotted
the overthrow of this our republic
by means of the refusal to wipe.
My journals aren't here, my right hand
that wrote them, my waist that strained
against so many leather belts and belts
of cloth that finally surrendered.
My enormous feet that carried me safely
through thirty cities, my tongue
that stroked and restroked your cheek
roughly until you said, "Cat." My poems,
my lies, my few kept promises, my love
for morning sunlight and dusk, my love
for women and the children of women,
my guiding star and the star I wore
for twenty-seven years. Nothing of me
is here because this is not my house,
this is not the driver's seat of my car
nor the memory of someone who loved me
nor that distant classroom in which I
fell asleep and dreamed of lamb. This

is dirt, a filled hole of earth, stone
that says return to stone, a broken fence
that mumbles *Keep Out,* air above nothing,
air that cannot imagine the sweet duties
of wildflowers and herbs, this is cheap,
common, coarse, what you pass by
every day in your car without a thought,
and it waits, this is an ordinary grave.

Choose

Sarah Messer

The first two weeks I search the sheets for blood,
lift my skirts in secret looking. Rolled apart
to bedside, I pound a desperate fist into my gut
each night, mouthing, *bleed, bleed,* while you

softly speak of choice—the former girlfriend
who had five and was all right. I try to imagine
their aborted lives, maybe nine or ten years
old by now, with scrubbed faces and shining shoes

ready to greet the big wide, and all the why's
to be explained: a mother too young,
who runs finger-in-throat to bathrooms,
a father on cocaine; the one-lunged, armless,

web-toed kids, blinded from a herpes kiss,
born with a tail curled like a pig's; or those slid
out wet and healthy, to slowly starve in a heatless
flat between potato bags and cans of instant milk.

Now we walk to a stirrup-horned place. Not knowing
what to say, you talk incessantly of women's swelling
bodies; skin stretched tight as fruit, swollen ankles,
strange hair growth, and how breasts jiggle,

grow to globes in pregnancy, spilling
milk like tilting bowls. But in the room
of white circle lights, still, it's only me
who lies during the pinch of a long-barreled

needle—legs spread in sheets
like a back-spun beetle—as the curled
nub of my cervix contracts and expands.
It's only me who bites the wings of cotton

that the nurse gives for the pain—
"bite down, look away—"
The lights, white globes jiggling, and the flutter,
"just a flutter" of the 45-second "evacuation—"

a butterfly in a dark jar. Still, it's me
who gets the red-candy pills, yellow ergotrate—
I who cannot unclench my cotton-crammed thighs,
or spread my jaws to speak of sores

left to my sex from birth, and all choices
carried behind me like a tail.

Still Life

Judith Ramos

Stone-still she sits, straight as
   vanity, good breeding and angled school chair demand;
Sweet empty face filled with
   kohl-shadowed painted puppy eyes, Cover Girl,
     cheek gel blush
   shiny red tiny red lipsticked lips;
Short-cropped curly black cap of hair warming the vacant
   cranium.
She smiles "I don't understand" to self-evident statements,
   shaking the bright head when asked a question,
Fills quarter-page essays with "This neat guy I know" who
     "really blew me away"
   and "Man, was it freaky!"
Stares at the clock but stolidly suffers through the class
   in silent graciousness.

What is your life like, lovely woman-child,
In that head where slumbering synapses becalm your perfect
   face?

Does your mystical passivity excite the males?
Do they cajole-tease, sweet-reason you?
   Lavish on you boutique baubles, blown-up Bowie posters,
     ready-made love
   letters with fuzzy-photo naked lovers
     running through dusky beaches and
   wildflower fields in drug store card racks?
And when your frozen flower face
   and quiet girl grace
Maddens them to urgent tumescence,
Do you perform the sacred modern hymeneal

and open pink petals
in Chevy vans and borrowed beds?
Are you—iceberg-like—crystal cool above and crackling
violent below?

Or can you be innocent as you look?
Sharing t.v. dinners with mom and dad,
Exchanging recipes for brownies and fascinating tuna souffles,
Confectioning puff-sleeved cotton frocks and crocheting
comforters for Christmas,
Collecting sea shells and plush bunnies and tinkly music
boxes whose rigid
ballerinas twirl to pop waltzes,
Lying in your Alice-blue cubicle on a dotted Swiss canopied
goldilocks bed
fantasizing chaste love scenes with Hollywood heroes while
McKuen's
poetry plays softly on your antiqued white wardrobe?

Stone-still she sits, weaving daydreams
through tedious lectures,
Dreams homespun of soap operas, cheap novels and the "good
life,"
Dark theater dreams of hot celluloid love and marrying well,
Marrying the Islander yacht, the Mercedes 450SL and the
annual station wagon for the kids,
Marrying the two-story six-bedroom house with electronic
garage door opener
and built-in Mexican maid,
the amethyst pool with short-hair pool service,
the crisp clipped yard with Japanese gardener,
the newspaper boy, the milkman, the monthly pest control,
the dry cleaner service, the diaper service,
the liquor delivery, the drug store delivery—Cutty Sark and
Seconal, Valium and vodka.
Marrying money. Marrying motion. Winnebago weekends in
Vegas, Aspen ski
runs, jumbo jets to Copenhagen, Caribbean cruises . . .
morning tennis doubles,
Mister Marcel coiffures, tipsy girl luncheons, health spa

massages . . .

meetings—neighborhood swim and racquet club, p.t.a.,
　　community playhouse,

Republican Women's Org. . . . Ceaselessly shopping,
　　chauffeuring afterschool kids

to orthodontist, swim lesson, riding stable, but
　　rewarded by

Beaulieu-Vineyard-Private-Reserve-Estate-Bottled suppers
　　for two and

diplomatic dinners with the boss.

Sweet concoction of male fantasy, cupidity and huckster
　　power,

All American dream girl.

Nativity

Stephen Sandy

Only husbands wearing gowns permitted beyond this point
                        —Maternity ward sign

A picture-windowed fifth-floor room:
above the rubble of delivery tables
the rubber sheets and terry towels
tray and stirrup, clamp and bolt,
a kind contraption shows the portal of your womb.
Among the arc lights everywhere
a convex mirror hung
above us like a shield
mediates, enlarging this far-flung
spectacle. May we not miss
the moment, paradise
of generation verified; *now* made minutely visible!

From slippery boards where we had danced
cobwebbed performers growing old
two seniors of Shalott feeling the cold
together we observed right breathing through the fast.
Suddenly lost
finding your own, as in a dream, you cry at last.
Dumbfounded spirits then, entranced
and hand in hand, a doubled Perseus,
behold this stun-
ning end of one.
The mirror returns

353

its image of
one love
becoming two; the utterly sumptuous
revolt.

You watch Medusa slowly wakening from sleep to flood
this gate of bone shifting to yawn in larger
gapes of you; and soon
the crown, like a shadow moon
through mist, appears
ghostly lanugo and bone, the chromium charger
with clamps like fangs, drenched hair
and plume of blood
and how you lost
—cried *No!*, your fare-thee-well to years
when the last great Hokusai wave, towering, tossed
you back, combed through us there
with rifling fold
furling along that shore
of incandescent light.
With distance doubled by the brilliant shield
we watch it yield
no stone, no harm, but suffered bliss;
Hard looking has afforded this.

The dazzled retina, then the Persian blue
sky I saw that shone above your head.
Stars and planets gleamed, spun
in one
boreal candelabrum,
shone out far from the saddle and the sheet
lighting a way, this exile from
ourselves, this passing through.

When all was done
twin cries declared what had begun:
your own, and this anomalous squinting incubus
a magnum of champagne uncorked
such great nothings-to-do-with-us!
Forgotten now in that hospital tumult

we were begotten too. Henceforward forked:
pinned on our astonished tines,
that business, this result:
one sociable camp meeting
or stairway of a summer night—
and now, surprised by her small muscular hello's,
we greet our own charisma, anodyne;
three rare birds flushed to flight
under one sign.

Fifteen More Essays:
An Editor's Choice

What follows is a recommendation for further reading in the nonfiction literature *MQR* has published between 1962 and 1991. One would like to add interviews with John Ashbery, Jorge Luis Borges, Maxine Hong Kingston, David Riesman, Isaac Bashevis Singer, and Leonard Woodcock, as well as archival material by R. P. Blackmur, Ezra Pound, Tess Slesinger, and Harvey Swados. An editor has as many favorites as there are issues, and more.

Francis A. Allen, "*Nineteen Eighty-Four* and the Eclipse of Private Worlds" (Fall 1983). A professor of law describes how the invasive procedures of our own government and media have eroded our private lives, as Orwell warned in his prescient novel.

Howard Baker, "The Tunnel of Eupalinus" (Winter 1976). When the author journeys to Samos to learn more about "one of the most haunting and evasive of ancient phantoms," Eupalinus of Megara, he rediscovers the classical Greek spirit in its full profundity.

Judith Laikin Elkin, "Recoleta: Civilization and Barbarism in Argentina" (Spring 1988). The Recoleta cemetery in Buenos Aires is an ideal location from which to assess the harrowing recent history of Argentina, as it is summoned here in documents and personal witness.

Edna Amir Coffin, "The Image of the Arab in Modern Hebrew Literature" (Spring 1982). The fateful encounter of Jews and Arabs in the Holy Land has been dramatized in many compelling literary works, here surveyed and analyzed with a sympathetic eye toward the authors' desire for peaceful reconciliation.

Brewster Ghiselin, "D. H. Lawrence and the Peacocks of Atrani" (Spring 1975). As the archetype of the phoenix, the peacocks painted in a certain Italian church visited by Lawrence in 1920 symbolized the life-renewing vision of his later masterpieces, a vision unfolded in this artful reconstruction by a poet and critic.

Lois Lautner, "Arnold Schoenberg in Kammern" (Winter 1967). "Do not hesitate to write what seems to be impossible for a given instrument to play," the great composer told his student in composition in 1933. His eccentricities and his genius are equally apparent in this admiring memoir.

Trevor Le Gassick, "The Image of the Jew in Modern Arabic Fiction" (Spring 1982). A complementary essay to Coffin's above, this commentary reveals that Arab literature "generally expresses deep antipathy and bias against Jews" rather than the more positive sentiments noted by Coffin in the Hebrew literature. Perhaps, the author hopes, a "more charitable and sympathetic view" will emerge in the future.

Carol Meyers, "The Israelite Empire: In Defense of King Solomon" (Summer 1983). By distinguishing between the careers of the two great kings of Israel, David and Solomon, the author implicitly indicates the options available to leaders in the Middle East today. Solomon emerges as the more attractive model because he was more willing to negotiate and cooperate with his enemies.

Toni Morrison, "Unspeakable Things Unspoken: The Afro-American Presence in American Literature" (Winter 1989). Already a classic, this essay recommends not (only) that the canon of masterpieces be enlarged but that the texts we cherish be examined in the light of new knowledge about African-American history; *Moby-Dick* is analyzed as an example. The author then applies her principles to her own work by explaining the origin and meaning of the first sentence of each of her novels.

James V. Neel, "Atomic Bombs, Inbreeding, and Japanese Genes" (Summer 1967). The distinguished geneticist calculates one generation after Hiroshima how severe the effects of radiation upon victims truly were, and how they were influenced by a culture of intermarriage.

Francine Patterson, "In Search of Man: Experiments in Primate Communication" (Winter 1980). The author describes her attempts to teach language to a gorilla, Koko, and speculates on the implications of achieving interspecies communication only imaginable before now in myths and children's stories.

Gilbert Ross, "The Auer Mystique" (Summer 1975). A detailed memoir of being a student of the violin master Leopold Auer, friend and performer of Brahms and Tchaikovsky, teacher of Elman, Zimbalist, Heifetz, and Milstein. The author was founder and first violinist of the Stanley Quartet.

Paul A. Samuelson, "Economic Forecasting and Science" (Fall 1965). Is economics really "the dismal science"? And if economists are so smart, Samuelson asks, why aren't they rich? The Nobel Prize–winning author explains with good humor how crises regularly upset the best laid schemes of grim scientists.

Wendy Steiner, "My Trip to Italy" (Summer 1984). Actually a report on a summer's stay in Czechoslovakia; the longed-for but always refused visa to Italy becomes the symbol of a governmental system unable and unwilling to satisfy its citizenry. This personal memoir tells us much about why the Party was voted out so decisively in 1990.

Maurice Zolotow, "'I Brake for Delmore Schwartz': Portrait of the Artist as a Young Liar" (Winter 1986). The author was a fellow undergraduate with Schwartz at the University of Wisconsin in the early 1930s, and here corrects the myths, both Schwartz's and his biographers', about that crucial year of the poet's intellectual and imaginative life.